LIBERTY *or* DEATH!

TATTERED
FLAG

Tattered Flag Press East Sussex

Liberty
OR
Death!

The Life and Campaigns of Richard L. Vowell

British Legionnaire and Commander –
Hero and Patriot of the Americas

Maria Páez Victor

The Author

Maria Páez Victor is a sociologist, born in Caracas, Venezuela, where she obtained her first degree. She has an MA from the University of Kent at Canterbury and a Ph.D. from York University, Canada. She lives in Toronto, and travels regularly to Venezuela and Britain. A lifelong enthusiast of Latin American and British history and politics, she participates regularly on Canadian and Venezuelan television, radio, and at public events, and has published numerous articles on recent and historical topics in both English and Spanish. As a curious anecdote, while researching for this book, a remote personal connection surfaced with Richard Vowell, who served under three revolutionary generals all of whom are in the author's family tree, among them José Antonio Páez, leader of the Llanero cavalry and later President of Venezuela.

Published in Great Britain in 2013 by
Tattered Flag Press
11 Church Street
Ticehurst
East Sussex TN5 7AH
England

office@thetatteredflag.com
www.thetatteredflag.com

Tattered Flag Press is an imprint of Chevron Publishing Ltd.

Liberty or Death!
© María Páez Victor 2013

Jacket Design and Typeset: Mark Nelson, NSW
Cartography © Tim Brown and Carmen Victor

British Library Cataloguing in Publication Data

A Catalogue Record for this book is available from the British Library

ISBN 978-0-9543115-8-2

Printed and bound in the United Kingdom by Henry Ling Limited, Dorchester, Dorset

For more information on books published by Tattered Flag Press visit
www.thetatteredflag.com

To my dearest husband, Peter A. Victor,

who accompanied me every step of the way in the search for

Major Richard Longfield Vowell

To our loving children, Carmen and Mischa, Marisa and Marc

and, to our wondrous grandchildren, Rio Gabriel, Sacha Elias,

Griffin Delfín and Acacia Marie:

hoping they will always be proud of their Venezuelan heritage

And to the memory of my beloved parents,

Delfín Enrique Páez Chataing and María Luisa Osuna Lucena de Páez

And to the memory of President Hugo Chávez, the second Liberator

∽

'We can speak of earlier ages only through the accounts of eye-witnesses...
For in the last analysis it is human consciousness which is the subject matter of history'

MARC BLOCH, *THE HISTORIAN'S CRAFT*, 1954

Contents

Acknowledgements

IT has been a daunting task to write a first biography, especially of someone about whom little has been written. I have relied heavily on the work of Major Richard Longfield Vowell, cross-referenced and complemented with the work of many historians to whom I am most indebted. I greatly appreciated the work of war historians, particularly that of the late John Keegan, which gave me insight into the world of the soldier, as well as that of the late Eric Lambert, historian of the British Legion which has also been of enormous help to me. Since my work entailed reviewing works in both English and Spanish, I have taken the liberty of translating when necessary and if there are any misinterpretations, these are due to my failings.

The search for more information on Major Richard Longfield Vowell led me, and my husband, on unforgettable visits to England, Ireland, Venezuela, Chile and Australia and along the way many generous people helped me to try to piece together a picture of his life.

I give my heartfelt thanks to the librarians at some great libraries and archives: the Bodleian Library at Oxford University; the British Library; the State Library of Victoria, Australia; the State Library of New South Wales, Australia; the New South Wales Archives in Australia; the Library of Congress in Washington DC; the National Library of Ireland in Dublin; and librarian Jorge López Falcón at the National Library of Venezuela. My thanks also to librarians in many smaller libraries: Sra. Cecilia Guzmán Bastías, Librarian and Archivist of the Naval and Marine Museum in Valparaíso, Chile; Bath Central Library, Bath; Guildhall Library; Gloucestershire County Office Archives; Mallow Library, and also to those at universities: Dr Cliff Davies, Wadham College Archivist at Oxford University; Keel University Library; Reading University Library; University of Toronto Library; the Map Librarian, Ms. Trudy Bodak at York University Library in Toronto; and Ivan García B. at the Museo Bolivariano in Caracas.

In Bath, I should like to thank Mrs Estelle Holloway, a member of- and a historian of the Vowell family, who in the autumn of 2001, over a delightful afternoon tea at her house, talked about the family history, parted with a copy of the Vowell genealogy chart and gave me her outlook on the Anglo-Irish tradition; and to family historians Mr Bernard Welchman and Mr Ken Smallbone for their help with my research.

In Australia, my thanks go to Jenny Stiles, great-great-great-great niece of Major Richard Longfield Vowell, for all her valued help and friendship. Also to Ian Black at the Hamilton History Centre, Victoria, for all the valuable information he discovered on my behalf, and for his much appreciated continued interest; to Cheryl Elmes and Janette Lier of the Casterton Historical Society, Victoria, who shared so much of their fascinating local history with us as we had coffee on Casterton's main street one sunny morning; to Mrs Denise Houlighan and Mr and Mrs Ross Davidson, of Bruk Bruk, Victoria who welcomed us warmly to their homes, as complete strangers, just to talk to us about their local history; to Mrs Joan Hunt of the Ballarat Archive Centre and Public Records Office of Victoria who, on Christmas Eve 2004, in the middle of her organization's office party, with interest and patience, helped us find Vowell Creek; to Australian historians, Dr Sue Rosen and Dr Ann Maree Whitaker, whose thorough and solid research was invaluable to me and greatly appreciated; in Lithgow, to local historian, Ollie Leckbandt, who on a Sunday afternoon, having never met us before, took us on an amazing tour of the remains of the Cox's River Stockade; my thanks also for all his generosity in sharing his knowledge and for his continued support for this project; to our friends, Cliff and Jean Hooker, for their warm hospitality and to Scott and Nara Chalmers for a delightful Christmas stay that seemed like a homecoming.

In Cork, Ireland, to Mrs Pat Foote who, one night, poured over old church papers with us in her kitchen and then took us on an unforgettable midnight tour by torchlight, of Kilshannig Church near Mallow, that had been on her family's estate for centuries, so that we could see the tablet on the wall honouring Rev. Michael Becher, Major Vowell's brother-in-law.

To the descendants of the Becher Family: Eileen Franchi and Alistair Gordon, who from the very beginning of my research, have given me many clues, information and encouragement; and to Vivian Harrison, direct descendant of George Laval Chesterton, for her kind interest in this endeavour.

To the distinguished Chilean historians, Dr Carlos López Urrutia, whose work has been an inspiration and who very kindly encouraged me in this project; and to Dr Armando Moreno Martín who also encouraged me.

To my dear friends in Toronto, Margaret Van Dijk, who set me on the path to writing this book and gave me unwavering support; to Maarten van Dijk who expertly deciphered ancient documents for me; to Liz Cox and Peter Timmerman for their welcomed comments and support; to Linda Cook for her inspiring example and to John and Judy Grant for their kind encouragement. A special thanks in England, to David and Patsy Franks for their support and the extraordinary hospitality and affection they have shown us throughout many years of friendship.

I am particularly grateful to my editor and publisher, Robert Forsyth, of Tattered Flag Press, who took on my work with such enthusiasm and helped turn it into the work you now hold.

In Venezuela, to my very dear brother-in-law, historian Gil Ricardo Salamé Ruiz, whose advice and help was invaluable to me; and to all my amazing sisters, especially

Alicia Páez de Velasco, Beatríz Páez de Salamé and Mercedes Páez de Corral, for their special help and for always having had faith in me.

To my dear daughters: Carmen, who was so helpful regarding the artwork, and Marisa for her help and counsel. And my gratitude and love to my husband Peter, without whose enthusiastic support and constant help I could not, and would not, have written this book.

María Páez Victor, M.A., Ph.D.
2013

AUTHOR'S NOTE

IN order to remain faithful to the writing and 'feel' of the period covered by this book, I have decided, wherever possible to retain the period writing and spelling as used by Richard Longfield Vowell when I cite his work written in 1831.

Readers may therefore notice some variation in spellings between the period style and contemporary spelling: for example, Vowell spells 'monkeys', 'monkies', and so on.

Similarly, wherever possible, I have decided to remain as close as possible to Vowell's syntax and sentence structure, even if, on occasion, it may not be similar to the linguistic styles we use today.

I ask for readers' awareness and understanding of this.

MPV
2013

INTRODUCTION

'Every town and village in South America contains a Plaza or principal square. In it is the church, government houses, and calabozo, or jail. Troops are paraded, public meetings held, and criminals executed there. It is the rendezvous for politicians and loungers, and usually the theatre of revolution.'

Richard Longfield Vowell, *Campaigns and Cruises*

SAN FERNANDO DE APURE, VENEZUELA, 1998

I was standing in the main plaza of San Fernando de Apure, the dusty, sleepy capital of the Venezuelan state of Apure, a region of seemingly endless tall grasses and enormous rivers, on a hot day in 1998. It was a plaza like many others in the country, with a statue of Simón Bolívar in the centre, perhaps more pleasant than most due to its many large trees and benches that invite the passers-by to sit in their cool shade. The government house and the cathedral stood on two sides of the square. The bright blue house of the Masonic Lodge graced another side, and outside it, like a sentinel, stood a life-sized statue of the favourite hero of Apure, General José Antonio Páez. He was the leader of the horsemen of the *llanos*, the great wide plains of Venezuela and Colombia, and the people who inhabit them, the *Llaneros*. They formed the ragtag cavalry of Simón Bolívar's Patriot Army which, against ridiculous odds, fought and triumphed over the seasoned troops of the Spanish Empire. He was also one of my ancestors.

A gentleman, seeing me staring at the statue, stopped to chat. This was a liberty that he could take because noting my business dress, stockings, and shoes, he could tell that I was 'from Caracas'. Rules of interaction can be bent with outsiders. 'Páez; he wasn't born here you know,' he pointed out, 'Many people think so. But he was born in what is now the state of Portuguesa. Apure was where he lived mostly and he had a ranch near here.' The man talked of Páez as if he was a mutual friend that I might want to look up. History is not quite dead in this land where past glories continue to give solace.

I stood there for some time, looking at his image, trying to reach some understanding of this almost mythical man whose exploits on horse and in battle I have heard of all my life. He died in 1873 and since then many books and articles have been written about his colourful public life. Two hundred years is not too long ago in the life of a family, yet ours retained only a few personal anecdotes about him. I had leafed through his autobiography and, like so many military narratives, it seemed that only military and political events were important enough for him to write about. It was disappointing how very little he referred to his family, the people of his everyday life, how people dressed, what they ate, what their daily customs were, the houses and places in which he lived, things he liked or not, and his thoughts about the llanos – his knowledge of which was key to his success.

So, I resolved to find out more about Páez and the times in which he lived – beyond the military image. I did it and along the way I encountered Major Richard Longfield Vowell, an Englishman who chose to live in South America and fight alongside Bolívar, Páez, Sucre, O'Higgins, and Lord Cochrane, against the Spanish Empire. It was Major Vowell who answered some of my questions and raised many more, yet left a fulsome and moving testimonial of those brave times in which they all lived.

This book is not a historical treatise, but rather a biography; the story of a man who lived and took part in events of historical importance. I have not only been interested in Vowell's military life, but also in the natural and social environments which he encountered and wrote about assiduously. However, my very modest endeavour cannot even begin to do justice to the thousands of instances of heroism, sadness and suffering, and also to the achievements and triumphs that occurred during the struggle of the peoples of Latin America and the Caribbean, as well as the Australian people, to liberate themselves from colonialism. Many scholarly historians have written about these struggles and from their books I have learned so much and am grateful.

This is Major Vowell's story.

MAPS

South America, 1817. (Library of Congress)

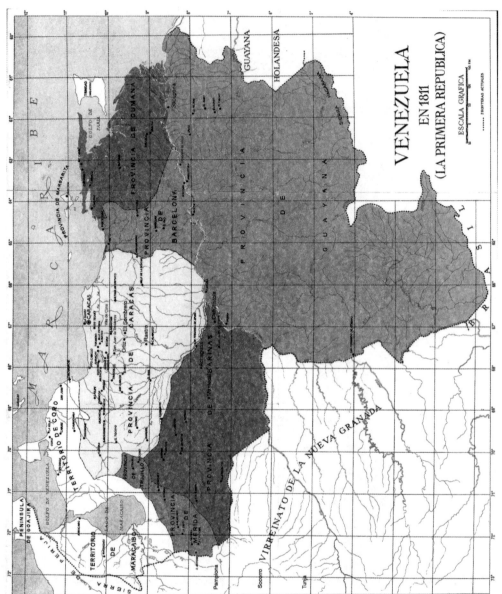

Venezuela, 1811.

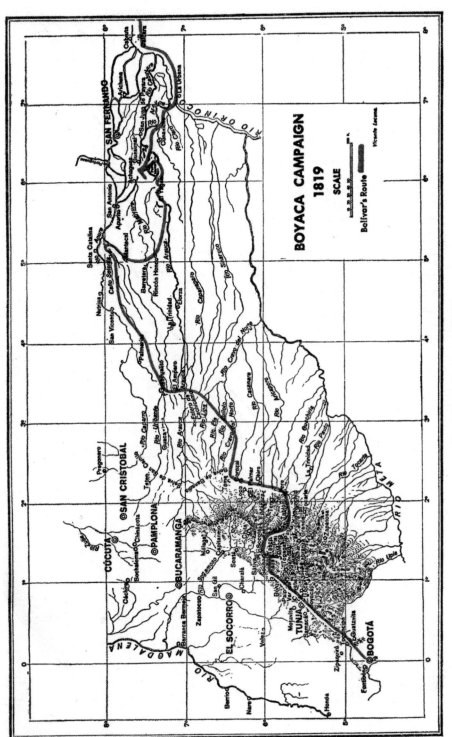

The Boyacá Campaign, 1819.

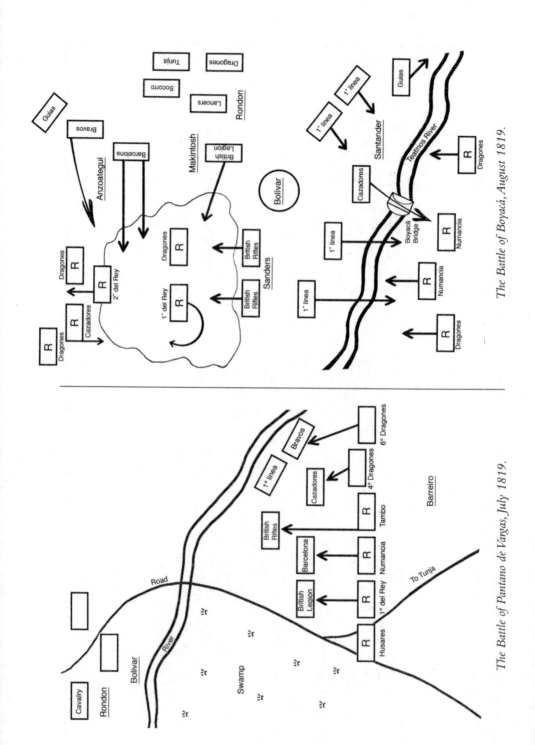

The Battle of Boyacá, August 1819.

The Battle of Pantano de Vargas, July 1819.

*Battle of Chiloé
Ancud Harbour
10-14 January 1826*[1]

Morning of 10 January: *Chilean soldiers disembark on the beaches of Puerto Inglés (A, B): they march to the battery at Balcacura (D) to take it.*

11 January: *the Chilean Squadron crosses in front of Fort Agui battery (C) towards Balcacura, where it picks up the Chilean soldiers and takes them to Playa Lechagua on 12 January.*

14 January: *Soldiers and marines capture the ships in front of Ancud Fort and the fort itself.*

[1]. Guillermo A. Toledo Leal 'La Infantería de la Marina La Armada de Chile', 1999 Revista de la Marina de Chile.

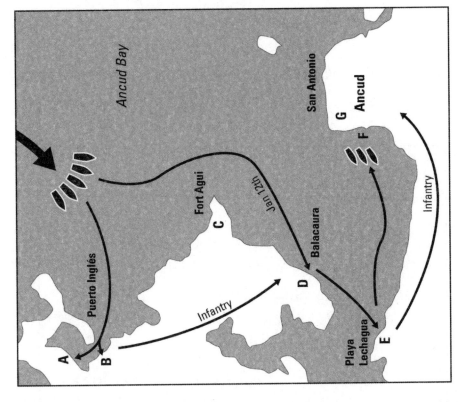

Ancud Bay

San Antonio

G **Ancud**

F

Fort Agui

Jan 12th

C

Balacaura

D

Infantry

Puerto Inglés

A

B

Infantry

Playa Lechagua

E

Infantry

Chile, c. 1870.

MAP OF CHILI

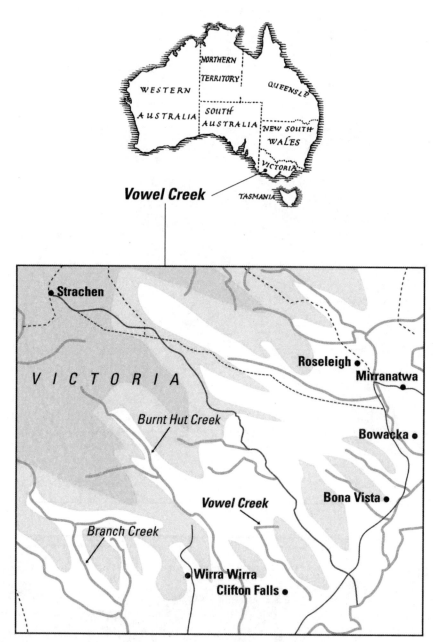

Vowel Creek, Mirranatwa, County of Dundas, Victoria, Australia.

Editor's note: According to regional cartographical references, the spelling is 'Vowel' with one 'l'.

PROLOGUE

'There is an especial glamour about men who have gone abroad to risk their lives in a cause which was not their own, either because they were impelled by an ideal or perhaps merely because they loved fighting for its own sake…'

Alfred Hasbrouck, *Foreign Legionnaires in the Liberation of Spanish South America*, Columbia
University Press, 1928

IN 1817, a young former Oxford student, Richard Longfield Vowell, joined the Venezuelan Patriot Army that was recruiting volunteers in London. He could not have known at the time that in joining he would go on to serve in the armies of northern South America and in the Chilean Naval Squadron; that he would survive brutal military campaigns in the harshest possible terrain and climates; and that he would take part in historic events and battles that liberated from the ruthless Spanish Empire, a vast territory many times larger than England.

Richard Longfield Vowell would prove to be not only an excellent officer, but also a well-educated one who could write – and write well. He wrote about his experiences in his book *Campaigns and Cruises*[1] which is composed of three sections. The first section, *Campaigns and Cruises,* relates to his thirteen-year experiences as an officer in the Venezuelan and Colombian armies and the Chilean navy. During that time, as an army officer, he took part in nine major battles and five minor ones, and as a naval officer, he not only took part in the capture of ships, naval blockades and actions, but also participated in the final naval battle that liberated Chiloé, the last bastion of the Spanish Empire.[2] About this section of the book one Latin American historian states that perhaps Vowell's best skill was in describing people, particularly the Patriot leaders; as well, he provides abundant material for the social researcher, particularly related to the men who liberated the llanos: *'Therefore his descriptions are of great interest to understand that historical time.'*[3]

The next two sections are historical fictions, considered by a Latin American scholar as being in the best tradition of Sir Walter Scott, who at the time had only just started on his literary career.[4] *The Savannas of Barinas* is a love story that takes place in the *llanos*, or plains, of Venezuela during the War of Independence. It is reminiscent of Geoffrey Chaucer's *Canterbury Tales* as the various characters in the plot each have a different tale to tell and, certainly, Vowell was well acquainted with Chaucer's work. Vowell paints a picture of a time, a place and a people that few had written about, and it constitutes an ethnographic treasure of Venezuelan *llanero* culture. The prologue to the *Savannas of Barinas*, as published by the Venezuelan National Academy of History, states that it is a book that deserves to be included among any collection of rare books because it deals with a period of Venezuelan history of which little is known, principally due to the place where it occurred, a centre of the nomadic life: the *llanos*. It further states that the significance of Vowell's book lies in the fact that it is the history of a period which was largely ignored, except in the military accounts of José Antonio Páez.[5] Another Latin American historian states that he recommends this book to all those '…who are eager for Venezuelan impressions, or who simply seek the emotional, the scientific or beauty, since through the *Savannas de Barinas* one will find a perennial fountain of history, novel and poetry.'[6]

The Earthquake of Caracas is also a fictional love story set against the 1812 earthquake which almost swept away the Patriots' chances for independence. It was based on the first-hand accounts that Vowell received from those who had lived through this event. It was the very first novel in which the leaders of the Venezuelan Patriots, Simón Bolívar and Francisco de Miranda, his precursor, appear as characters and, as one Latin American writer states, they are treated with respect and admiration.[7]

Campaigns and Cruises was praised in the British press at the time, receiving brilliant accolades from the most prominent newspapers.[8] It was also translated into French and published in Paris in 1837, also receiving press accolades there.[9] Thereafter, it was mostly ignored in the English-speaking world, except as a book of travels.[10] However, it remained highly regarded and repeatedly cited by Latin American historians as a reliable narration of an eye witness to seminal events related to the Wars of Independence in South America and as a unique record of Venezuelan culture of that time. Since Major Vowell's name did not appear on the publication, his authorship remained unconfirmed until 1919, when Luis Romero Zuluaga wrote a newspaper article about his research on Vowell.[11] In 1952 the Chilean historian, Carlos Sunyer, wrote a short article about Vowell, concluding: 'There are great gaps that remain in knowing the character and the life of Vowell.'[12] This is the first biography of Vowell, filling some of the most glaring of these gaps and providing hitherto unknown information about his early background and of his life after South America.

Latin American historians have high praise for the author of *Campaigns and Cruises*.[13] His book covers battles, campaigns and other military and naval actions which added to the knowledge of these wars and which was considered to be particularly interesting because it was a personal, first-hand account. Romero Zuluaga states that among military memoirs Vowell's book is infinitely more interesting than the rest because of the immense amount of data that he gives about the war in the *llanos* and life in general in that region.[14] Rufino Blanco Fombona has called him a 'heroic soul' and a '… heroic narrator whose heroism is evident in the very natural way of a modest man… a truthful man who did not idealize nor despise, but who wrote with acute descriptive ability in a serene and impartial way.'[15] Fombona also thinks Vowell, although sincere, appraised the leaders and officials with whom he shared his experiences in a cold, distant, and severe way. However, he also believed he did not have a critical sense of synthesis. This comment, coming from a modern day historian, betrays some hindsight logic from someone familiar with the whole military and political scenario of the time, whereas Vowell was writing, not as a historian, but as an officer in the midst of the action. Furthermore, Venezuelan and Colombian historians have not always welcomed Vowell's criticism of the military command.[16]

Nevertheless, he has been called the 'wise legionnaire' and historian Carlos Sunyer considers Vowell's work to be of undoubted historical merit and interest, and one that is '...honest, serene, objective... this work is outstanding for its objective honesty and truthful openness; it does not flatter, but neither does it slander, and it registers events just as the author sees them happening, and not a version deformed by passion or resentment.'[17] Chilean historian, Carlos López Urrutia, considers that there is no doubt about Vowell's historical narration; that he is an important player whose three tomes, totalling 700 pages, describe events that correspond to the reality of what occurred.[18] López Urrutia also refers to Vowell as a valiant officer.[19] His military narrative in *Campaigns and Cruises* is lauded for its impartial style of writing; for example, Manuel Segundo Sánchez states that 'This work, interesting beyond all pondering, was written with noticeable impartiality by an English officer... His judgement of men and events are eloquent and precise.'[20]

As to his historical fictions – *The Savannas of Barinas* and *The Earthquake of Caracas* – these are praised for the vivid prose and creative plots. Juán Uslar Pietri considered that his stories have '... the full force and interest of a vivid colourful picture.' He calls him '... a master storyteller; since the author is not satisfied with describing his own impressions, but also writes that of others and with the ability of an oriental storyteller, he starts to link together like a colourful necklace not of beads, but of human beings where one would find the monk, the servant, the outlaws, the slave, the *Llaneros*, the hierarchical lord, the hero, and others, and he does much more, because as he narrates their lives, he is also narrating the history of Venezuela with a clear and easy language.'[21]

Major Richard L. Vowell displayed an encyclopaedic interest in the New World in which he had arrived: the peoples, the geography, the flora and fauna, the social mores, songs, stories and traditions of these quite remote territories were all captured with keen detail in his book. He preserved in its pages, for posterity, the original songs of the Venezuelan Independence as sung by Patriots and troops, and which have been reproduced in the Independence Bicentennial Year (2010-11).[22] From his writings we know that he was fluent in Spanish and French, with such a flair for languages in general that he could pick up local accents and idioms; that he was an excellent horseman and swimmer; that he liked good food; that he had a particular interest in the medicinal properties of plants; that he liked women and enjoyed their company; that he was not particularly interested in money or wealth, and that he welcomed new experiences and took risks. He was a man savouring every minute of his grand life adventure.

For a good many years, the identity of the author of *Campaigns and Cruises* remained a mystery, but after it became known, there remained the puzzle over the character of the same. Why did he omit his name from his book? How did he maintain an observational attitude, yet so heroically make sacrifices for the sake of the liberty of others? Even after Vowell's authorship was known, there was so little known about his life and background that his persona retained an elusive character, thus prompting the historian, Carlos Sunyer, to lament the gaps in the knowledge of Vowell's character and life.

Much of his narrative and outlook suffered from the inconsistencies of the various translations that his book underwent – from English to French, and then from French to Spanish. His wry, British sense of humour, so salient in his original writings, goes largely unnoticed by those of a Spanish tongue. Eric Lambert, a historian of the British Legion in Venezuela and Colombia, comments in his book *Voluntarios Británicos e Irlandeses en la Gesta Bolivariana* that when Vowell left Bolívar's army to join Admiral Lord Thomas Cochrane in the Chilean Squadron, 'It is a shame that Vowell exited as narrator to all that took place during the campaigns, since he arrived in Venezuela mid-January 1818, since his contribution has been enormous, frequently wrapped up in a great sense of humour.'[23]

Vowell's book was translated into Spanish from the French by different individuals in three parts at different times; one part pertained to his service for Venezuela and Colombia while, done later, the final part covered only his service for Chile.[24] His book has an expansive quality to it: it is a military account, an ecological description and an ethnographic analysis all in one, possibly confounding modern readers so used to specialization. It is fair to say that his work has not been comprehensively, nor even adequately, translated into Spanish because it was not directly translated from the English. Some of the characteristics and expressions typical of his background, time, and culture were lost in translation also, and all this has added to the air of mystery.

One of the most noticeable characteristics of his narrative is that, unlike other foreign volunteers who also wrote about their experiences in South America, Vowell's was remarkably free of some of the extreme cultural and racial prejudices sometimes found among his contemporaries.[25] For example, one British volunteer wrote, '(I) feel for the situation of those brave men, whose misfortune it was, to be made the victims of treachery and injustice in the first place, and of ignorance, imbecility, cowardice and cruelty, in the second.'[26] Another recorded, 'Dirt, disease and famine were the reward of the services of men who had left their county to embark in the desperate cause of those who now so ill requited them.'[27] A British physician had this to say about the people, 'The population is made up of Indians and South American creoles, who show in all their actions, physical or mental, a great indolence. Many of them, do not want to take the bother of seeking an occupation, [and] allow themselves to die of hunger.'[28]

While Vowell dispassionately pointed out failings in the Patriot campaigns and its commanders, it was without an underlying depreciation of their cause, or spite towards leaders or common soldiers, or towards their race or religion. One Latin American scholar states that Vowell '…shows constant veneration and sympathy for the top leaders of Venezuela's independence which contributed to its defence on the battlefield.'[29] He was also particularly conscious of women, their role, and their sacrifices. His fluency in Spanish surely helped him understand the culture, but it was his own psychological disposition that gave him an avid curiosity of the unknown world around him and tolerance for those who were different to him.

As to why Vowell wrote at all, one could ask why does anyone write? There can be many reasons, such as money, recognition, or some psychological need to make sense of one's experiences. In Vowell's own words, as published in the *Bath Chronicle* in 1831, he was unaware until he had completed his work that many other volunteers to South America had also written memoirs: 'But may not one, who was among the earliest volunteers that assisted to clear the land with their personal exertion, be allowed to glean after the harvest has been gathered in? Especially as no single individual, as far as he is aware, has traversed the country to such an extent, nor resided in it for so long a period, and in such eventful times.'[30]

To do justice to his engaging and vivid writing style, and in view of the fact that his book was out of print for 127 years and somewhat difficult to find, I have included a variety of his passages which I cannot hope to improve upon.[31] However, very recently his three-part book has been published as three separate books.[32] In quoting Vowell I have retained, at times, his original 19th century spelling which is slightly different from that used today for certain place names, rivers, people, and where this applies, I have indicated so in the footnotes.

When embarking on writing a biography, the question of significance is unavoidable: what effect or impact did the life and work of the biography's subject have upon events at the time and on our understanding of these in the present time? With respect to the historical significance of Richard Longfield Vowell's life and work, there are some definite conclusions but also some unanswered issues.

The assessment of his work by Latin American historians confirms that he is considered to be one of the best narrators of key moments of the Wars of Independence waged by Simón Bolívar. He is unsurpassed in his descriptions both of the crossing of the Andes in 1819 by the Patriot Army, as well of the Patriot leaders. Such descriptions would have been lost to history if Vowell had not written about them. The unsuccessful campaign of the Patriot Army of the South led by General Valdez is a part of the war that has not received as much attention by Latin American scholars, mainly because it did not achieve its main purpose, which was to reach Quito. However, Vowell gives a detailed account from the point of view of an officer on the front lines – not from hindsight – as to why and how this mission failed. It is in this, in writing about a doomed campaign, that Vowell demonstrates especially even-handedness and honesty without spitefulness, which is remarkable. In comparison with the memoirs of other British legionnaires, Vowell's work is far superior not just because of his excellent writing, but because he attempted to be fair and dispassionate. Other legionnaires wrote with acerbic disdain on the lack of resources and shortcomings of the campaigns, and often criticised the quest for liberty itself; even a writer as good as Chesterton fell into this subjectivism.[33] Vowell never entered into such bias and never wavered in his belief in the ultimate benefit of fighting for independence.

From the point of view of Venezuelan ethno-cultural studies, Vowell's first-hand explanations of life in the *llanos* in the early 1800s, both in *Campaigns and Cruises* and in his fictional work, *The Llanos of Barinas*, are exceptional and distinct from that of others who may have travelled through the region as passers-by. Vowell's account of that subculture contains the insight of an insider. He participated fully, for a significant time, in the life of the *llanos* and was accepted as an integral part of the community due to his standing with Páez's cavalry, which explains the extent of his descriptions. For Vowell, the lives of the *Llaneros* were not limited to lives of battle, as was the almost universal prejudice with which they were thought of, but consisted chiefly of a hospitable, worshipful, music-loving, solid family and social network which went unremarked by others. These facts would have been lost to history without his work.

Vowell's description of life as an officer of the First Chilean Squadron is again the voice of someone with first-hand knowledge of early naval combat, and has been invaluable to the historians of the Chilean Navy. His capacity for observation comes to the fore again in Chile where he picked up the customs, sights, songs, and idiosyncrasies of the *Huasos* and Chilean cultures and society of his time.

As to his actions as an officer on the battlefield, it is difficult to state if these changed the course of battle or victory, as he does not dwell upon his own achievements. However, we can surmise the consideration in which he was held as an officer by the fact that Bolívar esteemed him personally and granted him the award of the Star of the Liberators, Sucre lauded his work as trainer of the troops, he was the only European on the army disciplinary board, and by his successive promotions (lieutenant, captain, major, commander).

As to Vowell's open-mindedness, religious tolerance, respect for women and interest in indigenous peoples, his attitudes may not have changed the path of history, but he likely had some influence over others who encountered him, particularly since he was, by all accounts, an amiable and well-liked man with many friends.

There is one overriding significance of Vowell's life and work. It underlines the importance of the role played by the small number of British officers and troops in Simón Bolívar's army and in Chile's naval forces, particularly in the training of troops and crews in the modern warfare of the time. Immediately after achieving Independence, for various reasons, their contribution, while never denied, was undoubtedly played down by the Patriots. Firstly, in the euphoria of the emergence of a new nation state it is understandable, and rightly so, that a war be interpreted through a patina of nationalistic heroism. It was crucial to recognize the triumph as something the people of the nation had achieved. Secondly, there were devious manoeuvres on the international political stage soon after the South American nations attained their independence, and these were not conducive to the Patriots sharing the limelight with England – a powerful country that did not, officially, back the struggle for independence and, after it was attained, conceded political interest in the region to the United States. So the voluntary contribution of the men who formed the British Legion, while wholeheartedly recognized and lauded by Bolívar and his officers, in later years was less mentioned. Knowledge of Vowell's life and work can change the way Latin America's history of independence is conceived and taught. It underlines the link between the British people, if not its governments, and the struggle for Independence of a continent.

The present book attempts to shed light on the life and character of Richard Longfield Vowell, who along with many other foreign legionnaires, fought valiantly for the independence of Venezuela, Colombia, Ecuador, Bolivia, Perú and Chile, and who left us an admirable account of his time and adventures. It may also spur reflection in this, our 21st century, about the struggle for human freedom and the desire for justice, about the exercise of power, about war as instrument for settling the affairs of society, its historical legacy and the grave costs it demands from those who wage it.

It may also serve to inform many in the Anglo-Saxon world about the struggle for Latin American independence during the 19th century, a struggle that received the contribution of many English and Irish volunteers who fought next to the South Americans and shared their fate. This historical perspective is the context of the transcendental events that are occurring today when Latin American countries are struggling to maintain their sovereignty and their democracies as they face a new, and more powerful empire.

CHAPTER ONE

The South American Mania

*'It seems that all the [British] population is engaged in this occupation of
sending one or another expedition to aid the insurgents.'*

Duke of San Carlos, the Spanish minister, in a letter to the British Foreign Office,
12 October 1817

B Y 1817, Napoleon had been defeated, the French had been kicked out of
Spain, Britain's streets were filled with out-of-work officers and soldiers, and
in Venezuela Simón Bolívar, the leader of the patriot forces, was almost
in despair.

Simón Bolívar was born of an aristocratic and very rich Creole family of Caracas
on 24 July 1783. He was given an excellent education steeped in the ideals of the
Enlightenment. Having married at the young age of 19, and having lost his bride to
yellow fever eight months later, Bolívar swore to dedicate his whole life to the liberty
of his homeland, a cause to which he applied himself so thoroughly that he spent his
entire and considerable inheritance in this indefatigable quest.[1] His leadership of the
forces that dared to challenge the Spanish Empire became well known in England and
Europe. He displayed unwavering determination to achieve independence, showing
political astuteness, strategic vision, and diplomatic ability to keep together discordant,
ambitious, and parochial local leaders. With extraordinary personal sacrifices, he was
tireless and ingenious in his struggle to obtain the funds and resources needed for his
armies. In spite of innumerable setbacks and outright defeats, he came back repeatedly,
picking himself and his armies up from defeat to fight another day. As one historian has
said, 'His superb and unquenchable spirit, refusing to be discouraged, kept him
planning and preparing, struggling and fighting, marching and winning victories until
the whole of the present republics of Venezuela, Colombia, Ecuador, Perú and Bolivia
had gained their independence. That is the reason why Bolívar is called "the father of
five nations" and why today the name of The Liberator is spoken almost with the
reverence due to a god, especially in Venezuela, land of his birth.'[2]

While today Bolívar's military deeds may be considered as just dates in the past, his
political thought, particularly his prescient political ideas of sovereignty and Latin
American integration, have kept him very much alive in the political discourse

throughout the continent. His contribution has been summed up this way: 'Bolívar gave the Revolution an intellectual core, a doctrine, which it had not before possessed. His passion for independence grew not from personal vanity or resentment against personal slights, but from study of the French prophets of liberty and reason, and from a romantic admiration of the supposed virtues of patrician republican Rome. He was a doctrinaire republican as well as a local Venezuelan patriot and an American revolutionary.'[3] Currently, political events in Venezuela have also centred on Bolívar's ideals and they have brought about a marked interest throughout Latin America.[4]

However, in 1817 Bolívar and his patriot forces were tasting, once again, the bitterness of defeat. Twice Bolívar thought he had achieved success – in 1812 and in 1814 – only to lose to the superior power of the Spanish. The danger to the independence movement had become even greater, because the Spanish Crown was now able to deploy troops seasoned in the Peninsular War, whereas the patriots lacked a professional army altogether. The patriots' poor military preparation was understandable, if regrettable, given Spain's policy of despatching only lesser militia units to its colonies. With few exceptions, such as General Francisco de Miranda,[5] creoles had very little war experience or training. Bolívar's 'ragtag army', as it was mocked, faced the daunting prospect of confronting a large number of trained troops experienced in fighting Napoleon's formidable armies.

At about this time, a twenty-two year old Englishman, Richard Longfield Vowell, was kicking his heels having abandoned his studies at Oxford, and was looking for a way to follow in his father's footsteps into an exciting military life. Unfortunately for him, but fortunately for Bolívar, the British forces were not recruiting, but dismissing its men, unlike the Venezuelan army.

But how and why would a young Englishman want to join a war in a far-off country of a different language and culture, and against terrible odds? On balance, it was perhaps not so unusual a decision for a high-spirited youth to make, considering that British public opinion, reflected in newspaper accounts and articles of the time, was decidedly on Bolívar's side and that would surely have influenced Vowell.

As soon as South American patriots started to challenge the power of Spain, the British press closely followed the events. The *Morning Chronicle*, the *Morning Post,* and *The Courier* regularly published news of Simón Bolívar's army. *Bell's Weekly Messenger* referred to this widespread enthusiasm as 'the South American mania'.[6] According to one official report: 'In the years after 1815, a war-weary Europe saw in the fabled lands of the Spanish Empire a new El Dorado…With the revolution, interest became intense. It is doubtful whether there has ever been so general a demand in England for information about this vast area and proportionately, so liberal a supply, as in the eighteen-twenties.'[7]

Indeed, during the first two decades of the 19th century, there was an extraordinary demand for information in England about South America, perhaps as never before or since. For most Europeans these lands were unknown, mysterious territories, but of immense natural wealth. Spain, an absolute monarchy, eager to extract resources, tried to keep a fierce control over its South American colonies, including a strict prohibition to trade with any other power except itself. However, much of Europe had a stake in Spain's colonies. Spain had a stunted productive capacity traced back to its expulsion of the Arabs and Jews from Iberia, which emptied the royal treasure and greatly diminished industry and agriculture. The exploits of Columbus came at a most opportune moment for the Spanish monarchy as it was on the brink of ruin when the wealth of a new continent, with new people to oppress, was handed to it. Unfortunately, the immense fortune that Spain obtained from Latin America was spent – not on industry or investment in the development of Spain itself, but by the idle aristocracy on conspicuous consumption and huge estates.[8] Therefore, Spain had to import the majority of manufactured goods it needed, and hence, most such goods it sent to the colonies were not made in Iberia but in other European countries. Soon Spain owed millions to Europe's bankers and traders – German, Genoese, Flemish, and Dutch.[9] The fortune in gold and silver plundered by Spain from Latin America and the Caribbean, extracted by the slave labour of indigenous peoples, as well as slaves from Africa, was the basis of the capitalist economic development of Britain and Europe.[10]

In the 19th century however, Spain could not quite control such a vast coastline as that of Latin America, especially when wars were being waged in Europe and brisk contraband flowed between British ships and the South American colonies. British traders had long desired formal trade with the Spanish colonies. During the previous century, Spain had allowed British slave traders to supply slaves to the Spanish colonies at the rate of one ship a year and under this abominable trade, many other goods were also exchanged.[11] When France took over Spain in 1808, the British led a determined campaign to disrupt trade between Spain and her South American colonies. By the 1800s, smuggling flourished between the eager colonies and British merchants; the latter were feeling hard done by, not only because of the Spanish monopoly but also because the very same British warships that laid siege upon Napoleon's mainland also blocked British merchant ships from European ports.

The British government entertained ideas of opening up these colonies, not so much for their own liberation as to gain British control and to compensate for the loss of Britain's North American colonies. So marked was the fascination for a South American foothold, that on June 1806 an expedition of 1,600 men led by Admiral Sir Home Popham, acting without British authority, but in accord with popular support, invaded Buenos Aires. This had more to do with attacking Spain and France than any sort of liberation.[12] Buenos Aires was vigorously and valiantly defended, not by Spain, but by the local inhabitants of the fair city, who were not about to welcome yet another imperial power. The British government sent another expedition, led by General Whitelock, to regain Buenos Aires, and again the colonialists prevailed.

These experiences made the cautious, but highly influential, Lord Castlereagh, British Secretary of State for War and the Colonies, decide that British military interventions in South America were futile.[13] He rightly concluded that they would not be welcomed unless they came bearing freedom, that they would awaken the colonists' ire and thus could even favour Spain. He preferred to continue '…the silent and imperceptible operation of our illicit commercial intercourse'.[14] Nevertheless, on

28 August 1817, Castlereagh announced, in a pointed memorandum to all European powers, that Britain maintained that only Spain herself might use force to retain her colonies. Thereby he blocked any intervention by the rest of Europe in aid of Spain. Historian Humphrey Milford gives a forceful interpretation of this declaration, stating that by refusing to allow Europe to intervene in support of Spain while the issue was still in the balance, Castlereagh made the triumph of the revolution certain.[15] In fact, Milford overstated the case and underestimated the extraordinary effort and sacrifices the patriots had to make in order to make that revolution certain.

The war with Napoleon brought two important advantages to the cause of independence for Spain's colonies. Firstly, the triumph of Admiral Horatio Nelson at the battle of Trafalgar saw the destruction of virtually the entire Spanish navy, which left Spain vulnerable and incapable of patrolling the enormous South American coastline. Secondly, when Napoleon invaded Spain, patriotic governing councils, or *Juntas*, sprang up throughout the colonies, supposedly to safeguard the rights of the Spanish Monarch. In effect however, these became the bedrock of the independence movement.

The British government conducted an undignified dance around the issue – at times expressing overtures of sympathy and promises to the colonial patriots, and later avowing neutrality to the Spanish authorities. Under George Canning as Foreign Minister,[16] a man of an idealistic and progressive temperament, the British government planned to provide troops for the liberation of Venezuela to General Francisco de Miranda, predecessor of Simón Bolívar. In June 1808, a force of 10,000 men was raised in Cork, led by Sir Arthur Wellesley, the future Duke of Wellington, and intended to sail for South America. Unfortunately, for Venezuela, Napoleon invaded Portugal and at the very last moment that force was redeployed to fight the Peninsular War.[17]

Two years later, in May 1810, the Foreign Enlistment Act made it illegal for foreigners to enlist, and for British men to join, foreign armies. The Act was an example of the Machiavellian flair of British policy, as, 'The bill passed through Parliament after a violent struggle, but its subsequent history shows that the government had no intent of enforcing its provision.'[18] This was evident as the British naval hero, Captain (later Admiral) Lord Thomas Cochrane, set off to help Chile without any official opposition, while in London and Ireland, Bolívar's emissaries were allowed to openly recruit men for the patriot army, and the enlisted men carried out training manoeuvres in public. This was the closest that any foreign government would come towards actively supporting the patriot cause in South America. Simón Bolívar did not receive aid from any European power or the USA during his extraordinary feat of liberation, nor did any other South American patriotic leader. While European nations rushed to help George Washington rebel against England, the glory of South American patriot leaders – Simón Bolívar, José de San Martín and Bernardo O'Higgins – and their armies and navies, would be theirs alone, as were their hardships, to be shared with no allied power, but with only their own soldiers and the individual foreigners who volunteered to follow their cause. One historian has observed: 'In the great adventure of freedom no outside country came to their aid. The independence of the United States was obtained with the help of half Europe. It may be doubted if they could have achieved it at that time had not the French and Spanish aided them... but no country declared war on Spain or Portugal in order to help Latin America to emancipate itself... there was no European fleet to stop Spain from sending to America the soldiers who had defied Napoleon.'[19]

There was one small country that did help Bolívar: Haiti, the first Black republic, which had already freed itself from France. In 1815, President Alexander Petión provided Bolívar with 6,000 muskets, ammunition, food, a complete printing press, some ships, money, and the strategic help of Haiti's military governor, Gen. Ignacio Marión, for an invasion of Venezuela. Upon landing on Margarita Island, one of the first things Bolívar did was to declare the abolition of slavery, as he had agreed with Petión. Although this invasion was not ultimately successful, it did allow the patriots to control significant parts of eastern Venezuela, which included the mouth of the immense Orinoco River.[20]

There were many progressive British public figures who supported the South American patriots, among them Sir John Tylden, Sir Robert Wilson MP, Lord Hawke, William Wilberforce MP, Henry Brougham MP, the Duke of Somerset, and Sir Benjamin Hobhouse.[21] Another supporter was George Gordon, Lord Byron, whose admiration for Simón Bolívar led him to name his sailing ship after him. Byron was on the verge of volunteering for the patriot army, but in the end decided to fight for the independence of Greece, where he is revered to this day.[22]

By 1817, the British government, under Lord Castlereagh, preferring its European interests, declared itself neutral with respect to Spain's colonial struggle, not wanting to antagonize the country which, after the expulsion of the French from the Peninsula, became an ally of Britain.[23] This was not well received by the British press. One London newspaper, *Bell's Weekly Messenger,* repeatedly published editorials chastising the British government for siding with Spain against the colonies, and declaring that in this position the government did not represent the sentiment of British people nor aid its prosperity, which depended on free trade with South America.[24] As one eyewitness of the time stated: 'The contest between Spain and her South American possessions had long excited the lively interest and generous sympathy of the British public.'[25]

The British public had not forgotten that it was only eight years previously that war between Spain and England had finally ceased.[26] There was sufficient 'historical baggage' in the relationship between the two countries to sustain an underlying public distrust of the Spanish absolute monarchy which contrasted very unfavourably to Britain's parliamentary monarchy. After regaining his country, the reinstated Ferdinand VII of Spain affirmed his reign by absolutism and, worse, brought back the Inquisition. Little wonder then that he spurred the unpopularity of Spain throughout Britain and promoted a '... real desire to see freedom triumph in South America, altogether apart from the commercial interests, which dictated policy.'[27]

Pragmatically, Spain's harsh rule over its colonies impeded any legitimate trade between British merchants and South America. The merchants, wanting new markets, bitterly resented such trade barriers, as did the colonists who had to pay Spanish merchants much higher prices for manufactured goods such as posts, nails, guns, and cotton cloth.[28] The progressive Members of Parliament championed their cause and pressured for official backing for the patriots. Indeed, it was the financial backing of a group of merchants that helped finance the recruitment ships for the army of Simón Bolívar.[29] Bolívar praised these merchants in one of his most important speeches which he gave to the Angostura Congress on 15 February 1819: 'Our troops can compare to the most select troops of Europe, as there is no longer inequality among the means of destruction. Such great advantages we owe to the unlimited generosity of certain generous foreigners that have seen humanity moan and have heard the call of reason, and have not remained passive spectators, but have sped with their protective help and have helped the Republic in everything that it has needed and thus their philanthropic principles have triumphed. These friends of humanity are the genial custodians of America, and to them we will owe eternal gratitude.'[30]

It was not a small consideration to the British government that the streets of their cities were awash with the former soldiers and officers of the Peninsular Wars who now, in peacetime, found themselves unemployed, (many were unemployable); most might be better off fighting in a distant land. Such is a common fate of soldiers then and now: feted and praised in war, but dispensed with in time of peace. So it was that the British government turned a blind eye towards the recruiting activities of the South American patriots, which had started seriously in London at the beginning of 1817.[31] The recruits, particularly those who had no prior military experience, such as Vowell, were trained and exercised to strict British army standards, quite openly, in public areas of London.

War as it was waged in 19th century Europe was a brutal endeavour. Artillery was crude and operated with only elementary precision. Most combat was face-to-face, with sword or, worse, the bayonet – a weapon which, according to anthropologist Harry Turney-High, has been responsible for the destruction of more human life than any other artefact in history. 'For the real work of war in the age of Clausewitz was butchery. Men stood silent and inert in row to be slaughtered, often for hours at a time…'[32] Bolívar's army had minimal artillery capacity as it was constantly short of funds. Most of its artillery pieces were captured on the battlefield from the enemy and its cavalry relied on fearsome native lances. Therefore, the patriot army could best gain advantages if it had disciplined troops and successful tactics.

It was a French officer, H.I.V. Ducoudray Holstein, who, joining Bolívar in 1815 as his chief of staff, advised him to recruit a 'foreign legion' of experienced soldiers supportive of the patriot cause, and who were now plentiful in Europe. Holstein believed that the native soldiers did not lack bravery, and with training in European military methods and tactics, they would become 'invincible'.[33] The recruitment of volunteers could not start too soon. On 7 April 1815, the Spanish general, Pablo Morillo, had already arrived on Margarita Island, off the north-eastern coast of Venezuela, with 18 ships, 42 transports, 500 officers, and about 10,000 seasoned Royal Spanish troops.[34]

At the beginning of 1817, Bolívar asked Luis López Méndez, a cultured and able man who had been stationed in London since 1810 as representative of the Patriotic Junta of Caracas, to recruit experienced officers and troops. Caught up in the spirit of the times and eager to find military service in a noble cause, Richard Longfield Vowell lost no time and enlisted in the Venezuelan patriot army.

CHAPTER TWO

Semper Fidelis

'There is properly no history; only biography.'

Ralph Waldo Emerson

A S well as experienced officers and soldiers, a small number of gentlemen with no military training, but with the funds to buy their commission, were also recruited by the Patriots.[1] Among these enthusiastic young recruits, Richard Longfield Vowell obtained his commission as a Lieutenant in the First Venezuelan Lancers.

In his book, Vowell does not say very much about himself directly, and gives no information at all about his background. There is only one account of him by a contemporary, George Laval Chesterton, who gives testimony of Vowell's experiences as well as his character. Chesterton enlisted in Bolívar's army but only stayed in the country for a year. He found little good to write about his sojourn with the Patriot Army, but he took a liking to Vowell and wrote about him.

'At Angostura I became intimate with a Captain Vowell of the Columbian army; an Englishman of amiable but thoughtless disposition, whose strange career has been rarely paralleled. He was an undergraduate in one of the universities, at the moment when the death of a relative put into his own possession 2000 pounds. Absolute master of that sum, he relinquished his studies, quitted the university, and, infected by a prevailing mania, resolved to bear arms for the emancipation of Venezuela. After expending 200 pounds on an outfit, he embarked with the possession of 1800 pounds. Such a capital in such a region would have constituted him a wealthy man; but alas! Vowell was improvident and indiscriminately generous, and consequently lent so much to certain casual friends, and absolutely gave so much to others, that when I met him in Angostura (after only 3 years of service in South America) he had been despoiled of all his gold, and possessed only his own good sword.'[2]

How did Vowell come to be such a man? Who was his family? What was his background? We can piece together a picture of the young Vowell by an appreciation of the circumstances in which he and his family found themselves.

The Vowells are a very ancient family from Somerset, one of the western counties of England, whose genealogy can be traced to the 16th century. Major Vowell was descended from a long line of English gentry that included military officers, clergy, Members of Parliament, scholars, and lawyers.[3] Among the most notable of his ancestors are three mayors of the city of Wells, a privateer who plundered French and Spanish ships (Thomas Vowell), another Richard Vowell (alias Hooker), who was an Oxford graduate and a learned chamberlain of Exeter, a canon of Wells Cathedral, yet another Richard Vowell, who was the last Prior of Walsingham Monastery before Henry VIII had it demolished, and Admiral George Rodney who won the only naval battle for Britain during the War of Independence of the United States. This prolific involvement of one family in English public life prompted the historian Victor Bonham-Carter to state that, 'History, in its true sense, is rarely absent from the Vowells.'[4] The core Vowell family left for Ireland around 1620 and lived in County Cork for over two hundred years, forming part of the Anglo-Irish society there.[5]

Just outside the city of Bath, in the county of Somerset, in a well-appointed, upper middle class house, lives a descendent of the Vowell family who pointed out to the author that one cannot understand the character of Richard Longfield Vowell without first understanding the people known as the Anglo-Irish.[6] The Anglo-Irish, Protestants of English descent, having lived in Ireland for centuries[7] distinguished themselves from newly arrived English people whom they often believed did not understand Irish reality and often opposed them politically. It is the duality of country (Ireland/England), of religion (Catholicism/Protestantism), of ethnic stock (English/Gaelic Irish) that made decisions towards a calling in life and loyalty paramount markers or constants in the Anglo-Irish tradition. This was a characteristic also picked up by Elizabeth Longford, a biographer of Wellington, who stated that one of the traits of the Anglo-Irish was their faithfulness: their loyalty, once given, was firm. They had an ethic of service to the State and felt themselves retained for life to the service of their king. Thus Wellington, quintessentially Anglo-Irish, whose family also came from Somerset, stated: 'I have eaten the King's salt, and, therefore, I conceive it to be my duty to serve with unhesitating zeal and cheerfulness, when and wherever the King or his Government may think proper to employ me.'[8] Vowell would also go on to demonstrate loyalty and good humour, not towards the British King, but towards the Patriotic army and navy that he joined in South America.

With the exception of the Anglo-Irish aristocracy, many Anglo-Irish intermarried with Catholics and it was not rare to see both religions represented in one family. Thus, Vowell's paternal grandmother, Thomasina O'Callaghan, of Castle Lyons, was Catholic, and a descendant of the Irish kings, the O'Callaghans. It may well be due to this Protestant/Catholic mixture in his family that Vowell did not exhibit the extreme religious and ethnic prejudices evident in the narratives left by several other English and Irish volunteers in South America. On the occasions that he expressed criticism of

Catholic practices in South America, it was directed at the imperfect men and women who represented Catholicism; his opinions were not expressed prejudicially and not without a reason. He was by no means an atheist, but he maintained a very personal British reticence towards addressing the subject of religion.

His father, Major Richard Vowell, born in County Cork, Ireland, began his military career in the British army as an ensign of the 65th (2nd Yorkshire, North Riding) Regiment of Foot and went on to become a Major of the 66th Regiment of the Royal Berkshire (1774-88) with which he saw service in the West Indies, specifically in Havana, Jamaica and Guadalupe. After concluding his military career, he became Surveyor General of Cork, later a Member of Parliament in 1783-90 for Newborough, alias Gory Borough, in County Wexford, and attended the first independent Irish Parliament sitting in Dublin. In 1791, he was Justice of the Peace. Richard Longfield Vowell's mother, Ann Evans Hamilton, was from an aristocratic Anglo-Irish family and we know little of her except that she was the great-granddaughter of Gustavus Hamilton, Lord Boyne of Yougal.[9]

By 1795, the year Vowell was born, his family had left Ireland. This decision may have been due to the increasing political unrest in Ireland at the time, where the Constitution of 1782 was being sorely tested, with gradual and peaceful reform becoming an illusive proposition. The examples set by the rebellion against England in the United States (1776) and the French Revolution (1789), were powerful incentives towards independence in Ireland. Unfortunately, the wealthy landowning class in Ireland undermined reform when they took the Constitution to mean the consolidation of their particular political control and '...were unwilling to share the fruits of their victory with the middle classes who had helped to win it, still less to extend any political power to the Roman Catholic majority.'[10] A result was that the Anglo-Irish were increasingly being seen as apart from the Irish fabric; not as Patriotic enablers of the Constitution, but as a despised colonial English ruling class. Vowell's father must have seen the political turmoil that was coming and led his family back to its ancestral homeland, Somerset, to take up life in Bath.

Richard and Anne Vowell settled at 19 New King Street. In the highly stratified English society of the time, it was an appropriate townhouse by Bath standards for a gentleman such as Major Richard Vowell.[11] Today, the house is beautifully preserved as the Herschel House Museum, primarily because, prior to the Vowell occupancy, it had been the home of the sibling astronomers, William and Caroline Herschel. In 1781, Herschel discovered the planet Uranus from the garden of the very house where later Vowell and his sisters played as children. While not situated in the most fashionable part of the city, it was not too distant from it. The house has five floors, with two reception rooms on the ground and first floor, bedrooms on the two upper floors and a basement where the kitchen, parlour and workshop were situated, and which opened onto the charming walled Georgian square townhouse garden. It is located at a walking distance to St. James Cathedral[12] where four of the Vowell children, Richard, Mary,[13] Ann, and Catherine (Kate) were baptized on the same day, on 24 July 1795 which, ironically, was the day Simón Bolívar celebrated his twelfth birthday in far-off Caracas.[14]

Perhaps it was because of the existing duality of religions among their family, that upon arrival at Bath the Vowells had all the children promptly baptized in the Church of England. At that time, membership in the Church could not be underestimated for securing the children's future, even for acceptance in 'polite' society.

Throughout Vowell's childhood, England had been engaged in war with France.[15] Boys at the time were brought up with soldiers and sailors as role models and British military exploits were upheld as paths to glory. Swords, sailing ships, and horses were staple items in boys' childhood stories and fantasies. Having a father in the army must have also spurred Richard junior's interest in and awareness of the military profession, and since the military career of the elder Major Vowell took place mainly in the Caribbean, it would have acted as a lure to his only son, both to be a soldier and, to see these faraway lands.

Vowell's childhood came abruptly to an end with the death of his father on 16 November 1806, followed a year later by that of his mother on 4 September 1807. The parents left a sufficient inheritance for their children, which included the house, silver, and furniture.[16] It would have fallen to Vowell's aunts and uncles to care for the orphaned children and Vowell was given an excellent education to prepare him for Oxford University where, upon graduation, he could enter the Anglican Church. Greek and Latin studies were required to enter Oxford as the classics were the essential basis for English education and Vowell had a marked natural facility for languages. His guardians did not consider an army career as a desired choice for him since, as Longford recounts, 'prejudice against the army was almost universal' because its actions at home as a police force were deplored and made it disliked. According to one historian,[17] 'The profession of arms might be admired in moments of national peril, tolerated when necessary, but was mostly regarded with priggish contempt.'[18] The navy was infinitely preferred, but advancement depended greatly on naval connections.

So, in 1814, Vowell entered Oxford University as a student at Wadham, a college that catered especially to the sons of country gentry and was the preferred academic destination of young men of good Somerset and Dorset families intended mostly for a life in the clergy.[19] As far back as 1386, four of his Vowell ancestors had attended Oxford. Despite his academic abilities however, which had procured him the status of scholar at Oxford, Vowell's passion for life was not geared towards the Church but towards military life, as his father's had been. The sober, Gothic style of Wadham's architecture reflected its austere atmosphere, in contrast to other more affluent Oxford colleges, and it was inimical to Vowell's youthful restlessness.

Young Vowell may have felt trapped with no other avenue but to follow the dictates of his family's expectations, until the year 1815 when, by good fortune, he received an inheritance of 2,000 pounds sterling, a very significant sum, roughly equivalent today to anywhere between 140,000 and 5 million pounds sterling.[20] Most likely, the inheritance came from his namesake, John Longfield of Longueville, who died in that very year. Both Longfield and Vowell's father were likely close friends, and possibly Longfield was Vowell's godfather as he was given his name, since in 1775, Longfield was

High Sheriff of Cork and Richard Vowell, senior, had at some point been Surveyor-General of Cork.[21] Some historians have been puzzled that Vowell would at times use the name Longueville, instead of Longfield, but no doubt the French name was easier to pronounce for Spanish speakers and also Vowell most probably felt he could use both names. Furthermore, his great uncle, Hornby Longfield of Longueville, married to his great aunt, Mary Vowell, was most likely related to John, which added to his feeling of entitlement to the name Longueville.

Vowell was nineteen years old and it was no wonder that his new found wealth went to his head. He began spending prodigiously and extravagantly, particularly making large purchases of beer, all of which led to his expulsion from the solemn halls of Wadham on 11 December 1815.[22] He was not the first Vowell to be so expelled. In 1467 his ancestor, William Vowell, was sent down for being a wild and rebellious young man – but eventually went on to become a rector in Dorset.[23] Vowell would probably have agreed with Edward Gibbon who said of his time at Magdalene College that they proved to be the fourteen most idle and unprofitable months of his whole life.[24] But Vowell would have been wrong to think so. His sound education would serve him well throughout his life. That he was well read is indicated by his learned allusions and the literary quotes with which he prefaced each chapter of his historical works of fiction.[25] His knowledge of languages is evident from his sprinkling of his text with French and Spanish words or phrases and it allowed him to master Spanish quickly, to the extent that he was able to translate songs and poems of the Venezuelan *Llanos*, or tropical plains, leaving, for posterity, an invaluable ethnographic record of a time and place no others had written about.

When he was sent down from Oxford it is unlikely that his preference was to return to Bath. During the late 18th century, Bath had become England's spa of choice; the principal resort during the Regency where the aristocracy and their emulators went to see and to be seen, and one of the foremost places in the country for the acquisition and expression of status.[26] Its impressive neo-classical buildings and avenues made it perhaps England's most elegant city and in the early 1800s it became a place of residence and retirement for an affluent upper middle class, as well as a magnet for the elderly and infirm who came to Bath to take its famous mineral waters for their health.[27] In 1815, however beautiful, Bath was not an exciting place that could hold an adventurous young man's fancy. Vowell's military ambitions were thoroughly thwarted by the triumph of Wellington at Waterloo on 18 June of that year. Peace meant the dismantling of the British forces. England's towns and cities quickly became filled with demobilized troops and half-pay officers. It was bad timing for any inexperienced young man who wished to obtain a British Army commission when so many other experienced officers were in abundance. Vowell was never to become an officer of the British army, but rather would become a British officer in Bolivar's army and in Chile's navy.[28]

Vowell would have been aware that leading men in Somerset, including the Duke of Somerset, backed the South American colonies' fight for freedom. It is most likely that Vowell visited London where he would have seen one of the many daily posters that were put up in the coffee houses of London, inviting officers on half-pay to join the Patriot Army.[29] Here was a call to arms for the cause of Liberty, the opportunity for adventure, camaraderie, the spell of excitement and danger, and a chance to see the world; a heady invitation for intrepid youths, then and at any time. His friend, George Laval Chesterton, recounted how he was recruited to Bolívar's army by a military acquaintance whom he encountered walking down the Strand in London who remarked: 'Now, my boy, for South America, flags, banners, glory and riches!'[30] Such unrealistic expectations were bound to disappoint.

In joining the Patriots, Vowell was not fleeing from any difficult circumstance, nor could the modest wages offered be any lure to him, as was the case for many of the other volunteers. His willingness to venture overseas was probably made easier for him because, having lost both his parents by the age of twelve, he most likely was sent to boarding school, a common practice for boys of his social class. This would have meant separation from his sisters and a life growing up without the succour of a strong home base. Susan married in 1818, but Anne, Kate and Mary remained single.[31] Vowell, being exceedingly generous, would have surely used part of his inheritance to assure his sisters' welfare, if they had not enough inheritance themselves. He must have had a sense of emotional independence – such that allowed him to embark on the risky military endeavour offered by Bolívar. He was going towards the unknown with enthusiasm.

Later, when Vowell arrived in Venezuela, he and his fellow officers would be questioned by Patriot officers as to the motives that had brought them to such a faraway land to fight at their side. He stated clearly his reasons for enlisting, as he wrote: 'It was easy to perceive that they had no idea whatever of any one being induced, by mere curiosity, to travel through a country so convulsed with war; neither did they give the least credit to our assurances, that our motive for joining them was the desire of assisting them in their struggles for liberty.'[32] It was with their subsequent actions in battle that the young foreign volunteers would prove their idealistic motives beyond a doubt.

The Voyage of the Two Friends

'Pride, pomp, and circumstance, of glorious war!'

William Shakespeare, *Othello*, III. iii. 351

A T ten o'clock in the evening of 31 July 1817, Lt Richard Longfield Vowell set sail out of Portsmouth in the 250-ton chartered ship *Two Friends* commanded by Captain Cornelius Ryan. Its 80 passengers, a full capacity, were comprised officers and soldiers destined to St. Thomas, West Indies, where they expected to rendezvous with agents of Simón Bolívar and then go on to Venezuela. Vowell does not dwell much on the events of the voyage to St. Thomas itself, but we can gather what happened from an account of one disaffected passenger who described this tumultuous trip with great detail in an anonymous narration and it is amply quoted in this chapter.[1]

For days, Portsmouth had been full of eager soldiers and would-be soldiers headed for the South American war:

> 'The streets of Portsmouth were crowded by my fellow adventurers, whose courage and devotion to the interests of oppressed human nature were designated as magnanimous and generous in the extreme. To doubt their complete success was at once deemed treason against liberty, and infidelity to a sacred cause.'[2]

The recruited volunteers had been offered pay equal to the same grades in the British army, the officers to be paid upon arrival, and the soldiers from the day of embarkation. In addition, officers would receive US $200 and soldiers $80 on arrival to reimburse equipment and travel expense, plus two shillings a day and rations, and at the conclusion of the war they were to receive $500 and an allotment of land.[3] Little did the volunteers suspect that these were all hopeful – or reckless – promises of Bolívar's 'man in London', Luis López Méndez, since the Patriots had a continuous struggle to obtain sufficient funds for the war. Historian Eric Lambert considered that it was amazing the confidence with which López Méndez inspired, to the point that the guarantors were willing to give credit – of a total of 200,000 pounds – to a rebel government whose situation was considered precarious in the extreme in England. [4]

The *Two Friends* had been delayed many days at Gravesend before reaching Portsmouth, and delayed again in that port while loading supplies. The ship was at a disadvantage since its captain and many of its passengers were short of funds. The volunteer soldiers had to pay for their own passage at a cost of 40 pounds sterling, plus the costs of an amazing amount of wine, spirits, and porter for the voyage. Vowell's generosity – or prodigality – lead him to pay for the passage of several of his fellow officers, some with whom he had only the merest acquaintance.[5] When Colonel Donald MacDonald, commander of Vowell's regiment, the 1st Venezuelan Lancers, arrived at Portsmouth, he was arrested for a debt of 30 pounds, which Captain Ryan paid for the sake of avoiding any further delays. The difficulties of procuring stores and dealing with irate debtors were overshadowed by rumours that the British government would soon arrest former soldiers for joining a foreign legion. Pressure was put upon the captain and he was persuaded to set sail and pick up whatever supplies were still needed in Madeira.

On board, '… all was hurry and confusion':[6] beds, bedding trunks and packages strewn everywhere with officers celebrating rowdily, smoking and drinking, as their grand adventure was at last about to start. Another passenger described the scene:

> 'Any gloom which may have been produced by melancholy leave-taking was soon dispelled by the bustle of departure and the excitement of making new acquaintances. As the anchors came up, all was mirth and happiness. Their thoughts were of a speedy return, and their hopes were brightened with visions of wealth and glory to be gained.'[7]

Not all the ship's officers were enlisted in MacDonald's regiment: most were independent volunteers who did not recognize his authority, and seemed to resent his regiment for the display on board of splendid dress and highly polished arms. Evidently, Vowell esteemed MacDonald since he, unlike others, did not write disparagingly about him. Others described him as a vain, weak, and uneducated man whose indiscretion placed the ship in a precarious situation: 'Vanity was a ruling passion and the adulation of some of his satellites had so far procured his favour, that he was lavish of his promise of distinction.'[8] In combination with Captain Ryan, a quarrelsome man prone to drink, bitter quarrels between the two were inevitable. Conflicts among the passengers were daily occurrences on board and there were several duels, '… the captain, mad and drunk as his passengers, raged at them.'[9] At one point Captain Ryan almost threw the ship's papers overboard during a drunken altercation with MacDonald. It was a miserable, crowded ship tossed about in foul weather with meagre quantities of rancid, worm-eaten food. One of the passengers wrote a letter home describing the voyage as a comedy of errors.[10]

Throughout his book *Campaigns and Cruises*, Vowell displayed consistently a stoic attitude towards personal hardships and, characteristically, did not mention incidents of strife that others brooded upon in detail. In his typical, understated style he summed up the voyage thus:

> 'Suffice it is to say, that the usual average number of quarrels took place, as might have been expected, among a party consisting, chiefly, of inexperienced, hot-headed youths, who now, for the first time, wrote themselves men. Many trifling misunderstandings, such as would have been explained away, "by virtue of an if", under any other circumstances, but those of feverish ennui under a vertical sun, were here brought to mortal arbitrament. One of the numerous duels ended fatally.'[11]

Foolishly, upon arriving at Madeira, MacDonald had his regiment alight in full gala uniform. The 1st Venezuelan Lancers' uniform was dark green with scarlet collar and cuff, ribbed with silver lace; the epaulettes had the rising sun of Venezuela; the shako was mounted with silver lace and gold cord surmounted with yellow and blue plumes. Then, and even today, uniforms were an important status symbol, and a military incentive. Costly, at 60 pounds each, officers were expected to foot the bill, the entire military kit including sabre, costing 200 guineas.[12] Notwithstanding splendid uniforms, the impression left in the island by the entire contingent of soldiers was less than gratifying due to the fact that all semblance of discipline was lost. There were nightly disturbances at the local taverns, wild horse races, and a duel in which, fortunately, no one was hurt. The British consul had to intervene on behalf of the '…unrestrained and uncontrollable licentiousness of these juvenile adventurers.'[13]

The 1st Venezuelan Lancers was the first of numerous regiments that Luis López Méndez organized to add to Simón Bolívar's forces. In London, there had been a good deal of competition among the commanding colonels of the several regiments raised by López Méndez to be the first to reach Bolívar.[14] MacDonald, eager to reach Bolívar first and so obtain a preferential position, departed hurriedly and well ahead of his fellow colonels, leaving the onerous task of finalizing his regiment to Colonel Gustavus Hippisley. The five ships that sailed later in the year, in December 1818, carrying the regiment, experienced a stream of misfortunes, storms, shortages, desertions and near mutinies. Hippisley commanded the 1st Venezuelan Hussars but left Bolívar's service shortly after arriving in Venezuela, demoralized at the lack of funds and equipment. Colonel Henry Wilson, who commanded the 2nd Venezuelan Hussars, was expelled within a year by Bolívar, accused of attempting to sow dissention and undermining his authority. Colonel William Hewitt commanded the 2nd Venezuelan Lancers, Colonel Peter Campbell commanded the Rifle Brigade and Colonel J.A. Gilmour commanded the Artillery Brigade, but this last formation was disbanded upon reaching the West Indies due to lack of equipment. Colonel Robert Skeene commanded the 1st Venezuelan Lancers (the regiment that had originally been assigned to MacDonald), but, tragically, its ship went down in a storm with all except five persons perishing. Vowell would have surely died also had he not sailed with MacDonald. It would be only one of the many strange circumstances of his life in which sheer good luck would intervene on his behalf.

On 26 September 1818, the *Two Friends* landed in St. Thomas, in the Windward Islands, at that time under Danish rule. By disembarking his regiment in full uniform, MacDonald raised suspicions and compounded them by announcing brazenly to the commandant of the island that he was commissioned by the Prince Regent to assist the Patriots in South America. The astonished but sharp Danish commandant asked for his credentials. Unable to comply, MacDonald simply avoided him thereafter. The presence of an armed contingent openly intent on overthrowing the Spanish Crown was a political problem for the Danish authorities as their island depended on Spanish possessions in the Caribbean, such as neighbouring Puerto Rico, for water and other provisions. The Danish authorities were further irritated because there was already a group of penniless, would-be volunteers for the Patriot forces that had arrived earlier in St. Thomas and, having nowhere to go, were practically vagabonds on the island. The Danish were not at all happy to see another such group on their doorstep, especially one that was armed and quarrelsome.

St. Thomas

From this eminence, Mama Chepita pointed out to the novice the enchanting scenery which it commanded, of both town and harbour, far below them. In the former, the flat roofs of the principal dwelling-houses, covered with white chunam, were contrasted with the picturesque palm and cabbage trees, and the dark coloured evergreens, which filled the surrounding gardens.
The calm unruffled bosom of the latter reflected a cloudless sky, and the tapering masts of the merchant vessels of different classes, which floated on it, with well-bleached sails hanging loose to dry, and the many coloured ensigns of their respective nations, drooping in the still morning air. Innumerable boats, and light canoes, were crossing it in all directions, scarcely dimpling the surface of the dark blue mirror over which they glided; while the wild sound of the conch-shell, blown in the foremost of a line of fishing piraguas, announced their return from a successful night's toil.

Vowell, *The Earthquake of Caracas,* 190-191

Vowell and his companions soon discovered to their dismay that, contrary to their expectations, there was no emissary from Bolívar to meet and guide them to the mainland. Added to this, they learned from the local inhabitants that Bolívar's forces were at a great disadvantage to the Spanish who controlled the mainland coast, the Patriots controlling only Margarita Island:[15] 'This intelligence came upon us like a clap of thunder, involving darkness and destruction of our golden day dreams, and prostrating in the dust all our brilliant anticipations.'[16] Some were deeply discouraged by the prejudicial reports against Bolívar and the people they sought to liberate: 'The mass of the population of the Spanish Main was described as yet unprepared by both habit and feelings for the enjoyment of rational liberty, and independence, [they were rendered] blind, bigoted, and infatuated, the ready victims of the priesthood and the instruments of designing men.'[17] Such prejudice was completely absent from

Vowell's outlook as he never mentions these allegations, nor was he discouraged by the absence of Bolívar's contact.

The volunteers were in a bind. Captain Ryan could not take them any further since his ship had been chartered only to St. Thomas and, in any case, their relationship with Ryan was such that they had lost all trust in him. So much so that most of MacDonald's officers left the ship for a French boarding house where Vowell, always attentive to good food, said that they fared sumptuously on turtle and iguanas.[18] They had no contact with Bolívar or means to rendezvous with him. Predictably, quarrels broke out amongst them. There was a duel in which one young man was killed and those involved had to go into hiding from the Danish authorities.[19] Meanwhile, Captain Ryan, again short of funds, avoided paying port duty by surreptitiously sailing off with about twenty of the officers on board, leaving Vowell and the rest of the passengers abandoned on land. Those twenty managed to return to Portsmouth. Of the stranded passengers of the *Two Friends*, two died on St. Thomas from fever, 24 remained with MacDonald, and the rest went to Trinidad.

MacDonald had letters of introduction addressed to generals Simón Bolívar, Santiago Mariño, and Sir Gregor MacGregor. During their stay at St. Thomas, Madam Marquesa de Tovar, a Patriotic Venezuelan, entertained MacDonald and his officers at her tropical evening soirées. She informed them that General MacGregor had recently taken Amelia Island, off the east coast of Florida, from the Spanish and suggested they go there to serve under him until they could reach their original destination on the mainland.

General Sir Gregor MacGregor was an eccentric Scottish adventurer who joined Bolívar in 1815 and made a real contribution to the Patriotic cause. However, he also engaged in making a profit by selling commissions in non-existent regiments to enable him to go off on independent expeditions not connected to Bolívar's plans.[20] Amelia Island had a strategic significance for the Patriots, who desired a port on the Florida peninsula that could serve as a safe haven to Patriots in Spanish-controlled Cuba, México, and Venezuela and also as a launching point for the liberation of mainland Florida from Spain. On 30 March 1817, Lino Clemente, a Patriot naval officer and agent of Bolívar in the United States,[21] instructed MacGregor, to occupy just such a port.[22] On 25 July MacGregor, with about sixty men, occupied Amelia Island on the Spanish-controlled coast of Florida, proclaimed it a republic, and established the small port of Fernandina as its capital. As expected, he encountered little resistance from its small garrison of about forty or fifty men.

MacDonald, with his twenty-four officers including Vowell, contracted a small schooner from the United States, *The Mary*, commanded by Captain Lane, to take them to Fernandina, in search of MacGregor. After two weeks, they arrived at the eastern coast of Florida. The Gulf Stream runs along this coast with a strong undercurrent, and it confused Lane to the extent that his vessel unknowingly entered the wrong river in a Spanish-controlled area. As Vowell recounts, having no pilot to help them over the sand bar, seven officers, including himself and MacDonald, keen to leave the confines of the ship, decided to take the jolly boat in themselves with only one sailor.[23]

Unfortunately, the surf was so heavy that the boat capsized half a mile from shore. Fortunately, all the men were able to swim, but they could not relaunch the jolly boat against such strong surf. To add to their predicament, their companions on *The Mary* presumed they had drowned or were captured and sailed away. They were stranded, again.

Struggling under a hot sun, on empty stomachs, they dragged the heavy boat ankle-deep in soft sand to calm water. They realized the precarious situation they were in, having landed in Spanish-controlled territory, wearing full uniform. Poignantly, Vowell recorded his thoughts at this time:

'We had before us the disheartening prospect of being imprisoned, perhaps for life, in a Spanish dungeon; all which places of confinement, and especially those in the South American colonies, are, I should suppose, the worst of any in the world. The further hardship also awaited us, in the event of our being taken, of being compelled to labour in irons at the public works; fortunate indeed if we escaped "*un petit pendement bien joli*" [escaping the scaffold], in the character of pirates taking in arms on the coast.'[24]

In later life, Vowell would discover that the South American prisons were not the worst – by far.

As fortune would have it, their small group encountered two black slaves from a nearby plantation who spoke English, the language of their master. The plantation owner, a Mr Fitzpatrick, was an Irishman who, delighted to meet his countrymen, hid them in his barn. Vowell, with his gourmet tastes, noted the food they were given as '… a hearty supper of fish, venison, wild turkeys and parrots which were sumptuous.'[25]

He also took time to sketch a fine view of the east coast of Florida.

It is, indeed, a perfect wilderness, where not a sound is to be heard, except occasionally the scream of a solitary waterfowl, disturbed in his fishing, or the slash of the small river porpoises, called 'toninos', as they gambol along in shoals. The banks of the numerous islands, formed by this labyrinth of creeks, are covered with mangrove trees, growing so close together as to render it extremely difficult to land. The branches of these trees, or rather shrubs, hang into the water, and give shelter to innumerable alligators and water snakes. Tree-oysters are found here in abundance, adhering firmly to the mangroves, on which they colonize, and multiply amazingly; although, as the tide falls, they are left suspended, at least half the day, out of their natural element. These oysters are very small, and are scarcely worth the trouble of opening. They form considerable masses, resembling masonry, as they attach themselves to each other by means of a firm white cement, which hardens like mortar. There are many old forts in the neighbourhood, built by the former inhabitants of this country, to protect them against the inroads of the Creek Indians. We saw several of this description, formed entirely of blocks cut from the masses of oysters.

Vowell, *Campaigns and Cruises*, 10–11

Vowell and his stranded fellow officers were guided to Fernandina and found it a chaotic place, full of smugglers, slave traders, pirates and privateers, its streets filled with liquor shops and dancing houses which '... kept the place in a continuous uproar.'[26] To their dismay, they learned that General MacGregor had left the very evening of their arrival. Whereas MacGregor was undoubtedly intrepid, he was not very judicious. His occupancy of Amelia Island was marked by superfluous activity and when he did attack the mainland, it resulted in the death of fifteen of his men and it had the effect of alerting the Spanish forces of his presence. His men subsequently became mutinous due to lack of payment and MacGregor decided to leave for Nassau, handing the command of the island to Louis Aury, a French officer who had briefly been in the service of Venezuela and who had arrived there with about 300 men.[27]

MacDonald and his men found MacGregor's abandoned forces completely demoralized and disorderly. Vowell describes Aury as being totally incompetent to govern such an island, exposed as it was to external attacks and riddled with conflict within. According to Vowell, Aury lacked the mental and physical energy to govern, not only because he was elderly and infirm, but also because of his distrust and jealousy of those now under his command, to the extent that he had his own guns spiked. This action was not so foolish to Vowell, as the garrison appeared to agree only on its expressed contempt and hatred for Aury and his men.

Vowell revealed that Aury offered to pass command of the island to MacDonald, '... but, from the specimen we had witnessed of the garrison's conduct, we begged leave to decline'[28] and resolved to seek out Bolívar as originally planned. By expressing himself in the plural, he implies that this was a decision that MacDonald took in consultation with his officers. Vowell further revealed that American naval officers who were in Fernandina informed them that negotiations were under way between the United States and Madrid to acquire the island, which prompted them to make their getaway as soon as possible. This they were able to do as, fortunately, they encountered *The Mary* in port and were happily reunited with their comrades.

Shortly after Vowell's departure from Amelia Island, Spanish forces tried to take it back but, having failed, retreated. This was the opportunity the United States took to take control of the island without directly attacking Spain.[29] The United States attacked the Patriots in December and, in view of its superior forces, Aury surrendered the island. The taking of Amelia Island was strategic for the United States, signalling the beginning of its control over the Seminoles in Florida and the takeover of the entire Florida peninsula, which had been previously under Spain's dominion.[30] While General MacGregor believed he had the approval of the United States for his incursion on the island, his biographer considers that he had been used as a stalking horse by the Americans who had long planned to take the Floridas from Spain, but had no wish to go to war with her: 'By encouraging the revolutionaries to use MacGregor in what seemed to be their interest, the State Department had actually been pursuing its own design, helping to plot an illegal occupation it could later use as the excuse to gain its first foothold in Florida.'[31]

Negotiations ensued between Spain and the United States over Florida and while these lasted, the United States declared itself neutral to the war of emancipation of the Spanish colonies, and would not recognize the new republics until it had sealed its business interest over Florida with Spain.[32] It was a questionable neutrality as American ships continuously ran the Patriots' blockade on the Orinoco River to supply arms to Spanish forces, despite formal neutrality. Simón Bolívar had little, if any, reason to trust the United States because of these incidences. Even when, in 1822, the US Secretary of State, John Quincy Adams, recognized the independence of the new South American states, he did a diplomatic pirouette wherein, at the same time, he also recognized Spain's right to its colonies: 'This recognition is not given to invalidate the rights of Spain, nor to impede the use of means that she is still willing to employ to keep those provinces within her dominions.'[33]

As for Vowell and his companions, they sailed into a severe gale, which damaged the ship and stranded them again, this time in Grenada.

CHAPTER FOUR

Terra Incognita

*'In none of the colonies of Spanish America was the struggle for emancipation
so stubborn, so heroic, and so tragical, as in Venezuela.'*

Bartolomé Mitre, Emancipation of South America, 1869

VOWELL and his companions, stranded in Grenada, learned that Simón Bolívar could be found up the Orinoco and were fortunate to locate a brig, *La Felicité*, in the service of Venezuela and bound for the great river. The French captain realized that Vowell and his companions could act as armed guards for his brig in the Spanish-controlled waters, so he eagerly gave them passage to Angostura, Bolívar's recently established capital on the banks of the Orinoco. The mouth of the Orinoco was patrolled by the royalist coast guard led by the dreaded Spanish commander Juan Gabazo, who had recently captured and butchered the chief mate of the *Two Friends* when he and his men were attempting to enter the river in an open boat. With such chilling news, enveloped in heat vapours, and with considerable trepidation since neither the passengers nor crew of *La Felicité* had previously entered the river, they sailed towards the treacherous and enormous entrance of the Delta which spanned 24,522 square kilometres with more than 300 channels, most of them not navigable. It was an extraordinary feat of navigation as they relied solely on soundings and had to keep a sharp lookout for shoals and numerous large tree trunks embedded in the mud.

The great Orinoco, a name given by the Tamanaco Indians meaning 'the curled snake', is among the world's largest river systems and is the third largest in South America. Its length is estimated to be 2,140 kilometres and its huge river basin covers about 880,000 square kilometres, which includes more than 500 rivers. It has been the home of over a dozen native tribes and the inspiration to many legends and mysteries. It was in the year 1500 that the first European saw the river.[1] Immediately after, European adventurers persisted in believing it to be the gateway to the mythical city of El Dorado. It is one of the most impressive ecological areas of the continent that has inspired a plethora of writers including among others, Walter Raleigh, Alexander von Humboldt, Pablo Neruda, and Alejo Carpentier. Although the renowned scientific traveller and geographer, Alexander von Humboldt (1769-1859) had explored half of the Orinoco a few years before, in 1818 most Europeans had little or no knowledge of the area, let alone direct experience of it. Its origins were only discovered in 1951 and, even today, the great river has never been quite tamed by urbanization.[2] The adventure for Vowell and his companions was doubly so: not only were they journeying towards war – but in unknown territory.

Vowell was dazzled by the pristine flora and fauna of the Orinoco as seen from *La Felicité*. He describes the howling of the *araguato*, the large red monkeys that roam in herds from tree to tree, as being so loud that Englishmen believed the noise came from tigers. He marvelled at the splendid plumage of parrots, macaws, toucans, darra or bell-birds, as well as pelicans, spoonbills and gigantic cranes.

The scenery in this part of the river is strikingly beautiful; and when viewed from a ship's deck, as she glides slowly along the smooth water, presents a magnificent moving panorama. The banks, on each side, are covered with impervious forests of majestic trees; chained, as it were, to each other by the bejuco, or gigantic creeping plant of South America, which grows to the thickness of an ordinary cable. These ancient trees, when decayed through length of years, (for the axe of the woodsman has never yet resounded in these wilds), are supported upright by these enormous plants, which bear a striking resemblance to the huge water snakes that lurk in the swamps beneath. There are many other parasitical plants, which bear flowers of various brilliant colours, forming festoons on the trees to which they cling… When to this is added the occasional appearance of that tyrant of the stream, the alligator, floating in conscious superiority among the bulky manatis, and the blowing in shoals, the scene altogether may be imagined, but cannot be adequately described.

Vowell, *Campaigns and Cruises*, 19

As they sailed the Orinoco, Vowell and his companions had no idea of the type of army that they were rushing to join. The patriot army was not tightly organized. It was composed of separate forces led by a number of military leaders who did not necessarily act under the rigid military rules expected in a formal European army. The lines of communication between them, essential to any army, were difficult to maintain in such harsh and vast terrains with few roads. They were also poorly armed and clothed. Nor, in 1817, was Bolívar's authority secure; his political power was being contested and challenged, whereas most contemporary leaders held sway over their own men and over territory with which they were most familiar. Vowell soon became aware of this situation: 'At this period, every general in the Venezuelan service had a separate army, and a guard of honour which was entirely under his orders, and would acknowledge no other authority, but his.'[3]

The one thing the patriot leaders shared was the collective desire to rid the country of Spanish rule which had become more tyrannical as the insurgency advanced.

The Spanish authorities, under the command of General Pablo Morillo in Nueva Granada and the Captain General Salvador de Moxó in Venezuela, had committed barbarous cruelties to such an extent that angered many royalists. There were reports of abuses in British newspapers, such as contained in a letter in the Jamaican *Morning Chronicle* of 24 January 1817 which reported:

'Since the arrival of Morillo, such numbers have died on the scaffold and battle, that the face of the population is completely changed. Everyone who could write or read has been held in the light of criminals… detachments of a thousand men enter the defenceless towns, bear away the inhabitants to mend the roads, and a miserable ration is all they are allowed to subsist on… Numbers die through this cruel treatment. Even the aged are not free from outrage and vengeance.'[4]

In 1817 the Patriots were really on the run as the royalists controlled all the main cities, all the forts, almost the entire coast, and the richest and most populated part of the interior of the country.[5] To wage a successful war, Simón Bolívar needed to consolidate Patriot forces in one strategic command, and that could only be done through persuasion of key leaders, and this he worked at most assiduously. Bolívar was the one Patriot leader who went beyond parochialisms. Having a strategic understanding of what was needed to gain the independence of South America, '… he towered above his class in knowledge, judgment and ability.'[6]

Needing a safe haven and a recognizable headquarters, one of his most sound military decisions was to campaign for the control of Guayana, a large area in the south-east of Venezuela that includes a good part of the Orinoco River, and which sheltered abundant horses for cavalry and cattle for food. This was a new and visionary strategy on the part of Bolívar – to base the revolution deep in the hinterland, among the great plains, and in the impenetrable vastness of their wide rivers and malarial swamps, a great barrier against defeat, a springboard for attack and a source of wealth in their rich reserves of livestock.[7] The Orinoco River would then become the main communication route, and to accomplish this the Patriots had to take the two main cities on the river: Guayana la Vieja and Angostura. Among the leaders whom Bolívar counted upon were Generals Manuel Piar and Manuel Cedeño.[8] In January 1817, Piar gained control of the missions, the Indigenous settlements on the Caroní River run by Christian friars, which were main sources of food and supplies for the royalist forces. Bolívar also counted on a small gunboat navy led by Admiral Luís Brión.[9] Originally from Curacao, he was wealthy, educated, Jewish and a loyal patriot who became a Venezuelan citizen in 1814, and proclaimed, 'I have become a Venezuelan citizen, adopting this country as my homeland for whose cause I want to live and die.'[10] In July and August of that year, Bolívar, with General José Bermudez,[11] the patriot leader of the north-eastern part of Venezuela, at the head of the troops and with Admiral Luís Brión and his gunboat squadron on the river, took both Guayana la Vieja and Angostura. Bolívar was prompted to declare, 'We are masters of the Orinoco.'[12]

Vowell's first landing on the mainland was at the Indigenous village of Sacopano. This was his first encounter with aboriginal people to whom he displayed henceforth remarkable acceptance and interest. Sacopano was one of twenty to thirty Christian settlements, or missions, which Capuchins and Franciscan friars had established in the countryside. Each mission had an elected mayor, a communal economy based on agriculture and handicrafts, with equal distribution of goods, and an annual tax paid to the patriot government at Angostura.[13] Vowell describes the settlement in some detail with implied approval. However, many missions were unproductive due to the ravages of smallpox, which had depopulated entire districts in Guayana. War also affected the settlements. According to Vowell, Bolívar had been driven by necessity to banish or even shoot some of the Spanish friars who insisted on preaching to the indigenous people the divine right of Ferdinand VII.[14] This was also the case in Caracas, where Capuchin and Franciscan friars – as opposed to ordinary parish priests – were decidedly against the Patriots since they were Spanish, not Creole. In Vowell's historical fiction, *Earthquake of Caracas*, he refers to inflammatory harangues with which the seditious Spanish friars of the capital incited the frightened mobs against the Patriots which, in turn, prompted Bolívar to strike a friar with the flat side of his sabre, and consequently he was forced to flee from the enraged populace.[15] However, in Guayana, once the monastic rule was removed, the Indigenous people in the missions took up the cause of independence and they became good suppliers of resources for the Patriots.[16] It was these liberated, patriotic missions that Vowell encountered.

Vowell's attitude to native peoples is synchronized with his times; that is, as people supposedly being outside of 'civilization', but Vowell was more complex in that he questioned the racist ideology of his time, having simultaneously a critical attitude towards what passed as 'civilization'. This was the basic tenet of colonialism – that the subjugated people were 'barbarians' and had to be 'civilized' with the values of the conquering people. He comments that the settlement natives had been 'civilized' by the missionaries and he distinguishes these from the 'wild or uncivilized Indians' who lived on the Orinoco.[17] He reveals his Anglican background, as well as his upbringing within the framework of the Enlightenment, when he expresses reserve towards Catholicism and a belief in human progress: 'As for their religious improvement, it is much to be feared that it is entirely confined to the observances of the ceremonies enjoined them by their Roman Catholic instructors. To these, it is true, they strictly attend; but the missionaries themselves cannot boast of any farther religious progress.'[18]

However, when in going aground upon a river shoal, they once encountered non-settlement natives, Vowell was impressed by their conduct. He noted that the Indigenous men behaved with the greatest propriety, never touching their possessions although very curious about them, cheerfully helped them push their boat off the shoal and he noted that they simply wished to trade fish and wild fruits with them. There was no presumption of their inferiority. Vowell wrote, 'They were fine looking, tall, muscular men; apparently very mild in their manners. Their long coarse hair hung down, nearly combed, so as to cover their shoulders; and their bodies were almost entirely naked.'[19] As well, in *The Savannas of Barinas*, Vowell displays deep sympathy towards aboriginal people as he tells a poignant story of the wife of a Tamanaco chief, Ancáfila, who tries to rescue her infant son from 'the power of those by whom the religion of their ancestors was considered a crime' – missionaries, who had kidnapped him. [20] Indeed, Vowell states that the Spanish purposefully killed the aboriginal inhabitants of the Caribbean islands and the mainland, using ferocious dogs, in order to bring about the supposed 'blessings' of civilization:[21] 'The numerous tribes of aboriginal inhabitants were, indeed, so effectually exterminated by this and other methods of wholesale butchery, that the wild beasts of the forest rapidly increased, as the race of native hunters became extinct.'[22]

Vowell was not wrong. One of the central aims of the Spanish Conquest and Colonization was the eradication of the languages, cultures and religions of the original peoples. The colonial historian, José de Oviedo y Baños, referring to the Province of Venezuela, expressed satisfaction that the indigenous cults had been exterminated.[23] The extent of the Spanish genocide against the original peoples of Latin America and the Caribbean has been extensively examined and we now know that thousands upon thousands of women were raped and many were killed by being thrown to ferocious dogs.[24] There is an especially horrifying incident recorded in the Aztec Law book, Códice Tudela, at the Museum of the Americas in Madrid, which tells how after Cortes's systematic destruction of Tenochtitlán, four Aztec wise men came to give themselves up, carrying with them the learned books of their people; they were thrown to the dogs, and their books lost to history, and only one of the men escaped.[25] Again, Vowell does not exaggerate as history has recorded that Christopher Columbus himself directed the massacre of the Taina (Arawak) original peoples of Haiti with a small detachment of cavalry, 200 soldiers and trained dogs, and massacred the original population of that island.[26]

Vowell and his fellow officers had the first clue of the type of war in which they would be involved when they arrived at the first town on the river, Guayana la Vieja. It was a small, unprepossessing town, yet Vowell was aware of its strategic location on an elevation at the bend of the river, an important post that could supply cattle and refreshments to the gunboats. He and his companions visited the former Spanish garrison, where the royalist troops, three hundred strong, had refused to surrender to the Patriots despite inevitable defeat. Upon seeing their remains still lying unburied around their abandoned fort, he wrote that it '…gave us the first specimen of the horrors of Guerra a la Muerte.' Here, he is referring to the proclamation of 'War to the Death' as issued by Simón Bolívar on 8 June 1813. According to Bolívar's Irish aide-de-camp, General Daniel Florencio O'Leary,[27] Bolívar received daily reports of savagely cruel murders committed by Spanish officers in different parts of Venezuela. Disgusted by such reports of cruelty and injustice on the part of the royalist commanders towards Patriot prisoners and civilians, Simón Bolívar issued his ominous proclamation. It stated that, from then on, he would wage a war of extermination towards those who fought against the Patriots.[28] The warning was directed not only to the royalist army but also to civilians, since many of them had switched sides at different times during the struggles. It is controversial even today, and Vowell records clearly that the English volunteers lamented this kind of war of attrition that was waged on both sides of the conflict.

The inhabitants of Guayana la Vieja warmly greeted and feted the volunteers being as they were, among the very first Englishmen who had come to join Bolívar's army – certainly the first the town had met. Its governor, the father of Bolívar's most able and celebrated future officers, Field Marshal Antonio José de Sucre, gave a ball in their honour and Vowell described it in great detail:

> 'Not only was every room in his house crowded, but the doors and windows were thronged with natives of all classes, and of every intermediate shade of complexion, between the so-distant white creole, and the coast-of-Guinea negro; a great majority being rather of the darker casts.'[29]

The entire event was an eye-opening experience for Vowell, as it was his first encounter with a very different culture from his own: the music, played with rustic musical instruments, was cacophonous to the ear, the songs seemingly shouted instead of sung,[30] and the dances – Babuco, Zjudian, Marri-Marri – were all very different from any dances he had ever seen before. Vowell saw maracas for the first time – 'rattles made of hollow calabashes containing some grains of maize.' The Englishmen danced readily with the ladies, ate the food, and were feted with shouts of '*Viva los Ingleses!*'[31] The volunteers made a good impression on the Venezuelans because, apparently, Spanish officers had been more fastidious and had not joined the local pleasantries. Vowell's description of the feast is highly amusing and in it he admits that they were happy to escape from 'this scene of confusion' to sleep on soft grass hammocks under the corridors of the Governor's house.[32]

We were as yet unused to breathe the atmosphere of tobacco smoke that invariably fills these ball rooms; every individual having, on these occasions, either a cigar or churumbela [pipe] in his or her mouth, which they do not think of laying aside, even while dancing. It is indeed, considered a compliment, to be presented by a lady with a cigar that she has half smoked; and it would be an unpardonable affront to refuse it... We were warned to beware of refusing anything offered us; and, in compliance with the fashion of the place, persevered most politely, in spite of fatigue, heat, and a total disinclination to a hot meat supper in this climate.

Vowell, *Campaigns and Cruises*, 26

The next day, the Governor provided them with launches, swifter than the brig, to proceed with their journey. They reached Santo Tomás de Angostura without further incidents.[33] It was a small city, 250 miles from the Orinoco Delta, and was the newly established headquarters of the Patriot government and forces. Its name appropriately means narrowness, as it is located at a stretch of the river no more than two miles wide with very turbulent waters at that point.[34] With a population of about 5,000, it was built on a rocky elevation on the south bank of the river with a fort at its highest point. Attentive as he was to his surroundings, Vowell notes, 'The views from this fort are beautiful, in whatever direction they are seen'.[35]

> *Some idea may be formed of the immense body of water that the Orinoco disembogues, by the fact of its rising, at the Angosturas, upwards of ninety feet above its usual level; and that the stream runs there, in the centre, at the rate of about eight miles an hour. The low country, on both sides, is overflowed at this time for many leagues from the banks, giving the Savannas the appearance of an inland sea. The wild cattle and horses, which abound in these plains, are driven by the flood from their accustomed pastures, to the higher ground, to sleep and rest.*
>
> Vowell, *Campaigns and Cruises*, 29

Vowell described Santo Tomás de Angostura with great detail. There were pleasant shady walks or promenades in the city whose streets ran parallel to the river and uphill. There was a main plaza with a shell of a cathedral, a one storey, spacious, brick building that served both as home to the Congress and to the Governor, General Santiago Mariño,[36] the barrack, a jail and next to it, a small chapel which was the only place of worship in the city. Most houses were typical of that tropical climate, made of bamboo and mud, while those of the more well-to-do were made of stone or brick, with flat, red-tiled roofs, and handsome balconies and verandas. Not far out of town was a hospital, and the burial grounds were on the very top of the hill.[37] Infectious diseases such as smallpox and yellow fever were endemic and Vowell attributed this to a nearby lagoon that he believed ought to be drained. This would not be the first time that Vowell would come face-to-face with infectious diseases while serving in South America. Food was not plentiful – except for beef – nor was it varied as the war had ruined agriculture; farmers had no incentive to plant when they expected their crops to be either taken by one side or other in the conflict, or even burned, and the overgrown fields near Angostura were littered with dried human bones.

The taking of Angostura became a turning point of the War for Independence. It helped Simón Bolívar consolidate his command over the patriot forces so that he could start his greatest campaign. By designating it the capital, he gave the patriot government of Venezuela a tangible form, a fixed anchor after four months of fighting and moving from bivouac to bivouac. The Orinoco became their communication route towards the interior, and Angostura became a viable port for goods and people. Another of Bolívar's most far-reaching acts was to buy a printing press, bring it to Angostura, and start a patriot newspaper, *El Correo del Orinoco*. It disseminated not only news of the war, but also kept alive a crucial political discourse with contribution to its columns by many distinguished intellectuals.[38] Angostura became a symbol of all that the Patriots fought for, the veritable centre of their cause of freedom and considered by them as a tropical Athens. As one writer comments: 'All the elements of the Spanish American drama were assembled in the little town with its simple architecture, the surrounding tropical jungle laced by the swirling currents of the Orinoco and Apure rivers. In this environment, only the hardy could survive. There was no pampering of the flesh.'[39]

On a number of occasions in *Campaigns and Cruises*, Vowell refers to events he did not witness. He assures the reader that his narrative can be relied on for authenticity for he relates only facts either that he could vouch for from his personal knowledge, or that had been obtained from unquestionable sources of information in the countries through which he travelled.[40] Two such events occurred in Angostura: an assassination attempt on Bolívar, and the execution of General Manuel Piar. Vowell relates that Bolívar had received word that a group of royalist women of Angostura would set out to stab him on a Sunday, after Mass, which he always attended with only one aide-de-camp, and was further warned not to trust the palace guard. Consequently, he fled to a nearby plantation guarded only by a handful of British soldiers led by Captain Raymond Edgar,[41] who had recently volunteered; from there Bolívar moved to Barcelona, a town on the northern coast. Undoubtedly, it would have been an embarrassing and difficult moment for him: if he stayed he could not, with honour, fight a group of women, nor could he imprison them without enraging the citizens – so he fled. To make matters worse, he had to rely solely on a few, new, English officers for his safety. This is noteworthy because it was recorded for history only by two people – Vowell and Dr John Robertson, a Canadian physician in Bolívar's army, and both of them were among the very first volunteers to arrive.[42]

The execution of General Manuel Piar is an event that to this day is controversial and still debated among historians.[43] It was a crucial time for Bolívar as he was facing challenges to his authority from Generals Piar, Bermúdez, and Mariño, each one acting individually. Bolívar realized that the lack of unity under a single command was the most serious threat to the cause of independence. Some historians think that Piar's insubordination was due to his desire for power; he resented Bolívar's order to allow Bermúdez to take Angostura, but more seriously, he threatened to start a conflict along racial lines. Piar, son of a Curacao mulatto woman and a Spanish merchant marine, began inciting the patriot troops about power for people of mixed races, or *pardos*.[44] Others believe his execution was a stain on Bolívar's record, that he made an example of Piar in order to impose discipline on his generals. It is probable that this affair embraced all of these aspects.

Vowell's version of events, gathered from the native officers and soldiers around him who witnessed it, was distorted and not reflected in the historical documents from the time or in eyewitness accounts. Vowell contended that Piar, who had a following of blacks, was a victim of jealousy, being the only general of colour among the Patriots, and that he was falsely accused of wanting to establish a black republic by killing whites. Vowell rarely expresses strong judgments, but in this case, curiously, he does not fault Bolívar for punishing insubordination, but rather faults General Manuel Cedeño's role in the affair, who was ordered by Bolívar to arrest Piar.[45] According to Vowell, Cedeño persuaded Piar to come unattended by his own guards to meet Bolívar, but upon arrival at Angostura, Piar discovered that instead of Bolívar, it was General Santiago Mariño, one of his most inveterate enemies, who was in charge of the court martial, which ended in Piar being executed on 15 October 1817. Vowell felt that the ruse was extremely dishonourable, particularly because Cedeño was Piar's *compadre* – that is, he was godparent to one of his children, and thus a sacred bond existed between them. Furthermore, Vowell labelled Cedeño a wretch because he was told that he once abused a Spanish officer, giving him a horse to escape, only to lance him in cold blood minutes later, and asserted, wrongly, that this incident was attributed to General Páez. However, this story appears particularly out of character for Cedeño because the historical record does not reveal him as a cruel or merciless man; on the contrary, he is depicted as a brave and loyal soldier, committed early on to the patriot cause, and was not despised in any way. Furthermore, Piar was not handed over to Mariño, as Bolívar was fully in charge at Angostura. In fact, Mariño himself was in rebellion against Bolívar at this time. Some historians believe the treatment of Piar was Bolívar's way of signalling to Mariño that he would brook no disobedience, since Mariño was also guilty of disobeying orders.

It is more than likely that the execution of Piar was such a disturbing event that the Patriot army was still reeling from its impact and, not wanting to seem disloyal to Bolívar, nor supporting insubordination, the discontentment of the officers and troops fell upon Cedeño, not for following orders, but for tricking Piar. Vowell's narration of these events – whether he got the facts right or not – reveals two features of his own character: his distaste for behaviour that he believed was dishonourable to an officer or to a family bond, such as betrayal, and strong dismay at incidents of wanton cruelty – even in war.

It is also clear that Vowell did not have all the threads of this complex incident before him. Piar's conduct indeed undermined Bolívar's authority among the troops since he had refused to obey Bolívar's orders. Bolívar feared that Piar's insubordination, unlike that of other generals, was extremely dangerous since it could lead to a civil war along racial lines, which would be a death blow to the Patriots' cause. Simón Bolívar knew, as no other before him did, that independence could not be a project of the '*mantuanos*', that is the white, upper class Creoles, the men of property, of one single social class, but that it had to be a profoundly inclusive task in which the diverse social sectors could see themselves reflected, and that it would coincide with their shared desire to liberate themselves from foreign domination. Bolívar understood that independence had to be a democratic project, despite the differences in class and race, and it had to be above the class struggle. Ironically, Piar was denouncing racism just as the Patriots were already granting equality to non-whites, such as Piar himself. As well, Piar was condemned, not by Mariño, who was not even there, but by a full court martial formed by eight top Patriot leaders, one who acted as his defender.[46] Piar was shot against the western wall of the cathedral in Angostura and it is said that Bolívar, upon hearing the shot moaned, 'I have spilled my own blood.' The impact of Piar's execution had the immediate effect of consolidating Bolívar's authority and putting a stop to other would-be insubordinates, particularly Mariño, who had been as rebellious as Piar.

The British volunteers were pleased to leave the heat of Angostura behind, and proceeded up the river with the Venezuelan troops in a small fleet of gun boats, launches and dugout canoes called *flecheras* ('shaped like arrows'), manned by twelve or more indigenous men. General Rafael Urdaneta was in charge of their expedition. About six years older than Vowell, of aristocratic birth and a well-educated man, Urdaneta had military training, and was one of Bolívar's most trusted generals.[47] Their destination were the *Llanos* near the river Apure where they would join the patriot cavalry led by General José Antonio Páez, renowned leader of the plains horsemen or *Llaneros*. Then, together, they would ride north to meet Bolívar and the rest of the army.

As they continued their voyage into the heart of the tropical plains, Vowell was entranced sufficiently by everything he saw to record it in writing. He detailed the unbelievably dangerous and rocky rapids, which obliged the group to pull its launches upstream with tow ropes. He described the evening campsites on sand banks, and the eating of delicious meals of fish and turtle provided by the indigenous people. He wrote about cheerful music around a campfire; it seemed to Vowell that most of the Venezuelans were natural musicians and singers. He noted the behaviour of the turtles, alligators, fish, electric eel, and the extraordinary manatee, and described the awful swarms of mosquitoes and other biting insects – gnats, sand flies, and ticks, nigua, jiggers – that tormented them.

The British, particularly, suffered from insect bites because they did not know how to properly care for the sores these left. Some of these insects burrowed into the skin to lay eggs and the sore they left led to gangrene.[48] What Vowell thought were mosquitoes were, in fact, *tábano*, a more vicious variety.

> [The mosquito] *This nightly tormentor is really a serious annoyance: and continues its attacks, without intermission, until the morning… another method* [to avoid them] *is to retire quietly, about a hundred yards from any company, and to lie down in silence. This expedient succeeds very well, but is not a very advisable experiment in bivouacs on the Orinoco, for apprehension of a panther lurking near, or of a visit from an alligator, or a water snake during the night. When the zancudo* [Mosquito] *retires, the diminutive sand fly begins its attacks, from which there is no chance of a respite during the day. A small spot is left by it at every puncture, remaining visible a considerable time, and causing great inflammation and swelling on the ankles and wrists, on which it principally settles.*
>
> Vowell, *Campaigns and Cruises*, 42-43

The alligators, Vowell observed, were enormous and abundant.[49] Not long after he had the horrifying experience of seeing one of his companions eaten by one of these creatures. It happened as Vowell and two Venezuelan officers, brothers, were carrying a dispatch to General Páez. One of the brothers took too long to cross the river and '…this dreadful scene, which passed before our eyes, without the least possibility of our rendering any assistance, terminated by the alligator, having previously drowned the unfortunate man, appearing on an opposite sand bank with the body, and there devouring it.'[50]

Few objects appear so truly farouche [wild] as a group of large alligators feasting on a horse while floating down the stream. The violence with which they tear off whole limbs, and the noise their tusks make, when they close their vast jaws in the act of chewing, are indescribable.

Vowell, *Campaigns and Cruises,* 53

Stark evidence of the war appeared in the form of the abandoned villages that they passed along the banks. Vowell called them a '…melancholy monument of the war of destruction and extermination carried on by the Spaniards'.[51] He refers to the royalist commanders, Bóvez and Yanes, as bloodhounds in human shape, and called the Spanish commander, Pablo Morillo, sanguinary, dismissing them all as merciless banditti. He faults them not only for their wanton destruction of defenceless villages, but also for their '…execrable plan of arming the slaves against their masters for avowed purpose of having under their command a set of miscreants, whose natural ferocity was inflamed by the desire of revenge for real or imaginary injuries.' Vowell thus distinguishes between fighting for political freedom and merely fighting for personal revenge, and again expresses his distaste for cruelty. Obviously, he had a strong sense of the rules of war: he accepted the harsh discipline (for example, execution for insubordination), but considered that fighting could only be honourable if it was between soldiers, not civilians, and that soldiers' arms should not be used for cruelty or human passions.

They had yet another danger to be aware of: river pirates. The river was home to fresh water pirates who made it extremely dangerous for lone boats to travel along the Orinoco. In his *The Savannas of Varinas,* Vowell mentions a local commenting that, 'Every stranger on the river is an enemy'.[52] This was soon made painfully clear to him and his companions. Colonel MacDonald, feeling cramped in his boat and wanting to shoot wild fowl, decided to board a merchant boat in the village of Caycara, taking with him only one young Coronet from his regiment. His boat became separated from the armed launches of the little fleet and was attacked by the river pirates. MacDonald killed three of four of them, but in the end was overpowered. All aboard were murdered except a boy who escaped by diving into the river. He managed to meet up with the Patriots fifteen days later at San Juan de Payara, where General Páez was quartered. Vowell referred to MacDonald as an active, vigorous man, in the prime of his life and obviously lamented his fate. Soon after, the pirates were caught having in their possession the special sabre that MacDonald was to present as a gift to Bolívar. General Páez ordered that they be blown from the muzzles of 18-pounder guns at the fort of San Fernando. Thus, the British volunteers got their first glimpse of *Llanero* justice.

CHAPTER FIVE

First Battles

'The banner of imperious Spain,
Trampled on th' ensanguin'd plain,
Has seen thy flag of brilliant dies,
The Tricolor of freedom, rise'

Vowell's translation of the *Song of the Libertador*, from Campaigns, 344

VOWELL, his British companions and the Venezuelan troops of Generals Rafael Urdaneta and Manuel Cedeño, journeyed about 300 kilometres from Angostura to the immense plains of the Apure River, where Bolívar and the rest of the Patriot Army awaited. At Caujaral, they left the Orinoco and continued on horseback for the rest of the way through forest and plains, past the great Arauca River.[1] Their next stop would be the small town of San Juán de Payara and then, twelve leagues north, the city of San Fernando, under Royalist rule but under siege by the Patriots.[2]

> *Immediately on leaving the river Arauco, there is a thick belt of trees to be passed, consisting chiefly of guadua, or bamboo. The underwood, which is at first luxuriantly thick, decreases gradually as the savanna is approached. Previous to entering the extensive plains, still farther inland, the forest opens by degrees, and leaves large grassy glades, surrounded by clumps of trees, which appear to have been purposely planted there to diversify the scenery.*
>
> Vowell, *Campaigns and Cruises*, 58

They were travelling through the Venezuelan *llanos*, vast flat and wide expanses of land broken here and there by clumps of trees and palms. These savannas were very sparsely populated, but teeming with freely roaming wild horses, mules and cattle. The *Llaneros*, the men of the savannas and expert horsemen, were not so much cattlemen but, as Vowell remarked, hunters of the cattle.[3] The *Llaneros* rightly obtained a reputation for fierceness in battle but Vowell, with his keen curiosity, goes beyond war to observe them in their daily life where they displayed a proverbial mildness of manner, not due to any lack of spirit but, he believed, because they lived in harmony with their elders who expected respectful and sedate behaviour.

Llaneros had not always, nor uniformly, supported the Patriots, significant numbers having supported Royalist armies from time to time with disastrous consequences to the Patriots. The explosive arrival into the *llanos* of that formidable Royalist commander, General Pablo Morillo, drove many *Llaneros* to the Patriot forces, to be placed under the leadership of General José Antonio Páez who managed to unite them into a Patriot cavalry of about 1,000 men, along with 250 foot soldiers, who included Cunaviche indigenous people.[4]

General Páez, the charismatic leader of the forces that fought the Spaniards in the *llanos*, attracted many to his side by his fearlessness and successful guerrilla tactics.[5] He was a rough and ready man, with only elementary education, but he was a natural leader of men, knew his terrain expertly, and, like the *Llanero* that he was, was an outstanding horseman. He has been described as a man of Herculean strength, skilful in the use of lance and sword, kindly, generous of nature and of very superior intelligence.[6] However, Vowell points out that he was also impatient and had a violent temper.[7] All Patriot leaders had, by 1817, accepted Bolívar's pre-eminent authority, except Páez, who acted independently and, while he had not opposed Bolívar, neither had he explicitly accept his leadership.[8] So it was imperative for Bolívar to get him and his cavalry onside.

In the spring of 1817, Páez had sent word to Bolívar that he would join his army and it was only at the end of January 1818 that the two leaders met face-to-face, when Bolívar rode into Páez's camp at San Juán de Payara with only about forty men with him: 'Páez became at once the first general of cavalry in Americas. He was the bond between the *Llaneros* and the Patriots.'[9] Vowell also revealed that the relationship between Bolívar and Páez was such that the *Llanero* leader was the only Patriot general who would dare argue with Bolívar, but that also he was the only one to whom Bolívar would explain his plans. This demonstrates the need they had for each other at the time. In later years however, Páez would put an end to Bolívar's dream of a united Gran Colombia by supporting a separate Venezuela.[10]

Before 1817, the deep *llanos* of the Barinas[11] and Apure areas were a safe haven from the war since most of the revolution's battles until then had taken place roughly in the centre-north or coastal areas of the country. However, that year after Bolívar's forces had suffered painful defeats at the battles of La Puerta, Rincón de los Toros, and Ortíz, they looked towards the *llanos* for respite. Morillo and his troops followed and he did so with vengeance, burning to the ground all the isolated haciendas on the way, defended generally only by women or boys since most of the men had taken up arms. Vowell commented that, 'The inhabitants of the plains of Varinas will long remember the year 1818, as an epoch, during which the horrors invariably attending civil war, under any circumstances, were experienced by them with greater severity, than at any other period of the eventful revolution in Venezuela.'[12]

The *llanos* had a profound effect upon Vowell, not only in terms of its geography, but also its people and their customs and stories. It compelled him to write a historical novel based on the *llanos* of Barinas, *The Savannas of Varinas*. Essentially, this was a romantic love story that took place amidst the War for Independence in the *llanos*.[13] Vowell, in writing this historical fiction, must likely have taken inspiration not only from writers such as Chaucer, but also from the works of Sir Walter Scott that were then very recent publications.[14] Historians have recognized that Vowell's work described a least known period of Venezuelan history, sketching life in the *llanos* with sociological as well as psychological insight. He is referred to as a 'master storyteller' with an able literary technique of maintaining interest in a plot, never waning, of renovating his narrative constantly with a diversity of characters, action-packed battles and forgotten legends.[15]

> *Silvestre Gómez, and his eldest son Felipe, were at that moment absent from the farm; having joined Páez's celebrated* Guardia de Honor *some months before. The second son, a boy twelve years of age, who had been left at Merricuri to assist his mother, having previously caught and hastily saddled the few horses that happened to be grazing round the farm, rode full speed to the Patriot camp at Caujaral, to carry Páez intelligence of Morillo's successful manoeuvre. The mother, and the remainder of her family, fled towards the* hato [farm] *of their kinsman, Juan Gamarra, without having leisure to save a single article of property; except a few ponchos, or men's cloaks, in which the females and children were wrapped; and that treasure to a Llanero, the family guitar.*
>
> Vowell, *Savannas of Varinas*, 8

The *llanos* have two seasons, rainy and dry, and when the rains arrive from April/May to October/November, the flat, clay plains become a gigantic marsh, almost like a sea or lake in many places. In the 19th century, the floods would have made travel impossible.[16] This had implications for military decisions as any fighting had to be conducted in the dry season, from November to March; furthermore, the flooded areas also could serve as defensive barriers for headquarters when the rains came in.

The town of San Juán de Payara was built on a low sand hill and was just one of those places that during the floods would be surrounded by water and thus protected from any attack. It was a run-down sort of place, built of mud huts, and yet even of here, Vowell has something interesting to say. He observed how cattle, the key component of life in the *llanos*, provided hides that were used for almost every commodity: doors, roofs, saddles, stools, boxes, cradles, beds, pails, even bottles. Vowell, knowing the importance of clean water, was critical of the inhabitants for obtaining their water from a nearby stagnant lagoon rather than taking the time to go to a running stream not half a league away. Vowell had a particular interest in medicinal herbs and in conditions leading to health. While the germ theory of disease was yet unknown, he held the sound views of the sanitation movement, that cleanliness of the habitat led to good health.

In this town, he encountered a nomadic tribe, which he called the Guagivis.[17] Traditionally, the women stuck long thorns through their under lips, and several used common pins instead of thorns, so he gave a woman a few pins he happened to have on hand.

She immediately called to her a girl of about twelve years old, (apparently her daughter), who had not as yet been distinguished by this ornament; pierced her lip, with equal indifference and dexterity, with a sharp instrument made of an alligator's tooth; and placed the pins in the orifice. The poor girl bore this operation with great patience; and appeared to be perfectly consoled, by the possession of her newly acquired ornament, for the pain it must have given her. She ran directly, "With a smile on her lip, and a tear in her eye" to display it to her companions.

Vowell, *Campaigns and Cruises*, 60

After a few days, in the first week of February 1818, the army started its trek north towards San Fernando. As they set off, the British volunteers became the object of amusement for the Venezuelan troops because they could not control their horses, and there was nothing of which *Llaneros* thought more highly than horsemanship. These horses had never worn an English bit or saddle '...to the great disorder of the ranks and the undisguised merriment of the *Llaneros*.'[18] The Venezuelan soldiers, not knowing how to secure the English packsaddles, cursed the makers of such complicated harnesses and those who were foolish enough to bring them. Vowell wrote about this, not as a complaint, but with his wry sense of humour, unlike several other British volunteers who wrote complaining of just about everything they encountered when they got to Venezuela including the food, uniforms, pay, lack of comfort, the customs of the place and the army organization itself. They treated the lack of resources as a personal affront rather than the general, and unintentional, state of scarcity of the Patriot Army.[19] By comparison, Vowell, however, displays sheer pleasure out of the adventure he was living.

We arrived, about midnight, at the banks of a small stream, where the army bivouacked; and lay down to rest on the grass in our cloaks. In fine weather, their mode of passing the night is delightful. The line of fire gives an appearance of comfort to the rude camp, and is also no contemptible protection against wild beasts, as we found in more than one instance. Each fire is surrounded by a party that has agreed to mess together; and, after the simple culinary process of roasting the beef, which has been served out on spits cut from the nearest bush, the ample ration is speedily consumed, without any complaint of the want of plates or even of bread and salt. A cigar, then, or a churmbela, is a luxury, after which follow as much sounder sleep than is perhaps often enjoyed in a bed, and under shelter.

Vowell, *Campaigns and Cruises*, 62

They arrived at San Fernando, the only town of note in the *llanos*, situated on the banks of the Apure River and well protected by Royalist heavy artillery. The taking of this town by the Royalists was a woeful and alarming event for the *Llaneros* because the enemy had managed to penetrate deep into the country: 'A few among them has occasionally visited San Fernando, on the solemn festivals of the church… and had brought with them on their return to their farms, such exalted notions of its strength and importance, that the report of its destruction was considered almost incredible.'[20] Bolívar, rather than lead a risky direct attack on such fortifications, had left troops laying siege to the town, expecting that eventually the enemy would be compelled to abandon it for lack of resources, and he had proceeded north toward Calabozo.

It is at this point that Vowell learned of an extraordinary feat of Páez's *Llaneros* that had just taken place on 12 February 1818, the day or so before their arrival, on the outskirts of San Fernando. Bolívar, determined to go to Calabozo, needed to get his army across the Apure River, but had no means of doing so. Seeing that the Spanish had an assembly of 14 gunboats anchored nearby, Bolívar half jokingly asked Páez if there was a man brave enough to get hold of the launches for him. Accordingly, Páez called a few of his guards over and ordered, '*Into the water lads!*' The *Llaneros* were not only fearless horsemen but, also coming from this land of enormous rivers, excellent swimmers. About fifty of them unsaddled their horses, stripped to their drawers, slung their light swords round their necks and under one arm, and rode into the water, a quarter of a mile from the gunboats. Vowell was told that when the Royalists on board saw the approach of the dreaded *Llaneros*, who never gave quarter, they fired upon them but their aim was inaccurate. Then, in a panic, they abandoned their boats and the *Llaneros* quickly took possession of them. However, although the *Llaneros* were excellent horsemen, they were no sailors, and needed the help of soldiers from the coast – the *Margariteños* from Margarita Island[21] – to join them and bring the boats in. Vowell commented: 'By this manoeuvre, which is probably unparalleled in military tactics, Bolívar obtained the command of the Apure.'[22] In later years it was recognised that this was probably the first time in history that cavalry had skirmished against armed gunboats.[23]

It was on 11 February 1818, at the San Pablo Ranch on the road between Calabozo and Ortíz, that Vowell finally met the famous man whose cause he had come to fight for – Simón Bolívar: 'We had long wished to see this celebrated man, whose extraordinary energy and perseverance, under every disadvantage, have since effected the liberty of a large portion of South America'.[24] The description of this meeting in *Campaigns and Cruises* has been endlessly quoted and referred to by Latin American scholars, as it is full of vivid details of Bolívar and his officers. Noting that Bolívar's clothing was a good indicator of the lack of resources of the Patriot Army, Vowell writes that he wore a helmet of a private light dragoon, given to him by a merchant from Trinidad, a plain, round jacket of blue cloth with red cuffs and gilt buttons, blue trousers and native sandals called *alpargatas*. He carried a light lance with a small, black banner embroidered with a white skull and crossbones and the motto: *Muerte o Libertad!* (Liberty or Death!).

He was about 35, but looked upwards of 40; in stature short – perhaps five feet five or six, but well proportioned and remarkably active. His countenance, even then, was thin, and evidently care-worn, with an expression of patient endurance under adversity, which he has before and since, given ample evidence of possessing, however his fiery temper may at times have appeared to contradict the supposition.

Vowell, *Campaigns and Cruises*, 66

Bolívar was surrounded by his officers whom Vowell described as '… men of colour, of lighter or darker shade, except the two generals, Páez and Urdaneta, who were white.'[25] Their uniforms were also eclectic; few had jackets, and their shirts were made of handkerchiefs of different colours, often of chequered patterns, ample, wide sleeved and worn outside the trousers which came down below the knees. Though almost all were barefoot, nevertheless they wore large silver spurs, stirrups, and silver scabbards for their sabres. On their heads they wore local wide-brimmed palm hats decorated with colourful feathers and, under them, handkerchiefs to offer protection from the sun. Vowell made the curious observation that although the officers had dark skin, they could not withstand the severe heat as well as most of the Englishmen.

As Vowell and his companions approached, these '…wild looking chiefs spurred forward to meet us with a shrill shout of welcome and favoured us with a profusion of embraces as is their custom'.[26] We can only imagine the embarrassment these reticent Englishmen must have felt at being thus greeted by complete strangers who happened also to be their superior officers! Bolívar returned their salute, and rode by with what Vowell described as his peculiar melancholy smile, but later that evening they were summoned to his presence. It was customary for Bolívar to meet with people while he sat on a hammock, and that is how he received his new British officers, politely apologizing for the poor accommodation but admitting that he was very pleased to have Europeans who would discipline and train his troops by instruction and example. Vowell stated that Bolívar greatly impressed them with his knowledge of world affairs and his impeccable manners.

At the end of the meeting with Bolívar, the tired Englishmen wished to retire after such a long march in hot weather, but the Venezuelans kept them from their beds, admiring and inspecting all their arms and equipment and quizzing them as to why they had left their country to come to Venezuela. The Venezuelans could not quite believe that these English travellers and adventurers had journeyed half way across the world because they supported the Venezuelan people's struggle for liberty; rather, they speculated that perhaps it was a scarcity of cattle in their homeland or perhaps due to Spain and England being 'ancient and natural enemies' that had brought them here. In any case, their new comrades-in-arms, surprised that the Englishmen had no lances, which was de rigueur for the Venezuelans, promptly gave each British officer a lance and a horse. The Patriot cavalry was armed only with lances, while just 1,400 of the infantry carried rifles, the rest having to make do with bows and arrows.[27] The *Llaneros'* lance, a formidable weapon measuring almost three metres in length, was much longer than the Spanish lances. It was made of Alvarico Palm wood (*Onocarpus Cubarro*), which had some degree of flexibility but with points hardened by fire.[28] William Miller, another English volunteer who arrived later and went on to become a general, was greatly impressed by the *Llaneros'* use of the lance as well as their horsemanship. In his memoirs, Miller describes how they controlled their horses with their legs by tying the reins above their knees, which left their arms free to wield the lance. They could spear their enemies with such force at a gallop that they would lift their foe two or three feet above the saddle.[29] It was a simple, but terrifying, weapon.

Next morning, 12 February, the Patriot forces left at dawn for Calabozo, having marched about 160 kilometres in three days.[30] Vowell noted that Páez and his *Llanero* staff rode along with much laughter and that whenever Bolívar was with the army he would never fail to '… pause there for an hour or so on his way to the front, for the purpose of enjoying the unrestrained, but good-humoured sallies of the *Llaneros* and their leader.'[31]

Vowell described the town of Calabozo as '… the largest and most populous city in lower Venezuela. The mud wall, which surrounds it, was built as a defence against the incursions of the Cachiri Indians, before a revolution in the colonies was contemplated as a possible occurrence. It is neither lofty nor thick, but was formerly considered by the native inhabitants to be so strong, that they called the city Calabozo, or, the dungeon.'[32] Here it was that Vowell and his companions took part in their first military action. Morillo was in Calabozo and Bolívar intended to take him by surprise. There were about 2,000 Spanish troops in the city and Bolívar had 3,000 men of whom 2,000 were infantry.[33] Since the death of Colonel MacDonald had left them without a commanding officer, Bolívar incorporated the British officers into his Guard of Honour and placed them under the command of one of his aides, Colonel James Rooke, a distinguished British officer who had served at Waterloo.[34] In this capacity, they had to stay close to Bolívar as they marched into the plains towards Calabozo, where a troop of the Spanish cavalry was attempting to cross towards the Indigenous missions. General Páez was allowed to lead the attack; General José Antonio Anzoátegui had his infantrymen to the right, while the cavalry of General José Tadeo Monagas[35] covered the rearguard, and the carbineers of generals Cedeño and Rangel cut off the Spanish retreat. Soon the Spanish cavalry was surrounded '… and quarter being unknown at this period of the war, they were cut off to a man, nearly 600 in number. When we reached the spot, the half-naked Creole soldiers were busy clothing themselves with the sky blue and white uniforms of the unfortunate *Husares de la Reyna*.'[36] Vowell makes no further comment than this, but one can infer that this sight affected him.

That was not the end of the day's horrors. When Morillo's forces retired into the city, Bolívar sent a young officer and a trumpeter, under a flag of truce, to offer the Royalists permission to bury their dead and to see if they would surrender. To the great consternation of the Patriots, the officer was shot dead and the trumpeter wounded.

Bolívar had to promise his troops that they would attack next morning, so great was their indignation at this atrocity. However, Morillo surprised them by attacking them first, at dawn, and cutting to pieces part of Cedeño's infantry which had bivouacked near a river. Soon a full battle developed, and only ended when the heat of the day exhausted both sides.

It was during this action that Vowell describes an amusing incident that allowed them to witness one of the very few occasions when Bolívar laughed openly. It was due to a large Scot by the name of Peter Alexander Grant, who 'found it very dull to keep in close attendance on Bolívar[37] and so went by himself to reconnoitre near the city. Grant duly caught a prisoner – a Spanish soldier leading a mule loaded with liquor. The man threw himself at his feet and pleaded for mercy, claiming he was a musician and he produced a clarinet from his pocket. Meanwhile, the mule with its prize cargo strayed away. So Grant tied the man to a tree and ordered him not to stop playing, so that he could be sure that the fellow's hands were busy and not engaged in the act of untying himself, while he went to recover the mule.

At midnight, Bolívar ordered a full assault on Calabozo. It was not a moment too soon as Morillo had managed to evacuate half his army already. The Spanish rearguard went into disarray as the Patriots made their assault. Vowell noted: 'We had here a specimen of that most awkward of all fighting: by night, in the intricate streets of a city, with which we were not acquainted.'[38] Páez and his cavalry cut off the retreat of the Royalists at the northern gate of the city. Vowell states that about 800 surrendered, but a great number were bayoneted before Bolívar could impose order. However, the historical record states that the Royalists' losses amounted to 220 dead and 80 wounded.[39] The town was sacked even though the officers went around breaking liquor jars and wine skins, trying to get the men in line.

They were able to rest for an afternoon in Calabozo. The British quartered among the many inhabitants who clamoured to the Quartermaster General, Carlos Soublette, for the honour of giving the English officers hospitality.[40] But Vowell was not deceived by their outward friendliness because, being overwhelmingly Royalists, these people simply wanted to avoid the insults the native troops would have hurled at them. Captain J. Sherwood was left in command of Calabozo and they hurried on their way to the town of Rastro, chasing after Morillo.

Vowell did not give further details of the English involvement in the battle of Calabozo, even though this was the very first battle in which he would have taken part and it is known that Bolívar's Guard of Honour was outstanding during this battle, along with the other corps.[41] During his narrative, Vowell would remain silent about the details of battle itself and about any feelings it may have roused in him. It has been observed that there is a common reticence of soldiers to speak about their actions, a sort of implicit agreement to shield others from knowledge of particularly violent actions, an aesthetic reflex, or a civilized distaste for discussion of what might shock or disgust, and possibly in this case, a peculiarly English reticence.[42] Later, in 1831, Vowell would explain to the British press that he had accumulated copious notes during his campaigns; it is evident that these diaries were not meant for emotional outlet or introspection, but as a record and interpretation of the events and places he experienced.[43] In English society of the 19th century, such discretion and reticence with respect to feelings was expected of a gentleman and an officer. Latin American historians have admired and puzzled over Vowell because of his lack of hyperbole and his attempt to be as dispassionate as possible, but one can only wish that Vowell had lost something of his inhibitions and left more of a record of his feelings as well.

On the way to Rastro, an incident occurred which elicited from Vowell a staunch defence of Simón Bolívar. The *Guerra a Muerte* (War to the Death) was a suspension of the customary rules of war such as they were,[44] and the Patriots contended it was initiated by the Spanish cruelty towards prisoners to which Bolívar responded in kind with his own proclamation.[45] However, Bolívar understood that this state of affairs was abhorrent in the eyes of his British officers: 'One thing is certain, that he had made incessant endeavours to induce Morillo to consent to a change, or exchange of prisoners; but this haughty Spaniard invariably rejected his overtures as insults, and spurned all attempts at intercourse, on this and every other subject, as if it would have been contamination in a Royalist to treat with an insurgent.'[46] Morillo, Vowell relates, fired at all who appeared before him with a flag of truce be they women or priests. Bolívar, stated Vowell, '… though justly incensed, did not give up the cause of humanity'[47] and in good faith, sent the Spanish commander twelve Royalist officers and twenty soldiers who had been taken prisoner in Calabozo with a letter asking for an exchange. Vowell commented that the manner in which this appeal was answered, would scarcely be credited. On 15 February, about three miles from Rastro, the Patriots found the butchered bodies of twelve Patriot officers and twenty soldiers lying in neat rows across the road. In his restrained way, Vowell simply writes: 'Such conduct requires no comment.' However, he bears witness that had Bolívar not retaliated '… his own troops would have torn him to pieces.'[48] In the presence of his troops, Bolívar dictated an order to Captain Sherwood in Calabozo to immediately execute all prisoners.

Vowell does not at any time give his approval to this conduct, although he attempts to explain it: 'These indiscriminate massacres, which disgraced both parties, during the first struggle for independence in S. America, sound dreadful in civilized ears.' He also objected to the guerrilla tactics of Páez of setting fire to the dry grasses to oust Royalist troops, resulting in their suffocation or being blown up by their own cartages. Yet he urges that the Venezuelans should not be judged rigidly since it was the Royalists – the 'civilized Europeans' conduct' – who taught *Llaneros* cruelty by their example.[49]

Invariably every prisoner was massacred in cold blood; villages and farms were ravaged and burned; and every species of cruelty and insult, without compassion for sex or age, were practised upon an unresisting, and often on an unoffending population – cruelties that emulated those practised by the discoverers of the New World, and which could only have been perpetrated by those miscreants, who were sent from Spain, under the name of soldiers, picked out of jails and condemned regiments, purposely to be a scourge to the insubordinate colonies; and who were supported and encouraged in their excesses by such as Morillo, whose name is mentioned with execration, even by his own countrymen.

Vowell, *Campaigns and Cruises*, 130

The troops themselves urged Bolívar to continue the pursuit of Morillo, who by this time had reached the town of Sombrero, twelve leagues away. They had a punishing march that evening and the next day, stopping only sporadically for water, but the troops were determined to catch up with the Royalists. Exhausted, they reached Morillo's army near Sombrero on 16 February. Vowell wrote that the battle that ensued was sanguinary, but short, and that here the first foreign volunteers came across a common tragedy of war – a nameless grave.[50] It is not known how many volunteers were killed, but it is known that the Patriots lost about one hundred men, including three officers of Bolívar's high command.[51] It was an indecisive battle for both sides – and both sides suffered heavy losses.

Morillo abandoned Rastro and sped to Villa de Cura. Bolívar allowed his troops to rest and sent Páez and Cedeño back to Calabozo, thus he was short of cavalry as he headed towards hilly terrain. Vowell was aware that it was a tactic of Morillo to lure the Patriots away from the plains to where the their superior cavalry was at a disadvantage. They marched through a series of towns and found them all but abandoned until they reached the pretty town of Villa de Cura where Vowell and his British companions were quartered in a lovely house which seemed like a palace to them after so many rough bivouacs. They continued on towards Victoria[52] but before reaching this city, they stopped for a while at Bolívar's sugar plantation, San Mateo. Although Vowell states that he was received by a number of female slaves still living there, in fact, these were former slaves since Bolívar had freed all his slaves long before he outlawed slavery in Venezuela in 1816, years before this inhuman condition was abolished in Britain, France or the United States.[53]

The views from the road, between this town and the city of Victoria, are beautiful beyond description. We marched all day through noble plantations, on each side of the road; and enjoyed, from every hill, extensive prospects over the well-cultivated valley of Aragua. This part of the country is famous for producing the excellent cacao, exported from la Guayra, under the name of cacao de Caracas, which bears a high price in the Spanish market... The inhabitants of the city of Victoria, who had been well known during the whole war for their Patriotic principles, could not contain their joy at the arrival of their old friend and general, Bolívar, at the head of an army,

which, they fully assured themselves, would defeat the Spaniards, and put an end to the war.
They raised triumphal arches across the streets, in the fullness of their exultations.

Vowell, *Campaigns and Cruises*, 78–79

They enjoyed for a while merry fiestas and entertainment and basked in the hospitality of Patriotic La Victoria, but joy would too soon turn to panic.

CHAPTER SIX

A Ragtag Army

'Life resembles a novel more often than novels resemble life.'

George Sand

IN his pursuit of Morillo, Bolívar divided his forces, sending the Patriot cavalry of generals Zaraza[1] and Cedeño north-east to try to cut the Spanish lines of communication with their commanders, Morales and La Torre. He took the rest of the army, Vowell included, on towards Caracas, his target.

On 15 March 1818, they reached the village of Cocuiza, a day's march away from Caracas, the capital. They were arranged in line formation ready to attack Morillo's rearguard which was close by when they received urgent word from General Urdaneta himself, who rode in to deliver the news personally, that on the previous day the Spanish troops of Morales and La Torre had inflicted heavy losses on the Patriot cavalry; worse still, two Royalist generals were coming up from behind to block the Patriot retreat in the hilly terrain. Under threat of being surrounded, the Patriot Army quickly turned around and headed back to Victoria. They took the most direct mountain road – a road so dangerous that it was known as the 'Road of Death'. They rode all night under a dreadful storm with thunder and lightning.[2] They passed through Victoria, warning the townspeople who were, at that very moment, celebrating a ball. The news of the retreat was as a death sentence to the locals who stood to lose both their lives and their properties when the Spanish arrived. They chose to run from their homes, to escape with the Patriot Army.

It was a dark stormy night; and the condition of the unfortunate emigrants was wretched beyond description. Husbands, who had no time to take leave of their wives and families; and delicate females, some with infants at the breast, ignorant of the fate of their husbands and fathers, and without a friend to assist them, were mingled promiscuously with the troops and baggage mules, on mountain roads, in many places knee-deep in mud. Several had rushed out of the ballroom, on the first alarm, and had joined the retreat, without the possibility of obtaining shoes or clothing better suited to such weather, than those they wore on the festive occasion. Although most officers belonging to the army, who were possessed of a horse or mule, especially the British volunteers, gave it up readily to these unfortunate females, yet several were obliged to hurry along on foot, without shoes, or sufficient covering. Many dropped during the night through fatigue and exhaustion, and either perished from the inclemency of the weather, or still worse, fell into the hands of the merciless Spaniards, from whom they could only expect the most brutal treatment.

Vowell, *Campaigns and Cruises*, 82

They marched the whole of the next day and on the 17th Bolívar realized he had to take a stand or lose all. According to Vowell, the Patriot commander had no choice as to the terrain. In a valley called El Semen, so named after a little river that flowed there, and before a narrow, rocky path called La Puerta (after which the forthcoming battle would be known), the Patriot Army lined up to face the larger, well-equipped and immaculately uniformed Spanish army. In comparison, Vowell describes the Patriots as having a completely ragged appearance, looking more like a rabble than an army. Only Bolívar's guard wore anything that bore a resemblance to uniforms – and they wore defective mariners' coats that the army had managed to purchase from London.

The rest of the army wore, literally, what they could get. Some were to be seen, in every corps, with Spanish uniforms, either with or without broad brimmed straw hats; but these few were so far from improving the appearance of the line, that they made it resemble a rabble, and displayed to greater disadvantage the miserable clothing of their comrades. Many were nearly stark naked; but for the greater part, they wore small, ragged blankets, and pieces of carpet, which they had plundered on the retreat, with holes cut in them for their heads to pass through. Straw hats were in general use; but some colonels had partially introduced into their corps a kind of nondescript shakos, made of raw cow hides of various colours. The firearms too, of this devoted army, were all old, and generally speaking, in a very bad condition.

Vowell, *Campaigns and Cruises*, 83

The muskets were carried for show, since without locks they were useless; many just carried lances. The Indigenous warriors, whom Vowell said were a timid, peaceful tribe, unused to the sound of firearms, had bows and arrows. He was dismayed that the Venezuelan army had no musical instruments with which to motivate its men as they went into battle, 'But, to do the troops justice, they behaved, in spite of every disadvantage, as well as men could do; struggling for victory long after the battle was evidently lost.'[3]

Bolívar placed the British volunteers in twos and threes among the different corps. Vowell and his friend, Lieutenant Braithwaite, were attached to the *Los Barloventos* regiment, composed of free black soldiers, mostly raw recruits, from Cumaná in eastern Venezuela, although Vowell attests, that they were totally fearless. His commanding officer was likely to have been General Pedro León Torres who was head of two companies of the Barcelona Battalion (by today's standards, it may seem unusual for a general to have commanded two companies but, equally, the structure of the Patriot Army was not as a modern army of the time would have been).[4] Because his plainsmen did not want to risk their mounts in hilly terrain, Páez did not wish to follow Bolívar north and actually refused his orders. Thus Bolívar left Páez behind at Ortíz. Vowell comments that this, in the end, was fortunate, because Páez managed to save the retreating army from annihilation.

Bolívar, Rooke, and the entire Patriot high command reviewed the troops and gave them words of encouragement. Vowell reveals that in the face of battle, Bolívar put aside his silence and despondency, donned a light leopardskin cap, became highly animated, and seemed to be in the thick of it everywhere, making incredible efforts to win the battle. According to Vowell, Bolívar's favourite rallying cry in battle was '*Firmes, Cachiríes!*' ('Steady, Cachiríes') – the Cachiríes being '… the most warlike and the most noble' of the Venezuelan Indigenous peoples – the Patriot leader honouring his troops by referring to them as such.[5] Lieutenant Colonel Rooke, who was by Bolívar's side and was twice wounded during the battle, said that he believed that Bolívar had lost his senses, or that he wished to die on the field, so utterly careless was he of his own safety. He seemed to court death recklessly. At one point, Bolívar grabbed the Patriot colours from one of his own regiments that was in the process of retreat, galloped forward, threw it down a steep section of the river bank where the enemy was located and urged his men to retrieve it. There was a desperate charge led by some of the British volunteers, who never returned.[6] The British gave a formidable demonstration of their skill and of the twenty who fought in this battle, and at the subsequent engagement at Ortíz, at least seven died.[7] Soon after these events, Bolívar was reported to have said that the effort and determination of the English officers astonished him and their bravery in the field was conspicuous.[8]

One English officer, Captain Noble McMullin, was wounded, taken prisoner and brought before General Morillo, who was bleeding from a lance wound. The ingenious McMullin was not put to death because he convinced the Spaniards that he was a surgeon and actually dressed Morillos's wound. He managed to escape that night.

The Royalist victory at La Puerta was decisive and the Patriots were forced to flee. La Puerta is considered to have been the worst military defeat that Bolívar suffered throughout his career, in which 300 of his soldiers died, 400 were wounded, as well as many horses, and the military baggage, including ammunition and documents, were lost.[9] The demoralized Patriots retreated to San Fernando which, fortunately, had been taken by Páez on 7 March 1818, and where they could count on the protection of his and Cedeño's cavalry. To top it all, Bolívar received the bad news that General Bermúdez had lost Cumaná, leaving the Spanish in control of all northern Venezuela.

The war was not going favourably for the Patriots and only remnants of their army were left in Apure and Guayana.[10]

Neither did Vowell fare well as a result of the battle of La Puerta, which saw him led into an exceedingly dangerous situation. At one point his company was ordered to dislodge a group of Spanish light infantry who were occupying a wood to the right of the main army, but their chances were slim as the enemy was not positioned on open, level ground and '…mere courage, without discipline, is of little avail against riflemen in a wood.'[11] Vowell praised black soldiers with whom he fought for their fearlessness and for standing firm, but they refused to retreat or to take shelter; consequently, following the skirmish with the Spanish, out of ninety, the company was left with only fifteen men. Lieutenant Braithwaite, who had been with Vowell from the start, lost his life but, curiously, Vowell did not mention this in his book.[12] The Spanish cavalry charged Vowell's company, cut them away from the main part of the Patriot Army, and then the Royalist riflemen advanced to finish them off. The Patriot soldiers broke their muskets and fled up the mountain in an attempt to rejoin their army. Vowell followed as best he could, but found that his boots and his sabre slowed him down as much as the fatigue of two days' march without any food; 'I therefore threw myself, exhausted, into a bush, where I lay expecting, every moment, to be bayoneted by our pursuers.'[13]

> *Finding, however, that several had passed without observing me, I began to entertain some hopes of being able to rejoin our army; and crept further into the undergrowth, to the brink of a rock, from whence the whole field could plainly be seen beneath me. It was thickly spotted over with bodies… men and horses were lying in heaps. Our army had totally disappeared, except a few stragglers who were still entangled in the broken ground, and whom the enemy had surrounded and was firing at, not choosing to encumber themselves with prisoners. A Spanish general, whom I believed to be Morillo, and his staff, were halted on a small eminence, which the Patriot Army had previously occupied. A few prisoners, apparently officers, were occasionally brought to him, and after a short pause, while by his gestures he appeared to interrogate and threaten them, were taken aside and shot.*
>
> Vowell, *Campaigns and Cruises*, 88-89

Here commenced one of Vowell's most extraordinary adventures which, for two whole months, would demand all his stamina and wits. With the Spanish army encamped before him, around midnight Vowell walked away towards the El Semen, a small river where a great deal of the fighting had taken place. The banks were strewn with bodies, which attracted wild dogs and vultures. He drank some water and continued up the valley, walking all night. He came to a cottage, the home of an old native man, his wife and four daughters, who, in greeting him, at first took him for a Spaniard. However, from his accent, they realized he was English and knowing there were Englishmen in Bolívar's army, they took him in. This was not surprising as most of the indigenous people in that part of the country were on Bolívar's side. The old man warned there was great danger from the Spanish troops who would come to look for food. As such, they hid Vowell in a thick copse nearby where one of the daughters spread out a mat and brought him water and food, and there he remained for several days. Knowing that the old man would be shot if he was found to be hiding an insurgent, Vowell felt guilty for endangering those who were being so kind to him. From his hiding place, he could see Royalist soldiers searching for fugitives, several of whom were found and shot. So, he decided it was time to move on. 'My worthy host endeavoured to dissuade me from this resolution, assuring me, that he did not apprehend any danger of discovery,'[14] but recognising that Vowell was decided on his course of action, his hosts provided him with a basket with provisions, flint and steel, and an Indian pipe with tobacco, and many embraces and kind wishes.

It is remarkable that in such a risky situation, lost in the forest of a land in which he was a total stranger, being hunted by enemy forces, he had the presence of mind and intellectual curiosity to take note of his natural surroundings including trees, wildlife, insects.

The trees in these mountain forests are chiefly the caoba, or mahogany, which grows to a majestic size, and affords a delightful shade. There are, besides, many different kinds of wild fruit trees, which are resorted to by the araguato monkey. Panthers inhabit these wilds; but although I often heard their yells, they never approached near enough to give me any serious apprehensions. When my provisions were expended, I was in the habit of going down, cautiously to the plantations, after dusk, and cutting sugar cane: this is well known to be nutritious enough to support life for a long time, without any other food... I found it difficult to guard against the depredations of the monkeys which frequently robbed me of my provisions. The mountains here abound with snakes and centipedes, which I used often to discover under the dry leaves that composed my bed. The former were, however, perfectly harmless, when not molested; although it was necessary to use caution on rising, to avoid touching them, as that would, of course, have provoked them to bite. The woods at night were brilliantly illuminated by the cucuis, or lantern flies, which, flitting in myriads from tree to tree, resemble sparks of fire. This insect is a small dark coloured beetle, similar to that which is found under rotten wood in England. It carries its greenish phosphoric light in the tail, and its lantern remains invisible, except when it is flying, as it is covered by the wings when in a state of rest.

Vowell, *Campaigns and Cruises*, 91–92

He wandered day after day, feeding on roots and berries, sleeping in trees, and slowly, but surely, gaining the appearance of a wild man. There is a certain passage in his book, which may seem a portent, but is also a clear statement of Vowell's values and attitude towards life: 'I soon began to find this solitary way of life too irksome to endure with any degree of patience. I even entertained serious thoughts of surrendering myself to the Spaniards, at all hazards, rather than lead the life of an outlaw, any longer, among these wild mountains.'[15] Evidently, the solitary life was not to his liking; even prison, or perhaps even death, were preferable to the profoundly distasteful life of an outcast.

Any idea of surrender was fortunately soon discarded. One night, as he was cutting sugar cane in the moonlight, he ran into a young man engaged in the same activity. They were, at first, suspicious of each other, but soon discovered that they were both lost after the battle at El Semen (La Puerta) and both were in search of the Patriot Army. Vowell's new companion was Vicente Artaóna,[16] a corporal from General Zaraza's army. The two men willingly agreed to travel together. Artaóna proved adept at finding provisions and at crossing rivers and Vowell noted that '… the days now passed much more agreeably than in my former solitude.'[17] They took refuge among the Victoria Patriot families who had fled the Royalists and were now hiding in miserable conditions on dry riverbeds. Stocking up with as much meagre provisions as they could, they decided to go south to seek their army, but having no idea where it could be.

> *While descending the mountains, we followed the course of torrents, as being the most unfrequented route we could take. This was attended by severe exertion, as we were obliged to leap from rock to rock, for hours together, and occasionally, to swim across any deep pool, to which we came. I was of course, under the necessity of throwing away my boots, with which it would have been impossible to proceed; but still my companion, the soles of whose feet were invulnerable, was obliged often to halt for me, as I was utterly incapable of keeping up with him, in walking barefoot over gravel and flinty roads. On reaching the more open country, we always concealed ourselves during the day, in some wood, and proceeded forward by night; carefully avoiding every beaten track, as well as all houses and plantations.*
>
> Vowell, *Campaigns and Cruises*, 94

Soon Vowell and Artaóna ran out of provisions and at one point necessarily approached a cottage which turned out to be a dairy. The dairyman was very reluctant to help them, but finally gave them some *arepas* (Venezuelan corn bread) and milk, and also informed them that the Patriot Army was only a few leagues away at Flores and was getting ready to march on the next day. Thus bolstered, they walked all night to reach Flores and at dawn, under rainswept skies, came upon a camp set up by what appeared to be a unit of cavalry. Artaóna, more astute than Vowell, insisted on first finding out which side these soldiers were on, so they crept among the bushes, the rain disguising any noise. To their dismay they realized that the colours of the cavalrymen's banners were the red and blue of the Royalists. They managed to back away and hide among a bamboo copse where they lay the entire hot day. Parched with thirst, they watched hour after hour as the soldiers bathed in the river. 'The *Godos* ['Goths' – a disparaging name for Royalists] passed repeatedly so near to our place of concealment, that we could distinctly hear the words of the Royalist songs they were singing, as they rode to and from the water.'[18] They found out later that the commanding officer of this Royalist troop had been a Colonel López known for his cruelty towards prisoners. Artaóna vowed he would seek full revenge on the dairyman who had so cruelly tricked them, to which Vowell remarked wryly about Artaóna: 'I am inclined to give the young creole credit for having kept his vows, in this matter, most religiously.'[19]

That night they managed to escape their confinement, following the shallow river course and concealing themselves from the Royalist camps they encountered. After walking two days without food, except for sugar cane, they reached the outskirts of the town of Ortíz. Artaóna, being a Venezuelan, was able to simply walk into town without causing suspicion, but Vowell had to remain hidden, as his appearance and accent were a giveaway. Vowell admits he spent an anxious day dreading discovery and fearing that Artaóna had been taken prisoner. But his comrade did return, bringing food and the good news that Ortíz was not under Royalist rule and that the local priest, Don Cayetano Guaxardo, was expecting them. This 'worthy man', as Vowell called him, was a venerable, elderly and stout gentleman who exhibited considerable kindness to them. He gave them some of his own trousers and shirts to wear – as their two months of wandering had taken a toll on their clothes. There was much laughter when the two lean men pulled on the well-built priest's oversize clothes. Don Cayetano also furnished Vowell with a pair of Royalist boots. He urged them to leave as soon as they could because enemy forces were expected in the area at any moment.

> Then dismissing us with his blessing, and hearty wishes for our safe arrival among our own people, he filled our haversacks with provisions, and gave me, at parting, a bundle of cigars, which were very scarce in this part of the country. I must not omit to mention, that on examining our stores at the first halt we made, we found a few dollars wrapped in paper, which the worthy old priest had put privately into each of our haversacks, to ensure us a supply until we should join the army.
>
> Vowell, *Campaigns and Cruises*, 99

They were now in territory familiar to Vicente Artaóna and not excessively worried about encountering Royalists. Next day, they arrived at the home of some of Artaóna's friends, who welcomed them and gave them a bed for the night. However, Vowell was startled when he heard the sound of many horses outside. Peering from a window, he saw no fewer than eighty horsemen surrounding the house. It was with some relief that he was assured by Artaóna that the riders were friends, not the enemy. Artaóna explained to them who the Englishman was, at which the entire party welcomed Vowell and embraced him (it must be assumed that by now Vowell was becoming used to this Venezuelan greeting). A bullock was soon slaughtered and a fire prepared for a feast. The leader of the *Llaneros* was a tall, strong, black man, with a scarred face and two missing fingers on his left hand: this was the famous Vicentico Hurtado who led the *Guerrilla del Palmar*. In reality, they were not guerrilla fighters, but bandits, whose exploits even Vowell had heard of. Hurtado favoured Bolívar, but would not heed his calls to join the Patriot Army and preferred to plunder the Royalists, probably because the Patriots had nothing worth taking.

Yet the bandits showed Vowell every possible kindness, giving him a horse and even coming up with an English saddle and bridle that they had likely purloined. They informed Vowell that Cedeño's troops were in Calabozo, but to get there they would have to go through enemy-controlled territory, and it would be better for Vowell to remain with Hurtado and his men as alone he could not hope to reach the Patriots. Next day, they all rode off to rendezvous with another group of sixty or more bandits near Ortíz and remained there for several days. The men passed the time drinking and gambling, and not surprisingly, quarrels broke out, accompanied by knife fights. Vowell noticed several guarded huts in the bandits' compound whose occupants were women, but Artaóna warned him not to ask any questions for fear of arousing the bandits' ire. The Englishman suspected the women were there under duress and that is why Hurtado's men would not allow him to remain in camp when they went out on their forays.

The bandits' principal tactic was to hunt out Spanish advance guards and plunder any poorly guarded baggage they could find, always careful not to injure the soldiers unless they resisted. Vowell felt no small amount of anxiety, and his writings reveal an important clue to his character, since he was reluctant to be associated with the illegal activities of the gang of desperadoes. This is an early indication of his sense of honour: 'Although I was obliged to accompany them, wherever they went, and to be an unwilling spectator of their lawless proceedings, they never urged me to assist them in any way.'[20]

Very soon and foolishly, the bandits irritated the Spanish forces beyond their tolerance when they rode, yelling, into the centre of Ortíz at midnight one night, in a raid of drunken bravado. The Spaniards were so insulted that they despatched a strong cavalry deputation after them. Luckily for Vowell, this meant that Hurtado and his men suddenly saw the necessity of leaving the area to join Bolívar, for no longer could they take for granted that the Spanish were going to turn a blind eye to their thieving. To Vowell's joy, they headed towards the llanos. He wrote, 'From hence I once more caught a distant sight of the Llanos of Varinas. Their immensity and perfect level, suggest the idea, when descending towards them, of approaching the seashore; and their appearance holds much of the calm sublimity and repose of the distant ocean.'[21]

Hurtado decided that he and his men would round up as many cattle and horses as possible to take as a peace offering to Bolívar. At this point, at last, Vowell was excused and was allowed to leave his shady 'friends'. They gave him an excellent horse, however, and with Artaóna guiding him, they soon arrived in Calabozo. Vowell had been lost for over two months.

A patrol of lancers escorted the two men, as if they were prisoners, to Cedeño who was camped in the town with his cavalry, two regiments of infantry and six field pieces.

A few hours after Vowell's arrival, the general was told that the Royalists were about to enter the city, and without further verification of this news, he ordered an immediate evacuation, leaving behind his guns and considerable military stores. It had been a false alarm. Shortly after, Vicentico Hurtado arrived at Cedeño's camp with two hundred of his men and even more cattle and horses. Thus bolstered, Cedeño ventured back to Calabozo but, not having scouts to check the area, they encountered the Royalists at a narrow pass called Los Cerritos. They had no time to form a line and were thoroughly defeated in the ensuing battle. Vowell does not give any further details of the battle at Los Cerritos. After this setback however, Cedeño ordered the cattle and horses to be driven to San Fernando where Bolívar and Páez were quartered. Vowell wrote: 'I was rejoiced to find myself detached on this duty: for I was anxious to be again among my own countrymen.'[22]

According to his friend, George Laval Chesterton, Vowell, a good writer of stories, seems to have also been a good oral storyteller too. Chesterton offered an interpretation of Vowell's adventures in his book[23] and commented, 'Vowell's miraculous escape was well known at Angostura, and is of undoubted authenticity. I have often listened to the recital of his erratic toils and providential extrication, and I narrate the story with the firmest conviction in my own mind of its truthfulness.'[24]

CHAPTER SEVEN

The Llanos

"The beautiful souls are they that are universal, open, and ready for all things.'

Michel de Montaigne, *Of Presumptions, Essays*, 1580

PON Vowell's return to the Patriot headquarters at San Fernando, together with the men bringing horses and cattle sent by Cedeño, he met with Bolívar who was astonished to see him, since the few survivors of the *Los Barloventos* regiment's actions at El Semen had reported him killed. Bolívar was eager to learn about the places through which he had travelled and the people who had helped him, and had the details recorded by his secretary. To Vowell's delight, the great man made him a guest at his table for all the time they were at San Fernando, which was no small favour since bread, vegetables and wine were in scarce supply. It may well be that Bolívar took pity on Vowell, for he must have lost much weight after his ordeal. Another sign of Bolívar's regard for the Englishman was his gift of 'a capital young charger' which Vowell lamented was lost with saddle, bridle, and blanket, disappearing into the savanna because he had not covered the horse's eyes before attempting to break him.[1]

Meanwhile most, if not all, of his British companions had left recently for Angostura with General Carlos Soublette.[2] Bolívar had just returned from that city where he had been reorganizing the army, since further regiments of British volunteers sent from London by López Méndez had just arrived. Their arrival at this time was a great boost to Patriot morale, but their voyage to Venezuela had been beset with calamity. Many men had been lost in the West Indies through desertion and a host of tropical diseases such as smallpox, yellow fever, typhus, malaria, and dysentery. The volunteers' long sea voyage had ended, not with an organized reception by the Patriots, but in hopping from one Caribbean island to another, trying to reach the mainland, and in the process exhausting their provisions and catching diseases. Typhus alone killed 250 of them in five weeks. Out of one thousand men, only 400 managed to get to the Orinoco, and half of them were ill.[3]

Bolívar grouped the volunteers into one battalion, the British Brigade, under the command of Colonel Gustavus Hippisley,[4] which greatly aggravated the long-standing animosity and rivalry between him and Colonel Henry Wilson.[5] This rivalry, based on personality differences, would cast a long shadow over the new brigade.[6]

Soon after Vowell's return to San Fernando, elements of the new British Brigade began to arrive. Lieutenant Daniel Florence O'Leary was one of the first arrivals; then Wilson, who refused to travel with Hippisley who arrived later with the rest of the British Brigade, having travelled by river boats accompanied by a few of the mens' wives and children. They arrived in May 1818, at a time when the city was 'in the greatest state of uproar and confusion imaginable.'[7] According to Vowell, this was caused by the presence of Cedeño who had arrived with what was left of his cavalry. He was greeted with hisses and accusations from the troops for having evacuated Calabozo needlessly, and for his defeat at Los Cerritos,[8] and his supposed role in the condemnation of Piar did not help his popularity either. Vowell stated that the tumult became so serious, that Bolívar locked himself away in his quarters and it was only the timely intervention of Páez, 'of whom all stood in awe... and whose decided character gave him the greatest influence over the minds of both officers and soldiers', that quieted the men and established order.[9] Cedeño was urged to leave for Cumaná. However, the 'frightful confusion' in San Fernando was most likely because the Patriot Army was in 'wild retreat' before the Spanish forces of Morillo.[10] What the British Brigade really encountered was a defeated army whose leader, Bolívar, was sick with fever, which is the real reason he remained in his quarters.

In any case, the rains were coming, so the troops in the *llanos* had to find a safe place until they ceased. Bolívar, intending to leave for Angostura, gave the British volunteers the choice of returning to the relative comfort of that city with him or to remain in the more rugged quarters of Apure with Páez. Hippisley, whose fastidiousness only found things to object to in San Fernando, did try to establish some sort of order among the British troops but, undermined and outwitted by Wilson, decided to leave with Bolívar along with a few of the British officers. He had been only forty-eight hours in San Fernando and soon after, on 25 June, he sailed back to England. Most of his troops objected to leaving Apure, wanting to see action against the Spanish. Wilson, who spoke Spanish, remained, and obviously obtained what he had longed for, command of the British Brigade – but not for long.

At this point a most obscure episode of intrigue occurred: it has been given several interpretations which has made it difficult to discern what actually happened. Essentially, once Bolívar had left for Angostura, Páez immediately marched out with the entire army to his winter quarters in the town of Achaguas on the Apurito River. There, Wilson proceeded to drill the troops. Lieutenant Daniel Florence O'Leary would later write that the British troops were given the place of honour on Paez's right when on parade, undoubtedly because of their flashy uniforms which contrasted with the rags and near nudity of the regular troops.[11] Then, on 28 May, according to Vowell, all the officers proposed to give Páez the title of Capitan General – a title apparently also held by Bolívar, Mariño and MacGregor.

O'Leary's version of events is that Wilson, having invited Páez and other officers to dine, and after much drinking had taken place, toasted Páez with the title. Wilson knew that this title was given in Spain to those in charge of a province, and since Páez was in charge of Apure, he thought it appropriate to address him so. He nevertheless then turned to Colonel Briceño, who was sitting next to him and who was cousin to Bolívar's secretary, and asked if he had acted correctly with this toast – to which, Briceño answered that he saw no harm done. However, Wilson believed this officer later, in some kind of sleight, 'betrayed him' and his actions to Bolívar. Those present seem to have reached a consensus that it was appropriate to convey this title formally on Páez. So it was that a week later, in front of all the troops, Páez was hailed as Capitan General. The general was delighted at first, but then thought it over and decided to send the document drawn up to that effect to Bolívar to seek his approval. According to Vowell, 'This occurrence, though unimportant in itself, was studiously misrepresented and exaggerated to Bolívar who was nervously alive to any appearance of intrigue among his generals, and expressed himself highly offended with Páez on the subject.'[12]

The episode came to a head a month later, on 22 June, when Wilson arrived in Angostura with documents for Bolívar and was promptly arrested, accused of attempting to undermine Bolívar's authority. Bolívar said that he spared Wilson's life in honour of his country, England. A few months later he was sent home and upon his arrival in England, Wilson defended his actions and motives, declaring that these had been misinterpreted and misconstrued, but he showered insults on Bolívar and the Patriots.[13] Many other rumours swirled around this event, even accusations that Wilson was a Spanish spy. In any case, Vowell's narration favours Wilson, but he could not have been entirely cognizant of all that had happened to the rivalry between Hippisley and Wilson, or of the possibility of appearing to bolster Páez against Bolívar; or, perhaps, he preferred not to write much about it. It would not be the last time that Vowell would encounter Wilson in his life. It would seem safe to say that Wilson's ambition, controlling character and desire to ingratiate himself with Páez, rather than any deeper duplicity or treason against Bolívar, got the better of him.

Despite the intrigues of Hippisley and Wilson, and the many complaints from the volunteers on their arrival in Venezuela, Bolívar was so pleased with the general conduct of the British officers who had arrived with Vowell, and others who arrived independently, that he awarded the First Venezuelan Hussars, now under the command of Colonel James Rooke,[14] the motto *Siempre fiel a la autoridad suprema* ('Always loyal to the supreme authority'); yet, perhaps this was both an honour and a warning. Furthermore, Bolívar asked Colonel James T. English to gather all those volunteers and deserters who were stranded throughout the West Indies.[15]

Vowell, in his cheerful way, proceeded to observe and enjoy as much as he could during his stay in Achaguas, a town turned by the rains into an island between the Apurito and Orinoco rivers. The streets were knee-deep in mud, making shoes useless. It was too wet to even visit surrounding plantations, so evenings were passed with Venezuelan families who had taken refuge there with the troops, and whose conversation he found highly interesting. Páez tried to make sure that the British soldiers were as comfortable as possible, even providing milk cows for them,[16] and whenever he managed to secure a quantity of *aguardiente* (liquor), he would invite the whole town to a party, with much dancing, of which he was very fond. Vowell describes a wild celebration on the feast day of San Juán Bautista, which involved horseracing, bonfires and, literally, much mud-slinging!

> The streets were excessively muddy; and the diversion consisted, chiefly, in everyone making his neighbour as dirty as he possibly could. This object was so easily effected, that the natural colours of both horses and men were soon completely undistinguishable. These that refused, or even delayed to join the revellers, were pulled out of bed, sans ceremonie, and rolled in the mud… they then separated to their quarters, to clothe themselves, and prepare to attend the general at breakfast, to which every officer at headquarters had been invited. What this dejeuné a la fourchette wanted in elegance, was amply compensated by the plenty and variety of the viande.
>
> Vowell, *Campaigns and Cruises*, 118

Vowell has left a vivid portrait of Páez, a man whom, obviously, he much admired. Others have repeated his description of him on innumerable occasions, although not always having given appropriate attribution to Vowell himself.[17] He describes Páez as a white man, who dressed simply like other *Llaneros* with a wide-sleeved shirt made of English handkerchiefs of a red cross-barred pattern, loose white cotton drawers reaching just below the knees. On his bare feet, he wore enormous silver spurs with four-inch diameter sharp rowels. He wore a palm leaf hat with a broad blue band tied under his chin. A twelve year old boy, his page, seated upon a large horse, carried his light black cane lance. 'Páez,' recorded Vowell, 'the dreaded *llanero* chief, showed no trace of the ferocity that has been attributed to him in his fair open countenance! His hair curled naturally and closely over his high forehead, and he wore small black mustachios, but no whiskers. His dark eyes alone betrayed indications of that quickness of temper which so frequently hurried him to deeds of extreme severity – to say the least of them – however they may be palliated, in his case, by pleading the expediency of retaliation.'[18]

Vowell refers to Páez as an extraordinary man whose leadership of the *Llanero* cavalry was such that Morillo was unable to deal with them and that Royalist troops greatly feared them. It is well known that Páez commanded the loyalty and obedience of his men, and that his plans were carefully thought out and rapidly executed.[19] But it was Vowell who revealed that when planning a military action, Páez did not just give out orders, but would call together a council of the elder *Llaneros* and ask their opinion on his plans of attack.[20] Vowell also praised an efficient mint that Páez set up in Achaguas intended to counter the dire lack of coin at that time, and which was readily accepted as such because his word was trusted in the entire region.[21]

In his even-handed way, Vowell also wrote of Páez's shortcomings: that he was proud, that he had a violent temper (he had Colonel MacDonald's murderers shot by cannon), that he openly defied Bolívar's order to march into hilly terrain, and that he may have been ungrateful to Wilson. Another criticism he had of Páez was his attitude towards his wife, Doña Dominga, whom for reasons unknown Vowell refers to as Doña Rosaura, which demonstrates how attentive Vowell was to the role of women during revolution, as well as his belief in marriage and romantic love. He paints a scene in *The Savannas of Varinas* too close to real events to be taken as fiction. Páez and his cavalry had led the *Llanero* families towards a refuge deep in the *llanos*, near the lagoon of Cunavichi, where they erected rough shacks, or *ranchos*, for shelter, creating a kind of temporary village. He wrote that, 'The *Llaneros*, indeed, showed on all occasions the greatest regard for "*La Señora*" as they generally styled her,' and the men of Páez's Honour Guard held his wife in the highest regard, not because she was the commander's wife but because, '… her education was so far superior to that of all around her, while at the same time, she was so unassuming and uniformly kind to everyone, that they looked up to her with feelings of unqualified respect and admiration.'[22] Vowell goes on to explain that Páez's wife did not follow the army – as many other women did – but remained in the couple's small plantation, taking care of their two infant sons. Páez rarely visited her '… for his pursuits and habits were so totally opposite to those of Doña Rosaura, that although he was incapable of feeling indifference towards her, there was an evident coolness and constraint in his manner, when in her company, that could not fail to give her, who loved him with an enthusiastic and devoted attachment, deep cause for sorrow.'[23]

> She was now surrounded by groups of Llaneras, who had been always accustomed to apply to her for advice and assistance in their minor afflictions; they accordingly felt confident that her presence, although she was involved, no less than them, in the common calamity, was in some measure a protection to them. With the assistance of the Cura [parish priest], de Guasdualito, she gradually succeeded in calming the excessive apprehensions of the emigrants, who had been terrified by the loneliness of the wood in which they had sought shelter.
>
> Vowell, *The Savannas of Varinas*, 69

There is no doubting Vowell's sense of romance, so in tune with the Romanticism of his century. This is illustrated, for example, in the tender love story between the characters of Juanita and Andrés in *The Savannas of Varinas*, '…when Juanita, who at once recognized his voice, stepped forward and stood before him. He sprung from his steed, and clasped her in his arms, before she had the presence of mind, or perhaps even the wish, to avoid the close embrace.'[24] Or, for example, in the melodramatic scene in *Earthquake of Caracas* when, at the very moment of a terrible earthquake, María del Rosario, a character who was about to have her luxuriant hair cut off in the rite of becoming a nun in the Cathedral, is rescued by the hero, Carlos, who '… thought only of her whom he had just been on the point of losing for ever. With a desperate effort, he seized and tore down the latticed screen, and caught the fainting novice, as she lay insensible on the *atahud*.[25] And, although there is no evidence as to whom Vowell himself may have loved, there may be a hint of love lost in his historical fiction, for as one of his characters states: 'Ah, *Señorita*! You are now happy in your own family: may you never know what it is to be separated from one you love!'[26] This reoccurs in another passage: 'For if there be one pang more keen than that inflicted by the sense of unrequited love, it is that which a generous heart feels, when it is forbid to return the affection with which it is sought.'[27] So there may have been, after all, another reason why the young Vowell had left England.

Vowell did not entirely approve of some of the guerrilla tactics adopted by Páez. He described an occasion when Páez had surrounded a detachment of Morillo's infantry in a llano of dry grass. The Royalists were close to the town of Mantecal, where they could be safe, but they dared not leave the relative shelter of the grassland, so great was their dread of the *Llaneros*, even though they were equipped with firearms and the *Llaneros* only lances. To coax them out, Páez tried driving a herd of cattle into the troops, but without success. Then he set fire to the dry grass which did dislodge the Spaniards, but not before many were suffocated or blown up by their own cartages. Vowell considered this an indiscriminate massacre, typical of both sides during this time of *Guerra a Muerte*, but he faults the Spanish for having introduced it 'in an evil hour… and which was long carried on with unrelenting fury by both parties.'[28]

Most British troops admired Páez – but not all. For Alexander Alexander, a British artillery officer who was, for a short time, in the Patriot Army, the very qualities that were pleasing to others, were to him quite the opposite:

'Páez is a strong little man of an active aspect with an agreeable and very expressive face; he is a good musician and dancer, daring and brave to excess, but too rash by far, who throws himself into combat without any other idea but to crush everything that opposes him by pure animal force. Lacking all culture, he scribbles with great effort "P–a–e–z".'[29]

Páez decided to show off his new British officers to the surrounding *Llanero* families, so he invited six of those with the best command of Spanish and who were able to swim well, to accompany him on a local tour. Vowell was one of them, and it was during this tour that he was able to gather so many impressions, anecdotes, and observations about life in the *llanos* which he included in the second part of his book, *The Savannas of Varinas*. His descriptions of the *llanos* are the most lyrical and the most detailed written during that period and they are considered by Venezuelan scholars to be an ethnographic treasure.

The herds of wild horses present a beautiful spectacle, when they are alarmed in their native wilds, by the intrusion of an army. Instead of flying, as the deer and other timid animals, they gallop round in compact masses of many thousands, apparently for the purpose of reconnoitering the strangers; and frequently advance boldly to within a few yards of the line of march, where they halt to gaze at the troops, snorting, and shewing every sign of astonishment and displeasure,

especially at the sight of the cavalry. These droves are always headed by some fine looking old
bashaws,[30] *whose flowing manes and tails, plainly show that they have never been subject to*
man's control; and in the rear, the mares and colts follow.

Vowell, *Campaigns and Cruises,* 120

Vowell's description of the *Llaneros* and their families is completely different to that generally given by others. They have been painted usually as wild, primitive and unprincipled men, and described as the '… ferocious herdsmen of the plains, primitive and predatory'.[31] Also,

'…South America's equivalent of the Tartars or the Mongols of central Asia, living in the saddle, they were the cowboys of Venezuela, but there was nothing romantic about them. Largely black, Indian or mestizo, they rode mostly naked except for rough trousers, and broad-brimmed hats… their diet consisted of raw beef, tied to their saddles in strips and salted by the sweat of their horses, washed down by the brackish water of the *llanos'* and '… half-breed desperadoes and thugs… vicious, uncontrolled forces.'[32]

Another writer called them '… these lawless half-breeds, accustomed to no restraint for plunder'[33] and even O'Leary, who fought with them, calls them 'rough and ferocious'.[34] Sadly, they are assigned the epithet 'half-breeds and mestizo' as an insult or disgrace.

Quite in contrast to these authors, Vowell took the time and had the interest to look beyond the *Llaneros'* ferocity in battle, to observe and appreciate their culture and customs. He described in detail the ranches of the *Llanero* families and their daily customs, food, industry, the soil and grasses of the plains, the types of wood they used, their use of sugar cane, their making of sugar and liquor, the fruit they ate, their types of tobacco, the way they tamed their horses and milked their cows – in short, everything about the life he was experiencing in the *llanos* was of interest to Vowell. He recounts how, during the rainy season, the *Llaneros* passed their evenings on their ranches dancing to their traditional tunes such as *El Bambuco* and *La Zambullidora,* and how '… the *Llaneras* are famous for their skill on the guitar and harp, as well as for singing their national airs.'[35] He was also struck by their generous attention to visitors '… where hospitality is exercised as a matter of course, and the visitor is considered as a person conferring the obligation.'[36]

On arriving at one of these farms, no ceremony whatever is used, except the usual salutation of
Ave Maria Purisima! (Hail Mary) The traveller's horses are immediately unsaddled, and
turned loose, for it is quite a matter of indifference whether they stray or not, as there are always
plenty of horses close at hand, which are considered completely public property. Water is then

brought to wash the stranger's feet, after which, everyone spreads his cloak or blanket in the shade, and lies down using his saddle for a pillow. Meanwhile, one of the family has already saddled a horse, and set out in search of a calf, or young heifer, for which they have seldom far to ride... In less than half a hour, an abundance of roast beef is set before the visitors, and sometimes, but very rarely in the remote haciendas, some arepa (corn bread)... Although these people, secluded as they are from society, must naturally be very desirous of hearing news of any kind, their innate sense of politeness forbids them to annoy their guests by asking questions until they have satisfied their appetite. They retire to rest soon after sunset and, previous to lying down, the patriarch of the family, who has probably scores of young descendants on the farm, working in company with and in no way distinguished from, the peons, recites the Rosario, or evening service to the Virgin, every one present standing, and joining in the responses. This religious ceremony is scarcely ever omitted by the South Americans.

Vowell, *Campaigns and Cruises*, 123

Vowell returned with Páez to Achaguas in March 1819, after having visited all those areas of Apure accessible during the rainy season. When a trading launch with hides and tallow appeared on the river, Vowell and a few others who had been longest in the service took the opportunity to obtain Páez's permission to travel with it to Angostura because they were in dire need of clothing. Travelling along with Vowell were the Irish lieutenants, Daniel Florencio O'Leary and Ambrose O'Daly and one wonders how these two Catholic Irish officers got along with the Anglo-Irish Vowell. The Venezuelans referred to both English and Irish officers as 'English' without distinction, or awareness, of the religious and political divisions that could exist among them.[37] For his part, O'Leary never mentioned Vowell, nor the officers, as his memoirs are typically narrow in that they refer only to politically important events and personages, especially Bolívar, upon whom he lavished praise.

The swollen rivers allowed them to reach Angostura in just twelve days. Upon arrival Vowell met the many recently arrived British volunteers who had been organized into a new corps known as Bolívar's Dragoon Guard and placed under the command of Colonel James Rooke and Adjutant General Soublette, and to which Vowell was promptly assigned. Their orders were to head for Barcelona, the east central part of the country, travelling by brig and later overland by horses, to the headquarters of General Monagas at the town of Concepción del Pao.[38] At this time, Vowell was promoted to Brigade Major for the two regiments – the *Lanzeros de Victoria* (Lancers of Victoria) and the *Carabineers del Oriente* (Rifles of the East).

The *llanos* of Barlovento were different from those of Apure, and Vowell's observant nature came to fore again as he described the low savannas, the many different fruits that grew there (including guayava, mericuri, maniroti, guanabana) and the very complex process of making cassava bread.

An incident occurred here that nearly killed him. In the *llanos* there is a fruit known as *coco de mono*, or 'monkeys' nut' (*Lecythis ollaria*), which birds and monkeys may eat, but which is poisonous to humans. Not knowing this fact, one day while commanding a party of cavalry out reconnoitring ahead of the army, and with his men being fatigued and hungry, Vowell's formation ate the fruit which, subsequently, made them violently sick. The army had no medicines and they had only muddy water to drink. Unfortunately, three of the soldiers died that evening and others lost their hair and remained ill for many weeks.[39] Fortunately, Vowell's strong constitution once more did not desert him.

Shortly after, Major Vowell and Bolívar's Dragoon Guards, now under the command of Generals Monagas and Mariño, withstood a ferocious attack by a division of Morillo's army near the town of Cantaura. They were able to rout the Royalists and gain their military chest and baggage, and even their enemy colours. Although Vowell's cavalry suffered heavy losses during the assault, they still had to guard the Patriot outposts during this time and were subsequently 'harassed day and night, with little intermission, until the end of the rainy season; the whole of which we passed in bivouacs, without once sleeping under a roof.'[40]

Thereafter, Bolívar, whom the Congress at Angostura had declared President of Venezuela, left that city for San Juán de Payara where Páez had his headquarters. He ordered his Dragoon Guards to leave Monagas' division and to join him there. Thus it was that Vowell returned once more to the *llanos* of Barinas and to yet another brush with death.

CHAPTER EIGHT

Escapes and Epidemics

'Throughout the period, disease killed more soldiers than human agency.'

Richard Holmes, *Redcoat*, 2001

AS the year 1819 commenced, Bolívar's revolutionary forces were on the verge of a breakthrough in their war aims, although they did not know it, nor would anyone have seriously suggested it at the time. Morillo's army numbered 17,000, while throughout the entire country Bolívar could count only 7,200 men.[1] Help was to come from Patriot forces in neighbouring Nueva Granada (today the Republic of Colombia), and from overseas in the form of some 1,500 British and Irish volunteers.[2]

Vowell relates that it was at this time that General Francisco de Paula Santander, the twenty-seven year old military leader of the Patriot forces in Nueva Granada – the present day Colombia – assembled a large force of cavalry in the *llanos* of Cazanares in Nueva Granada, to the west of Apure. Bolívar had promoted Santander to general a year earlier and had made him governor of the province of Casanare, with orders to liaise with Patriot forces operating on the other side of the Andes. The Patriot forces in Casanare urged Santander to invite Bolívar to enter Nueva Granada promising their support.[3] The relationship between Bolívar and Santander was a thorny one – that of colleagues, not friends, with Santander being considered '… a severe, humourless and touchy man, with a strong interest in money and a streak of vindictive cruelty, seen in his unconcealed delight at the execution of Royalists.'[4] For his part, Morillo did not overlook the strategic conjunction of Bolívar and Santander and, according to Vowell, 'The insurrection now assumed such a formidable appearance, that Morillo saw the necessity of making a desperate effort to crush the army which Bolívar had collected in the plains of the Apure and to cut off, if possible, his communication with Santander.'[5] Three Spanish divisions headed by Generals La Torre, Calzada and Morales, were sent to take San Fernando de Apure, the strongest outpost in the *llanos* and where the forces Páez and Bolívar had gathered were – and also where Vowell was stationed.

Bolívar realized that his infantry and artillery would not stand a chance against the formidable Spanish army, so he led his forces back across the Arauca River to a missionary settlement near Cayara and then, in February, he went to meet with the Congress at Angostura.[6] Páez, whose forces were much too small to make a stand against the Royalists, was instructed not to take the Spanish head-on, but to harass them. Vowell and Bolívar's Dragoons, to which the former belonged, stayed with Páez doing just that.

On 19 December, Páez had San Fernando evacuated and then burned it to the ground rather than let the Spanish have it. When the Spanish marched against San Fernando in January, it was a charred city. Páez was well aware that the enormous setbacks that the cause for independence had suffered between 1813-1814 were due in large part to the ability of the Royalists to use the resources of the *llanos* against the Patriots, including luring *Llaneros* to their side.[7] Perhaps Páez did not want to emulate Cedeño, whose reputation was hurt when he abandoned Calabozo and the Patriot equipment to the Spanish. In any case, the burning of San Fernando was a shocking event that made clear to all who lived in the *llanos* that the Patriots were deadly serious in their fight for liberty. It certainly made an impression on Vowell, who described it in detail. However, historians have tended to mark the taking of San Fernando by Páez on 6 March 1817, but not so much his burning of the town two years later.

The Patriots retreated to San Juan de Payara, but they kept going, taking the people of that town with them, as well as those from San Fernando. Vowell once more focused not on the military manoeuvres as much as the impact of war upon the citizens. He describes the chaos as the inhabitants were caught between the Patriots' retreat and the advance of the Spanish.

> The town and road to the Arauco were crowded with old men, women, and children, flying from their homes into the woods, very few of whom had time to save a single article of their property. The shopkeepers were running about in despair, offering any sum of money for horses or mules to save their goods. They met with very little sympathy or assistance from the soldiers, who were incensed against them, on account of the shamefully exorbitant prices which they had uniformly demanded for every article and the insolence with which they had been in the habit of treating all belonging to the army, without reflecting that they depended on it for protection.

> Vowell, *Campaigns and Cruises*, 146

They reached the settlement of Caujaral where Páez had every available man build trenches and defensive structures of casks of sugar, salt, rice, as well as the limbs of trees, and mud so that a few of Colonel Ferriar's artillery guns could be mounted to block the Spaniards from crossing the Arauca River.[8] The city was evacuated and the townspeople joined the Patriot exodus.

Páez carried out a scorched earth policy, as recalled by another volunteer, Alexander Alexander, of the Rifles:

'We swept everything in our path, destroying and burning every dwelling, herding before us immense cattle herds and inhabitants, and even burning the grass to stop the Spaniards. The scene was too distressing to describe; mules and donkeys hurrying to keep up with us; pigs, chickens and children tied together with hides to the same animal; mules and horses with two or three riders; the women always at the front, with one or two men behind them; women of strong legs and dark complexion dressed as men, with straw hats, shirt and knee length trousers; in short, the mass of the people of every age, sex and colour were marching before us, the Indian or negro women of the soldiers would ride or walk alongside them. The confusion and variety of languages could only make me think of the tower of Babel.'[9]

Together, the Patriot army and the civilians, with about 30,000 head of cattle, swam across the wide river and headed south, towards the Lagoon of Cunaviche, where they would find safety, since Morillo had no canoes. Obviously, based on his experiences here, Vowell drew a picture of the makeshift settlement in his *Savannas of Varinas*. In a remote wood, they set up camp for the displaced families, who built huts for themselves, creating a large, busy settlement; dogs barked and cattle grazed nearby, while women cooked, wove or milked the cattle. Their safety lay in that the only access to the camp was through a winding labyrinth of marshes, swarming with alligators and reeds. One day they held a *fandango* (party), creating a sylvan ballroom fenced in by cane screens on the banks of the lagoon. As Vowell recorded:

'Lamps formed of the pink-coloured caracol shells found in the savanna, were ranged at short intervals along the screen, and, being fastened round hoops of pliant *bejuco* (vines), were suspended, in lieu of chandeliers, from the branches extending across the salon. There was no want of music, for guitars and *vihuelas* (a small guitar) were as common among the emigrants as in the army.'[10]

Eventually Morillo managed to cross the river using a different route. By that time however, Páez had moved the army to the centre of the plains, which was exactly where he wanted to lure the Spanish troops. There he had the advantage and was able to weaken the Spanish with his constant guerrilla attacks. According to Vowell, this he accomplished admirably. One of Páez's tactics was to set up bonfires that would trick the Royalists into thinking the Patriots had settled for the night, but then in silence, his lancers would sneak up to the Royalist camp's rear guard and cause mayhem.

The Spanish army gradually became weaker. They encountered difficulties in carrying artillery and baggage through the *llanos* and across the rivers, whereas the Patriot troops did not carry any baggage at all. The Spanish cavalrymen grew afraid of the *Llaneros'* lances, so much so that eventually they hardly moved from their camps. Their horses, accustomed to a diet of maize and cane tops, became weak because they were unused to eating the grass of the *llanos*. Their troops, made up mostly of Spaniards or natives of the northern, hilly part of the country, were unused to the climate, terrain, or steady diet of beef, without bread or salt. There had also been *Llaneros* among the Royalist troops, in varying numbers, at different times of the war, particularly before Páez became the *Llanero* Patriot leader, and these men were key in helping the enemy army cope with the terrain, food and shelter. The Spanish supplies tended to come from the north of the country and were constantly intercepted by the Patriots, so they had little else. But then, even beef became scarce because Páez ordered cattle to be driven deep into the centre of the *llanos* beyond Spanish reach. Even if there had been cattle available, Vowell explains that the Spanish troops did not know how to hunt wild animals. Without daring to venture outside their camp and unable to forage, they began to eat their own horses and mules, and occasional chiguires.[11]

> *Chiguires are found in droves in the marches. These animals are a kind of amphibious river hog (some say a small species of tapir) with coarse black bristles, having very short ears, and no tail; but in other respects it resembles the pecari, or wild hog of the woods. They graze in herds on the borders of lagoons and small streams, to which they retreat on any alarm, and are capable of remaining as long under water as a seal, or cayman (alligator). Their flesh is tender and fat, but except in a young chiguiri, it has a strong fishy taste, which render it a very disagreeable food.*
>
> Vowell, *Campaigns and Cruises,* 150

Disease was also debilitating Morillo's troops. During the revolutions in South America, of the 40,000 troops Spain sent to its American colonies between 1811 and 1818, very few returned to their homeland, most having died of diseases such as dysentery, smallpox, scurvy, tropical fevers – particularly yellow fever – or sexually transmitted diseases.[12] It has been calculated that from 1810 to 1824, Spanish troops fighting in Venezuela and Nueva Granada suffered an astonishing overall fatality rate of between 90 and 96 per cent, attributed to the climate, disease, insufficient food, and primitive health care.[13]

Morillo continued to search for Bolívar, but he had very little chance of gathering intelligence as to his whereabouts because, as Vowell pointed out, in such a close-knit *Llanero* society, a spy would immediately be discovered. Morillo must have been quite desperate, because the Spanish king had given him 160 days in which to finally defeat the Patriots. That deadline was now long past.[14] Finally, at the end of February 1819 with a considerable number of his troops ill, Morillo retreated across the Arauca River, losing much of his baggage to the Patriots and having to blow up his own powder, because he had lost many of his horses and mules to sickness or had killed them for food. Eventually, he took a strong position in Achaguas on 8 March, where he hoped to prevent Bolívar from crossing to Nueva Granada. The Spanish troops suffered a setback near Cazanares from Santander, and Páez also maintained his guerrilla attacks, so that when the rainy season arrived, Morillo retreated to Caracas believing that it would be impossible for Bolívar to cross the Andes to Nueva Granada, so dangerous would be the passes from the torrents of the season. He greatly underestimated the man.

The British Brigade, consisting of Bolívar's Dragoon Guard commanded by Colonel James Rooke, the 1st Rifles commanded by Colonel Robert Pigott,[15] the 2nd Rifles commanded by Colonel McIntosh, and Colonel Farrier's artillery, retreated to winter quarters at Mantecal. In August 1819, Bolívar ordered Vowell, as Brigade Major of Bolívar's Dragoons, to Angostura with dispatches to the Vice-President, Francisco Zea. While there, fresh and anxiously awaited British and Irish troops arrived, 'and landed in all the pomp of new uniforms and a complete regimental band.'[16] They soon used up all the supplies they had brought from England and their fancy English uniforms were useless in the tropics. Upon enquiring about the 200 dollars per officer and 80 dollars per soldier that they had been promised in London, the Patriot army officials duly informed them that they knew nothing of promises made in London.[17]

However, not all complained, but actually understood that scarcity was not wilfully visited upon them by the Patriots, such as one captain, who wrote, 'The troops which left Ireland in 1819 for South America and which landed at Margarita were, though not expected, treated with as much kindness as they from the nature of things, could possibly expect.'[18] The British troops also brought yellow fever, which they had caught along the Orinoco settlements.

No place in the world could be more admirably calculated to foster and mature that fatal disease, than the sultry city of Angosturas, with its stagnant, half putrid lagoon; its matanzas [slaughterhouses] and its thousands of raw hides drying on the pavement in front of the stores, in preparation for shipment. The fever spread like a pestilence, and the unfortunate newcomers were swept away daily by sections; for the burial ground was beyond the fort, on the hill, and every funeral became the primary cause of sickness in the attendants, who were suddenly affected by it, either at the Campo Santo, or on their return from following their countrymen to the grave.

Vowell, *Campaigns and Cruises,* 152

The day before Vowell was due to return, he had to command the firing party at the funeral of Captain Brown of the 2nd Hussars, who had just succumbed to yellow fever:

'When we reached the cemetery, we found that the Indians had opened many of the foreigners' graves in search of the clothing in which they had been buried; and the scene was shocking beyond description. I felt convinced, at that moment, that I could no longer escape the fever.'[19]

His presentiment came to pass as the next day; Vowell was struck with the fever.

Yellow fever periodically struck the towns along the Orinoco and, this time, it left a significant toll among the new British volunteers, who died two or three a day. A person could be healthy one day and the next they would be dead. The epidemic of August 1819 was particularly severe. One correspondent noted: 'The number of persons who have fallen victims of this horrible pestilence is so great that it has not been possible to find wood in sufficient quantities to make coffins, and several bodies have been buried without them.'[20]

In general, the conditions of the military hospitals were exceedingly deficient for lack of Creole, English or Irish doctors, even though many British physicians served the Patriot army.[21] There was a lack of medicines, the torment of insect bites, and always the heat.[22] Hippisley describes the hospital in San Fernando most starkly:

'The miserable hovels, under the name of houses, afforded scarcely any covering for man or beast: they were all open in front, and the old and almost worn out inmates were wretchedly suffering under the various evils of poverty, distress and disease. So miserable a scene I had never before witnessed; and the horror I experienced on visiting the building set apart for an hospital, whither my poor countrymen must go if sick or wounded, was beyond expression. The unfortunate Patriots who were inmates of this place, sat or lay along the benches or flooring, waiting patiently the approach of the medical attendants. Some held up the stump of an arm, shattered by a ball, or lopped off with a sword; others lifted up a thigh, the leg belonging to which had suffered amputation by a similar process; others lay bleeding to death, with shots through several parts of their limbs or bodies; and my soul was sickened by beholding some, who, having lost the scalp or upper part of the skull, exposed the action of the bare brain to view. Yet hardly a moan escaped from the poor miserable sufferers, some of whom seemed to endure the agony they were undergoing with all the stoical indifference and resolution ascribed to their North American brethren when put to the torture by their conquerors. The only cry that I heard was for water.'[23]

As a sick patient, Vowell had the advantage of speaking Spanish; therefore he could communicate with the Venezuelans who attended him in the hospital. Being an officer, he had a personal servant, customary at that time in the British army, as well as in the Venezuelan army, who could bring him food and water.[24] Evidently, he had good friends who cared for him, because two of them, who came to say farewell to Vowell believing his death to be imminent, succumbed to the disease themselves, and died along with the three orderlies who attended him. Fortunately for Vowell, his strong constitution helped him to recuperate – and with little medical help. As soon as the army surgeon allowed it, he returned to headquarters at Mantecal.

Disease, lack of medical knowledge to cure wounds, lack of medical supplies and medical personnel were the harsh conditions faced by the Venezuelan army as a whole, but especially by the foreigners among them. What ailed the Spaniards of the Royalist army, also affected the British and Irish volunteers with the Patriot army. They were weakened, disastrously so, by the abrupt changes to climate and by local food.

They were fed the standard fare for Venezuelan troops: chunks of beef with no salt or vegetables. Each volunteer was given two pounds of beef per day which he had to roast himself, without even plantains (large bananas that are cooked before eating), maize, or any kind of bread. The ubiquitous food of the Patriot army was '*tasajo*' – strips of beef cured by hanging them out to dry, after which they became very dry and thus preserved. This extraordinary diet, together with dysentery, yellow fever, insect bite infections, and other tropical illnesses, played havoc with the ranks of the British and Irish volunteers, even though most of them were seasoned soldiers. When they first embarked upon the strenuous marches of the Patriot forces, day after day, they died by the wayside; others pitifully clung to their horses. As a result, a recently landed battalion consisting of 300 men was reduced to 150 men after two or three months. [25] The Venezuelan troops also suffered from disease, but Bolívar affirmed that the Royalists suffered more severely. The Royalists were in the further unenviable position of being unable to replenish their troops as Venezuelan men were less apt to sympathize with their cause, nor were they trained for soldiering, and it would take months, if not years, to obtain further troops from Spain.

However, the health situation of fighting troops was not unique to the arena of South America, as disease and lack of medical attention also was the lot of the soldiers in the European wars. In the Peninsular War, the British army lost 24,930 men to disease and 8,889 to enemy fire; in the Crimea, 2,255 men were killed in action, 1,847 died of wounds and there were 17,225 deaths from disease. According to historian, Eric Lambert: 'Ignorance of the process of infection and appalling sanitary conditions in military hospitals meant that death from infection was the outcome of many wounds and operations.' [26]

It is evident that upon arriving in Venezuela with his twenty companions from *The Two Friends*, Vowell was able to adapt himself quickly to these conditions. In his narrative, although he often mentions the good food he was served at different occasions, he did not overly complain about the local food and he gave no details or complaints at all of his illness, recuperation or the attention received. His strong physical constitution and staunch stoicism would become his salvation later in his life as well.

Vowell and his fellow British officers in Bolívar's Dragoon Guard had distinguished themselves not only in battle, but also in training and transforming local troops into a disciplined army. In a letter to Santander, two of Bolívar's senior officers lauded this work, calling it a miracle that the *Llanero* troops now had some discipline.[27] Repetitious drill and rigid discipline were indispensable in the battles of the 19th century, where handling of muskets, powder, and bayonets could cause terrible accidents, and where orders on the battlefield had to be obeyed without delay. As well, there was the underlying realization that only drill and discipline enabled a man to tolerate the severe stresses of the battlefield.[28]

At this time, Bolívar conferred upon all the British officers and privates of his Dragoon Guard who had fought with Páez in the *llanos*, including Vowell, the ribbon and star of the order of *Estrella de Libertadores de Venezuela* (Liberators of Venezuela).[29]

Vowell felt proud of this distinction. Bolívar created this decoration in 1813 and it was so highly prized because it was considered to be the highest award to which a soldier could aspire.[30] The official notice in the Patriot newspaper, *Correo del Orinoco,* stated:

'In the most difficult circumstances, and confronting the greatest dangers, the English officers demonstrated the most noble perseverance and fidelity to the cause they had embraced.' [31]

CHAPTER NINE

The Impassable Pass

Aut inveniam viam aut faciam

(Either I will find a way, or make one)

MAJOR VOWELL was about to experience – or suffer – one of Bolívar's most daring military manoeuvres: the passage of the Venezuelan Patriot army through the Andes. It would also make Vowell known to posterity as the eyewitness who best described it. The march took the Patriots through barren, desert-like lands, across swollen *llanos*, and the cold and 'magnificently wild' Andes mountain range.[1] No one, not even O'Leary, who was also there, described this march better than Vowell, in an episode in which the army overcame nature, before nature claimed any victory over the army.[2] One writer states that no other historian of the time was able to paint such a perfect picture of the forces of nature that hurled obstacles in the path of Bolívar's army as Vowell did; Vowell 'described and painted in vivid colours the scene of action and the distinguished exploits of the Patriots.'[3] Indeed, Luis de Terán points out that Vowell's narration – so very important in understanding the crossing of the Andes in 1819 – has been transcribed by some historians word-for-word, without acknowledging the author.[4]

In March 1819, Bolívar combined all his foreign volunteers into a 'British Legion', commanded by Colonel James Rooke, to which Vowell was assigned, and a Rifles Brigade, commanded by Lieutenant Colonel Arthur Sandes.[5] These formations included the volunteers who were left from the original five ships of 1817, as well as those who had arrived in February 1819. About 4,600 British and Irish volunteers arrived at that time, the British arriving early in the year and the Irish in July. They had been recruited by Colonel James English[6] who had managed to acquire 2,172 volunteers from England, including some Hanoverian veterans of the King's German Legion. Following in July, John D'Evereux's[7] 1,700 Irish volunteers arrived on Margarita Island, a significant number of whom were inexperienced in war. It was they who left soon after arrival, while many others died of the typhus they brought with them. It is fair to say that English and D'Evereux were negligent in not giving the volunteers a more realistic appraisal of the conditions they would have to endure in joining the Patriot army, and the Patriots, particularly in Margarita Island under the commands of Generals Arismendi, Urdaneta and Mariño, had not prepared, at all, the resources needed to receive a large contingency of foreign troops.[8]

The 'Irish Legion' was formed with those that remained and it saw action in the eastern and central parts of Venezuela. It became known more for its bravery than for its discipline and was regarded as '… an unruly lot, who had been duped into enlisting by unscrupulous officers and hated the whole affair.'[9] Nevertheless, the Irish fought bravely and solidly at the Battle of Rio Hacha, although later they sadly mutinied because they were not allowed to pursue the defeated enemy and because there was no water and no pay. Among those of the Irish Legion who did remain with the Patriots was Francis Burdett O'Connor,[10] godson of reformist Member of Parliament Sir Francis Burdett, who became one of Bolívar's trusted aides.[11]

In less than two and a half years, some 5,500 English and Irish volunteers sailed to Venezuela along with arms and supplies. There were, as has been recounted, many deaths due to illness and desertion, but many more died in battle. By 1821, there were about 3,000 survivors.[12] The Patriot army received an important boost with the arrival of these seasoned, yet scarcely paid soldiers. As testimony to the extent to which Bolívar regarded his volunteer troops is the fact that from 1815 until his death he was rarely without a British or Irish aide-de-camp.[13]

Major Vowell and the British Legion left with Bolívar for Apure on 10 March 1819 bound for Mantecal, their 'winter' quarters. Vowell and the Patriot army arrived at Mantecal at the beginning of the rainy season and expected to be there until its end in October, training the troops. To Vowell's surprise and that of all the army, on 27 May they began to march towards Casanare to meet Santander's forces. Casanare was the only region of Nueva Granada that had managed to resist Spanish control, and it was under the control of Santander.[14] The union of Santander and Bolívar's troops would greatly augment the Patriot forces. At this time, the Patriot army consisted of four infantry battalions, a rifle battalion, the *Bravos* of Páez, the British Legion, and 800 cavalry – in total 2,500 men.[15] When united with Santander's two infantry battalions[16] and two cavalry squadrons, the Patriot army would then total 3,400.[17] Generally, and when available to the Patriots, the infantry was armed with smooth bore muskets and the Rifles Brigade had early muzzle loading rifles. The Patriots had very little in the way of artillery and in any case, the terrain did not favour its use.[18]

Unbeknown to Vowell, or any in the army except those of the highest rank, Bolívar's plan was to cross the imposing Andes mountain range, to destroy the army of 4,500 men of the Royalist General Barreiro, and to liberate Nueva Granada. Then, he planned to double back quickly to destroy Morillo's forces before they could aid General José María Barreiro, in attacking Páez or Angostura. On 15 May 1819, General Jacinto Lara[19] arrived at headquarters to join Bolívar and to bring him important information from Santander on the state of the Royalist army which helped the Patriot leader to take this decision. Bolívar only revealed this audacious plan at a council of war held in a shack in the small, poverty-stricken town of Setenta on 23 May. With him were most of his senior generals – Briceño, Anzoátegui, Soublette, Carrillo, Irribarren, Rangel, Plaza, Lara, Manrique, and Rooke. Upon hearing that Bolívar intended to cross the mountains during the rainy season, two *Llanero* generals refused to join the venture and withdrew with their troops, believing that Bolívar's plan would end in disaster, and because, as plainsmen they were loathe to risk their horses on hilly terrain. Rooke, undaunted by this outrageous scheme, affirmed his loyalty to Bolívar and assured him that 'he would follow with the British Legion even beyond Cape Horn'.[20] Generals Bermúdez and Urdaneta were instructed to create a diversion by attacking Calabozo and Barcelona respectively, while the main part of the army would secretly cross the Andes into Nueva Granada. Páez was not present at the meeting at Setenta, as he had orders to march to Cúcuta to cut the enemy's lines of communication but, controversially, he followed his own counsel, not Bolívar's orders, and consequently did not get that far into hilly territory. General Pedro León Torres, in charge of the security of Lower Apure, was combating the Royalists in Achaguas, so he too was absent from the council of war – and was unhappy at missing it.[21]

The Patriots first had to cross the upper *llanos*, between the rivers Apure and Arauca. Vowell described this land as a barren, sandy area with little vegetation, except for a thorny plant that was the bane to the mostly barefoot infantry. The heat caused mirages that Vowell noted, remarkably, did not fool the animals, since they could smell when real water was near and hastened their gait. Some of the troops had to abandon their thirsty horses and carry their saddles on their backs, so debilitating was the lack of water to the horses.

An army, on approaching water, after having suffered much from thirst, exhibits the picture of a complete defeat. It is extremely difficult, upon such occasions, to preserve any subordination for every individual leaves the ranks, and rushes forward, with that wild look which peculiarly characterizes excessive thirst. It would indeed, in most instances, be certain destruction to an army to find an enemy in possession of the water which they themselves were approaching under these circumstances. Such as have never felt the sensation of extreme thirst, cannot possibly form an idea of the welcome refreshment the first long draught of water affords, although the tepid fluid in these pools would disgust any person who was not really and painfully thirsty. It is, in general, of a greenish colour, swarming with insects, and frequently containing the bodies of horses, and other animals, that have just had strength sufficient to reach the water and die. Add to this, that the bullocks and mules, which are driven with the army, rush at once into the pond and, when their thirst is quenched, lie down and roll in it, and some idea may be formed of the polluted draught, that awaits those who arrive latest.

Vowell, *Campaigns and Cruises*, 156

Even under these conditions, Vowell's curiosity prevailed and he managed to observe the various wild animals encountered on the way: the *cachicamo* (small armadillo), red deer, spotted antelope and the antics of the *aguaita-camino* (a small owl) that would observe from the wayside.[22] It seems that Vowell was just unable to ignore the new features of the surroundings through which he travelled, no matter how difficult the journey.

Upon crossing the Arauca River and entering the *llanos* of Casanare, the troops experienced exactly the opposite conditions to those they had just endured. Vowell wrote:

'It is impossible to give an adequate idea of the hardships that the troops suffered during this journey, at a time of the year when it is always considered that the plains cannot be crossed, even by cavalry.'[23]

The infantry had to march for hours with water up to their waists, falling into holes or becoming stuck in mud, and then, at night, they struggled to find even a small area of dry land on which to rest. When fording rivers, they were attacked by small, but fierce caribe fish which, in large swarms, are more frightening than alligators, and capable of eating men or beasts in a very short time. The expeditionaries had to make rafts of driftwood or hides to keep their ammunition and supplies dry as they crossed rivers.[24] O'Leary, another chronicler of this march, states that the rains fell in torrents, soaking already worn uniforms, which were used, in vain, to protect arms and ammunition.[25] The Patriots struggled through this veritable swampy lake for seven days.

As they approached Casanares, the waterfalls and mountain rapids increased the strength of the waters so much that the cavalry had to carry the infantrymen's packs to allow the foot soldiers to form two lines, with hands grasping one another, in order to cross the raging currents without being swept away. Vowell attested to the kindness Bolívar displayed to others during this ordeal.

Bolívar passed repeatedly across, at several of these torrents, carrying soldiers who were weak, and women who were following their husbands … He was, indeed, invariably humane in his attentions to the sick and wounded on a march; and quite as much so to the female emigrants and others, whose sufferings and privations, whether following an army from necessity, or choice, were truly pitiable.

Vowell, *Campaigns and Cruises*, 159

It is not too much of a stretch to surmise that Vowell, in observing such admirable conduct in Bolívar, would have followed his example somehow.

Bolívar had the option of two paths across the Andes, and he chose the steeper one, which had no Spanish threat since it was deemed impassable at this time of the year. As the terrain became steeper, the soil became stony and hard. The horses, used to the plains, became weak and lame, and were the reason an entire corps of *Llaneros* under

Colonel Carbajal, deserted. Vowell recorded:

'Carbajal's men, who bore with cheerfulness their own fatigues could not look with indifference on the hardships and loss of their horses: and left the army in bodies at every halt, until none but a few officers remained.'[26]

Conversely, Colonel Rangel led a corps of men from the mountainous region of Mérida who were in no way deterred by the terrain and did not object to riding mules, which Vowell affirms was 'a degradation to which no true *Llanero* could think of submitting.'[27] Rangel's corps had been 1,500-strong four years previously, but Vowell calculated that by the time they trekked across the mountains, they numbered barely 400 since so many had been killed in the war. Vowell continued his observation of the land and its people throughout this ordeal, commenting on the beauty of the valleys and glens, on the crops and food the mountain people consumed and even comparing their physical constitution unfavourably to that of the robust, beef-fed *Llaneros*. Then, the snowy peaks of the Andes became visible, and they seemed to him to be an inaccessible barrier, impossible to pass. But before reaching them, they had to pass through a rain forest.

The narrow paths leading to the Paramos [moors] *wind among wild mountains which are totally uninhabited and covered with immense forests, overhanging the road, and almost excluding the light of day. The trees are of a vast size; being constantly watered by the clouds they arrest in their passage, which perpetually hang on them, causing an incessant, drizzling rain. This had rendered the paths so slippery, when our army passed, they became excessively dangerous, especially to the few tired mules and bullocks that yet survived the fatigues of the march, and a total privation of sustenance; for nothing whatever grows under these forest trees but ivy, moss, and lichens. In many parts, the torrents that rage from rock to rock, almost perpendicularly beneath the narrow pathway, were so far below, that their roar was scarcely heard; and, as the wearied animals fell one by one, they could be traced in their descent by the rushing of the shrubs, growing in the clefts of the fearful precipice, until they were seen to roll down the foaming stream.*

Vowell, *Campaigns and Cruises*, 161-162

Vowell describes how, in crossing waterfalls and deadly torrents, often they had to use old, flimsy, wooden bridges, or worse, *tarabitas*, a type of woven basket hanging from greased ropes that could hold two people, pulled by lines from one side of a stream to the other. They would transport horses and mules in this way also, with a sling tied around their girth – as Vowell described: 'These *tarabitas* are frequently forty or fifty fathoms across; and the tremendous depth below renders it advisable, for those who have rather weak nerves, to close their eyes while crossing.'[28]

In passing through the rain forest, the army became completely drenched, but not cold. However, on entering the *páramos*, the treeless, barren, unsheltered mountain moors, the cold weather became a serious enemy. As related, the army was poorly clad and Vowell states that those who had started the expedition with shoes certainly had none by this time: 'Many, even of the officers, had literally no trowsers, and were glad to cover themselves with pieces of blanket, or whatever they could procure.'[29] The wind was incessant, there were no paths and the ground was icy.

> *It is not difficult to find the way; for it is strewed with the bones of men and animals that have perished in attempting to cross the Páramos in unfavourable weather. Multitudes of small crosses are fixed in the rocks, by some pious hands, in memory of former travellers who have died here; and along the path are strewed fragments of saddlery, trunks, and various articles that have been abandoned and resemble the traces of a routed army. Huge pinnacles of granite overhang many parts of these passes, apparently tottering, and on the point of overwhelming the daring traveller, while terrific chasms that are appalling to the sight, yawn far beneath, as if to receive him. A sense of extreme loneliness, and remoteness from the world seizes on his mind, and is heightened by the dead silence that prevails; not a sound being heard, but the scream of the condor.*
>
> Vowell, *Campaigns and Cruises*, 164

They pushed on, often enveloped by mist which increased the danger of becoming lost or falling off the mountainside. According to Vowell, at times the wind was so strong that it forced the masses of Patriots to lie on the frozen ground just to avoid being blown over. The men were weak from marching for days without food, and they began dying from the drowsy mountain sickness that compelled them to simply lie down and sleep. Officers would try in vain to stop them from doing so, knowing that once they did, it was the end:

'A night passed on this *Páramo*. The army not being capable of crossing it without a halt was dreadful in the extreme, for the inclemency of the weather. It was impossible to procure fuel for a fire; and had there been any, the continued violent gusts of wind would have prevented it from being kindled. Officers and men, therefore, sat down, huddled together, indiscriminately, in close groups, to keep each other warm. Many died during this truly fearful night.'[30]

Vowell, obviously touched, mentioned that the widow of one Patriot officer, returning home under the protection of the army, died that night along with all her children.

He does not mention that more than a hundred men died of exposure to the cold, oxygen starvation, or by drowning or falling – and fifty of them were British.[31]

All the horses died, which gives credence to the opinions of the *Llaneros* who had refused to march into the mountains with the army. O'Leary wrote that the horses had lain down on the trail and, refusing to move, obstructed the march of those who followed. Even the sure-footed mules lost their balance when forced to carry the loads of the horses plus their own, and they tumbled headlong into the precipices.[32] The Venezuelan soldiers suffered even more than the British because most of them, certainly the *Llaneros* among them, were quite cowed at seeing huge mountains for the first time. Furthermore, the cold weather was a new, and terrifying, experience particularly since most were practically naked.

They were tired, barefoot, sick, hungry, and ill-clothed. It is remarkable that amidst all this danger and suffering, Vowell was, once again, able to observe the beauty of the night skies. Later, as they descended the mountains, in much less discomfort, he remarked on the delightful temperature, the different types of ponies, and the appearance of cultivated fields.

> During this night, the heavens appeared of a dark blue, inclining to black; the number of the stars was either really, or apparently, much increased, and their twinkling evidently a great deal brighter. The moon was also much more prominent and globular in appearance; almost of a metallic lustre; and the dark map on its surface was far plainer to the naked eye than when seen from below. We saw several very brilliant shooting stars; but little difference was observable, except in the greater apparent length of their course, and rapidity of their motion.
>
> Vowell, *Campaigns and Cruises*, 166

At last, on 5 July 1819, the army vanguard reached the town of Socha on the lower western slope of the Andes and to its joy, was greeted warmly by the inhabitants who offered food and support. The army had been on the march for forty days, had travelled 600 kilometres since Mantecal, and was in a pitiful state. A rather novel way of aiding the Patriots was concocted by the parish priest of Socha, Tomás José Romero, and the mayor, José Ignacio Sarmiento: they gathered the people of Socha in the church for a party that was supposed to start with a religious ceremony. After they had entered the church, doors were shut and people were asked to take off any non-necessary item of clothing to donate to the poorly clothed troops. This was done with much hilarity. It was then rightly said of the ensuing battles of Pantano de Vargas and Boyacá, that much of the cavalry wore clothing that had graced the bosoms of the Patriotic women of Socha.[33]

The British Legion was the rearguard in charge of ammunition and supplies, and it was about three days behind the Venezuelan vanguard troops, struggling with its loads. So Bolívar sent General Jacinto Lara to gather as many mules as he could and go to its aid.

Apparently, 'The morale of the troops received encouragement from the buoyant spirits of Col James Rooke who now commanded the British Legion and whose optimism was irrepressible.'[34]

Rooke's optimism and good humour was evident a week later when, in conversation with Bolívar, he was asked how the British Legion was faring. Rooke answered that it was in excellent state, and had not suffered from crossing the *Páramos*. This was met with disbelief from the officers around the table since it was known he had lost two officers and a quarter of his troops, so he admitted the losses deadpan: 'I cannot deny it, but they deserved it – those were the most undisciplined lot of them all.'[35] This stoic black humour brought a smile to Bolívar's face.

The Patriot army's crossing of the Andes is considered to be one of Bolívar's major military achievements.

'It was an undertaking that has few equals in military history; seldom have men been called upon to overcome such obstacles; one cannot but marvel at their courage and admire the tenacity of purpose that upheld them.'[36]

How to feed, how to shelter, and how to move an army in the field remain today the most immediate and most persistent problems that a commander has to solve.[37] It is not clear whether, in 1819, the improvident state of the Patriot army as it faced the rigours of the Andes was due to a genuine lack of resources or because it had not thought to prepare for the risks by taking on more food and clothing. If Bolívar had not succeeded in facing up to, and overcoming this ordeal, thus ensuring that the crossing was hailed as a brilliant tactical accomplishment, it would certainly have gone down in history as a folly and a blunder. But succeed he did, even with an exhausted army; such can be the force of an army's high morale and a sense of purpose believed worth fighting for.

CHAPTER TEN

The British Legion

'Yet, Freedom! Thy banner, torn, but flying,
Streams like the thunder-storm against the wind.'

Lord Byron, *Childe Harold's Pilgrimage*, Canto 4,1

MAJOR VOWELL was now assigned to the newly established British Legion, whose motto was '*Die or Conquer!*' The Legion, together with the British Rifles Brigade, had travelled to Mantecal and across the Andes with Bolívar and the main arm of the Patriot Army, positioned in the rearguard commanded by General José Antonio Anzoátegui.[1] Bolívar had high hopes for the British troops as is evident in his proclamation to the people of Nueva Granada on 30 June 1819:

'From more remote climates, a British Legion has left their glorious land to obtain the fame of Saviours of America!' [2]

Since they had been busy training the native troops, as a unit, the British Legion had not yet been under fire. Now, the moment had come for Bolívar to witness his British formation in battle for the first time – and he would not be disappointed.

Vowell reveals that the Patriot Army reached the valley of Sogamozo before the Spanish realized that it had crossed the Andes. However, the commander of Spanish forces in Nueva Granada, Colonel José María Barreiro, who had referred disdainfully to Bolívar's troops as an 'army of beggars', learned they were there, and on 25 July 1819 he placed his 3,000 troops and 500 cavalry in an elevated area of *pantanos* (swamps) above Pantano de Vargas, between the mountains and the key city of Tunja. Here he engaged the Patriot Army. Bolívar very much wanted to take this city, the provincial capital, where he knew the Patriots had a great deal of support.

Vowell describes succinctly the ensuing Battle of Pantano de Vargas. He was in the very thick of it and, in his usual self-effacing way, does not express his own personal experience of the fierce hand-to-hand combat that ensued.

Although Bolívar's forces were in a very weak state, from the recent severe fatigue and privations they had undergone, and were labouring under the accumulated disadvantages of the bad condition of their firearms, and a deficiency of ammunition, he did not hesitate for a moment to attack the Royalists in their position. They had at first some slight advantage, in consequence of their superiority in numbers; but the fortune of the day was eventually turned in favour of the Patriots, by a few hundred English.

Vowell, *Campaigns and Cruises,* 168

At this battle, Bolívar counted on 2,200 soldiers. Under a hail of bullets and with lightning speed, the British Legion, led by Colonel Rooke and apparently comprising between 80-90 men, stormed the heights where the main corps of the Spanish troops was positioned. Their example spurred the Rifles and the Barcelona Battalion to follow.[3] Vowell records that Rooke was wounded at the beginning of the encounter and subsequently lost an arm. His place was taken by Major John McIntosh[4] who then '... led the soldiers up a very steep hill, under a heavy fire, which they did not return, until they had reached the heights, from whence they drove the Spaniards in confusion, at the point of the bayonet.'[5]

Colonel Arthur Sandes of the Rifles Brigade was twice wounded, but he continued fighting until his horse was shot under him; he supported himself against the dying animal, refusing to leave the field until victory was declared.[6] The Legion had forced the enemy to retreat with its bayonets and gained the summit.[7] The Battle of Pantano de Vargas was a ferocious battle that lasted from 11 a.m. to about 7 p.m., but it boosted the morale of the Patriot Army and sapped the confidence of the Royalist army. General Anzoátegui, a very brave and able young man, but also an overly serious one, had not been content with having to handle the new British volunteers but, after the Battle of Pantano de Vargas, he admitted that the British, whom he had considered not worth their rations, were now worth their weight in gold.[8] Bolívar said of this encounter:

'Three battalions of the enemy (*Numancia, Tambo* and *Dragones Regente*) were attacked by the rearguard headed by the British Legion which attacked the enemy with all intrepidity and they beat and dispersed them.'[9]

During the Peninsular War, the British army had focused on training its troops to charge with the bayonet. The effectiveness of this type of fighting was evident when the British Legion and Rifles charged at the battle of Pantano de Vargas, and later at the battles of Boyacá and Carabobo. When British officers were distributed among other battalions, they trained their men in British tactics and in this method of fighting, which became increasingly common throughout the Patriot Army.[10] Once again, as throughout history, technology and its methods give the upper hand in warfare.

There are not many surviving first-hand descriptions of the battle, but those that have survived are not in disagreement. The area was a narrow defile. The Spanish had the advantage of having positioned themselves on a higher ridge and of having superior numbers. Bolívar was hemmed in by the swamps on one side and the heights occupied by Barreiro. It seemed that the Patriots were in a trap until the British Legion's surprise charge. Then, when the British, and all who followed them, were almost surrounded and being fired at from every angle – at the very moment when it seemed they started to give way, Bolívar ordered the Venezuelan cavalry into the fray, exhorting the cavalry commander, Colonel Juán José Rondón, 'Coronel, save your country!' Rondón, accompanied by Lieutenant Carvajal, led the cavalry charge, and, amazingly with just 18 men, routed the Royalists. The battle lasted about six hours. The Patriots lost 104 men, among them many British, but the Royalists lost 500 men.[11] Major MacIntosh later said about the battle:

'In the battle of Vargas, from my battalion, were knocked out of combat one *coronel* with an amputated arm, my aide was killed, a lieutenant badly wounded, seven soldiers killed and twenty wounded, all in all, thirty: there were eighty of us when the action started, including officers and men.'[12]

The Patriots took many prisoners, about 1,600, plus arms and ammunition.[13] It was a significant victory for the Patriots considering they had the smaller force of which only a half were experienced soldiers. They fought with little clothing, in cold weather and on fog-shrouded heights, against a well-clad, well-fed and organized European army.[14] Vowell was well aware of the immediate consequences of this victory.

This was an important advantage gained by Bolívar, for he had now obtained a strong position, in a country where all were friendly to him; where there was also plenty of provisions to refresh his exhausted soldiers, and an ample supply of clothing, of which they stood greatly in need. Recruits soon flocked in from all quarters, and Bolívar found himself, in a short time, at the head of an army, respectable in number and appearance, and anxiously desiring to be led against the enemy.

Vowell, *Campaigns and Cruises,* 169

The loss of Colonel Rooke was greatly lamented. Vowell attributed blame on the friars of a small monastery in Tunja in whose hands he was left after the English army surgeon had amputated his arm. The friars, according to Vowell, had removed Rooke's bandages and applied their own concoction of oil and wine, which resulted in the onset of gangrene and the good colonel's swift death. As military historian John Keegan describes such occurrences, 'For at work now were the principal enemies of the wounded soldier of the period: shock, peritonitis, dehydration, loss of blood – much of it by artificial bleeding.'[15]

As his arm was severed, Rooke remained impassive, '…with his usual cheerfulness and courage.'[16] Then he took the limb, raised it, and said '*Viva la patria!*' (Long live our country!). Upon hearing this, the surgeon asked him: 'Which country, England or Ireland?' to which Rooke replied: 'The one that will bury me.'[17] He died the next day.

Rooke's stoic death is a classic example of the 19th century 'cult of the sword' which '… stressed two supreme ideals – fidelity and an indifference to physical hardship.' It was not only how he faced death, but in what manner a soldier endured wounds that increased his honour.[18] This may also explain why Vowell, in his writings, hardly dwelled upon his own hardships or wounds. Colonel Rooke was missed and highly praised by Bolívar. The Patriot Army Bulletin that day, 25 July 1819, published the following account:

> 'A rearguard column, led by the British Legion, charged the enemy with such intrepidity that it was beat and dispersed… All the army corps have distinguished themselves, but particular mention should be made of the conduct of Commander Rondón and Lt. Carbajal, and the British companies, to which, even though it was the first time that they fought under our flags, they have been given the Star of the Libertadores as a reward for their constancy and valour.'[19]

This was the second time Major Vowell merited the coveted Star of the Liberators.

Meanwhile, for ten days following this battle, at Corrales de Bonza, Vowell, along with his fellow British troops, made enormous efforts to train the 800 volunteers from Nueva Granada that had now joined the Patriot Army – all inexperienced men, who had never fired a shot. There was little time. Vowell would have taken part in the subsequent action in which the Patriot Army took over the town of Paypa (3 August) and, after a 21-mile detour marching in silence, the town of Tunja (5 August). Here they availed themselves of Royalist arms and ammunition, much needed food, clothes and medicine, and were able to rest for almost forty hours.

The defeated José María Barreiro needed to block the Patriots' way to Bogotá, the capital, where the Viceroy of Nueva Granada, the tyrannical Juán José de Sámano had his headquarters. By skilful manoeuvre however, and after marching from dawn until noon, Bolívar caught up with him before Bogotá, positioning his troops between Barreiro and the capital. The armies met before the bridge of Boyacá, south of Tunja. Boyacá was a small, hilly, valley with a very narrow bridge over a river that ran through it. On 7 August 1819, the river was swollen from the rains and its banks, thick with bushes and trees, were overflowing. The road meandered through steep hillsides. There were low ridges of barren rock and shallow ravines. Vowell, always attuned to the culture around him, explained the symbolic importance of this place of battle:

'This place was remarkable, as being the spot where the last battle had been fought, and lost, by the ancient inhabitants of Cundinamarca[20] against the Spanish invaders. It was now destined to witness the last struggle, and total defeat of the Spaniards in New Grenada.'[21]

Both armies were tired, but the Spaniards had just spent the last forty-eight hours hiking though rain, making detours to avoid Bolívar. The Spanish troops numbered 3,000, while the Patriot Army had about 3,000 to 3,200 men, but only 2,000 were veteran soldiers. Bolívar kept in reserve, out of the battle, the recently recruited, untrained recruits from Nueva Granada. The Spanish vanguard positioned in front and to one side of the bridge, was cut off from the main army by the Patriot rearguard that had positioned itself between the Spanish, the bridge, and the rest of the Royalist army, which was advancing towards the bridge. The British Legion blocked the bridge and engaged the Royalist vanguard, while Santander and the rest of the army attacked the main Spanish forces. Soon Barreiro surrendered. He was later executed along with his officers by an unnecessary order of Santander.

Bolívar's losses were 13 dead and 53 wounded, whereas the Spaniards suffered 200 dead and 2,000 prisoners. It was Bolívar's greatest victory and the most celebrated of the battles of independence because with the success of the Battle of Boyacá, Nueva Granada – soon to be Gran Colombia – was liberated from Spanish rule and it would become the springboard for the liberation of Venezuela, Ecuador, Bolivia, and Perú.[22] Boyacá is considered to be one of the great battles of the revolution in northern South America.

Success at Pantano de Vargas and Boyacá would not have been possible without the timely arrival of the British legionnaires. Bolívar needed disciplined infantry; the cavalry of the *llanos* alone was not able to hold territory, and cavalry is useless in mountainous areas. With trained infantry, Bolívar strengthened his army and also obtained greater mobility as detachments of foreign legionnaires were able to aid the generals in the northern-central and eastern regions against Morillo.[23]

Vowell does not provide details of his personal role in the battle. One historian unfairly criticizes this impersonality and believes he lacked synthesis about the transcendental actions that he himself contributed toward.[24] Another historian even doubts he was there.[25] A rather more insightful interpretation of Vowell's account should make the distinction between the battle accounts of a military historian and that of a soldier who actually does the fighting. The historian generalizes and dissects, qualifies and particularizes, perhaps even simplifies, but his or her main focus is a battle's outcome. The soldier's view is the entangled, confusing, roaring, smoky, perilous, horrific event that is a battlefield. This experience is more complicated to describe than the narrative of a non-combatant historian focusing, with hindsight, on outcomes or strategies. The experience may be so complicated that the soldier may not deem it possible to later write about it. As General S.L.A. Marshall has said, the battlefield is a place of terror;[26] it presents circumstances of extreme personal danger in which the soldier or officer confronts the battle's confusion by acting or giving urgent, but simple, commands such as *'Forward!'* or *'Form a square!'* or *'Fire at will!'* under tremendous stress.[27] Lieutenant Brown, a veteran of the Napoleonic Wars, wrote to that effect:

> 'The smoke, the bustle, which I fear is almost inseparable to Regiments when close to the enemy, and more particular the attention which is required from the company officers to their men, intercepts all possibility of their giving any correct account of the battles in which they may be engaged.'[28]

Major Vowell, as an officer, would have been too concerned with the immediate military goal before him and the survival of his men and himself during the battle, to obtain a detailed view of what was happening elsewhere, but he certainly understood and he wrote about his corps' role and the significance of what was achieved. He simply chose not to use florid language, which was not in his character, but which latter-day historians would amply use to depict these battles.

> Barreyra, on finding his capture inevitable, threw away his sword, to avoid the mortification of being obliged to surrender it to Bolívar, whose military talents he had always affected to treat with the greatest contempt in his proclamations. He was taken prisoner, with all his surviving officers, among whom was his second in command, Colonel Ximenes, a Spaniard, well known to the Patriots for his inveterate hatred and cruelty to them. He was distinguished by the appellation of *El Caricortado* (Scarface), from a sabre wound he had formerly received in the face. His favourite mode of putting prisoners to death, was by having them tied back-to-back, and thrown into a river, while he stood by, delighting to witness their struggles for life.
>
> Vowell, *Campaigns and Cruises,* 170

Vowell, who very much believed in army discipline and codes, laments that it was difficult for the army to protect the numerous Royalist prisoners from the vengeance of the peasantry that was now armed with the weapons that the Royalists had abandoned in their flight for, '… they held them in detestation, on account of the system of cruelty and robbery that they had exercised towards them.'[29]

The war between Spain and her colonies was not just a disagreement between a European and a Creole elite, as could be said of the war for independence in the United States. Four hundred years of imperial, and mostly brutal, Spanish domination had become increasingly onerous to the colonial populations, creating a true, but ultimately, deplorable rift between peoples that even had shared elements of culture, language, and religion, at least among the non-indigenous colonials. As for the Indigenous peoples, during the Conquest a small number of well-armed Spanish soldiers were able to systematically exterminate a population of 70- to 100 million indigenous people in Latin America. None of the wars and conflicts of the 20th century can compare to this genocide.[30] Two centuries after the Spanish Conquest, in 1778, the chronicles of a priest, Fray Felix de Villanueva, relate that in the indigenous missions in Venezuela the natives never forgot the cruelties that the first Spaniards visited upon their ancestors.[31]

Vowell sketches a vivid picture of what happened next. After the Battle of Boyacá, Bolívar force-marched his army to the capital and only when advised of his imminent arrival, did the Bogoteños realize that the Spanish army had been defeated. Vowell reveals that Viceroy Sámano had kept from the population, and even his own officers, news of the total defeat of his army because he wanted to escape to the Magdalena River and did not want the road to be crowded with refugees. He did escape, at midnight, disguised as a Capuchin friar, along with all the other Spanish friars of that order. Vowell describes that many Royalist officers were running around the streets trying to get horses and cursing Sámano, who had assured them that Bolívar's men had been cut to pieces and that 'with his old sandals he could annihilate the miserable remnant that had escaped.'[32]

The city of Bogotá erupted in joy and hailed Bolívar as its liberator and his troops as heroes. The British Legionnaires, as well as their Venezuelan and Nueva Granada comrades, wore local sandals or 'alpargatas' as not one of them had a pair of boots or socks.

> Crowds of all ranks thronged the streets, congratulating each other on an event that they had hardly dared to hope for; and while some busied themselves in preparing triumphal arches in the Plaza and principal streets to receive the victorious army, others hastened out to meet Bolívar, and to conduct him into the city. The army entered Bogotá, proceeded by the band of music that had formerly belonged to the Spaniards, and hailed by the acclamation of the inhabitants, who vied with each other in expressions of joy and gratitude… Every principal inhabitant was desirous of securing one or two officers, as inmates of his house; more especially Englishmen, to whom they expressed the highest gratitude, for the share they had in the last victories.
>
> Vowell, *Campaigns and Cruises,* 177

It is interesting that in describing the triumphant entry into Bogotá, Vowell highlights, not a heroic action of the army, but the death of a young Patriot woman of Bogotá, Doña Apolinaria Zalabarriata, who was shot to death by Sámano along with her fiancé just before Bolívar's victory.[33]

Vowell obviously admired women, not only in terms of their charms, about which he certainly wrote, but also their courage as protagonists in time of war. And he displays his attention to the role of women by poignantly reporting this young heroine's death. She was:

'...enthusiastically attached to the cause of liberty; she devoted herself to the hazardous task of obtaining and transmitting to Bolívar, secret intelligences respecting the force, disposition, and plans of operation of the Royalist army.'[34]

Doña Apolinaria Zalabarriata and her fiancé were bound and led together before a firing squad, she having refused to be bribed into confessing the names of her collaborators and she urged her lover not to do so either.

> She implored him as her last request, if he had ever really loved her, to shew, by his death, that he was worthy of her choice, assuring him that the tyrant, Zámano, would never spare his life, whatever disclosures he might make, and reminding him that he ought to derive consolation from the reflection that his death was shared by her he loved. The friars then retired and the firing party made ready. She then, for the first time, felt dread, and exclaimed '*Conque, verdugos, teneis valor de matar una mujer!*' (You have then the heart, butchers, to kill a woman!) She immediately covered her face with her *saya* (tunic) and, on drawing it aside for that purpose, the words '*Viva la Patria!*' (Long live our land!) were discovered embroidered in gold on the *basquiña* (skirt). The signal was then given from the Viceroy's balcony, and they were both instantly shot.
>
> Vowell, *Campaigns and Cruises*, 175

It is rare to see in a military narration a writer really aware of women as an integral part of the whole scene. Vowell also believed in romantic love, as idealization can be seen in his fictional and non-fictional writing to that effect. The Patriot soldiers had no scarcity of women; wives or sweethearts would follow the army just as they did in Europe. Bolívar, after the death of his young wife, was famously promiscuous, and did not encourage his officers to marry; indeed, those that were married left their wives in the towns. Vowell wrote wistfully that when Bolívar was a young man in Madrid, he '... had the fortune... to captivate the affections, and receive the hand, of a daughter of the Marqués de Uztaron.'[35] As for the British officers, they were men of the lenient Regency period, not the prudish Victorian, and would have no scruples in engaging in relationships with women; although coming from a very class-conscious culture, they would have had different rules of conduct with respect to 'ladies' of their own class. The Rifles had quite a reputation, not just for renowned heroism, but also for disorderly conduct and for their 'gallantry' in monopolizing girls.[36] But Vowell does not equate the high jinxes of his regiments with any lack of moral standards; indeed, he criticizes the Spanish army for '...those scenes of dissipation and licentiousness, for which the armies of modern Spain are notorious.'[37] What is interesting is that Vowell displays awareness for women by including in his narrative descriptions of the women he encountered, their ways and customs and, most importantly, their role in the war of independence, as can be seen in his sketches of women in Guayana, the *Llanos*, Caracas, Bogotá, Guayaquil, Santiago, Lima, Valdivia, and the mention of women such as Páez's wife, Doña Apolinaria, and a native woman, Ancáfila.

There was joy among the inhabitants of Bogotá with the overthrow of a viceroy who was 'sanguinary and covetous to an extreme.'[38] Nothing succeeds like success, and those who still harboured fealty to Spain, changed allegiance completely in favour of the Patriots, and almost all the native-born who had fought for the Royalists changed sides to the army of the liberators.[39]

As for the British volunteers, they continued training the newly raised Colombian troops, with such effectiveness that five years later, the Rifle Battalion consisted of 1,200 Indigenous warriors and only 10 British officers.[40] Many historians have referred to them as 'mercenaries' and never was such a word so ill-used nor a corps so misinterpreted. At the time of Boyacá, the British officers and men had not received a penny since they had arrived, so poor were Bolívar's coffers. The native-born Creole troops were fighting for their homeland and did not expect any payment, unlike the foreign troops. While it is true that many foreigners joined the Patriots thinking of riches, most of these deserted shortly upon arrival; but for those who stayed, it was not remuneration that lured them into battle.[41] The British Legion and the Rifles, along with the Creole corps who fought that day, were given the honour and the right to place the name of '*Boyacá*' on their banners.

In the end, they gave their lives for South American independence. According to one writer:

> 'Most of the British Legion perished in the war. They joined an army of almost naked men, destitute of baggage, tents, commissariat and ambulance, fighting in a tropical country of indescribable difficulty; where capture meant probable death, and victory was usually followed by a general slaughter of prisoners; where the path of war led across plains which turned from desert to swamp with the change of season, through a labyrinth of deep rivers infested by crocodiles, mosquitoes and caribes (man-eating fish) and over a vast mass of frozen mountains.'[42]

Many more, thousands more, of native-born Venezuelans and Colombians died heroically in this war also, but it can be said that they did so for their own homeland. There is something extraordinarily generous about foreigners who chose to face death for the sake of someone else's country. Today there is a plaque at the entrance of the Colombian Parliament honouring the British Legion; a plaque also at the National Pantheon in Caracas where their banner has a place of honour; and monuments to the memory of Colonel Rooke at the bridge of Boyacá and outside the Colombian monastery where the hero died.[43] On 19 February 1820, the Patriot newspaper, *Correo del Orinoco*, published a poem honouring the British Legion and Colonel Rooke, which, translated, reads,

'Also the loss we mourn
of brave Rooke whose daring
led him breathe his last
among the enemy.
Deserved praises
To the Britons in his company
Who left the banks of the Thames
To defend our dear Liberty
Their new adopted nation
Shall know to crown
Their efforts and their pains
Their triumph will not be less admired
Than that at Waterloo plains.'

To honour the brave British volunteers who helped to secure their independence, the government of Venezuela gave British troops the singular military honour, in perpetuity, of being the only foreign troops allowed to parade on Venezuelan soil with drawn bayonets. To this day, that promise is kept by Venezuela.

CHAPTER ELEVEN

The Albion Battalion

'Good morning; good morning!' the General said
When we met him last week on our way to the line.
Now the soldiers he smiled at are most of 'em dead,
And we're cursing his staff for incompetent swine.'

Siegfried Sassoon, *The General*, 1918

MAJOR VOWELL rejoiced in Bolívar's uncommonly complete victory over the Spanish army in Nueva Granada and the capturing of all its military equipment. He and his British comrades were now paid for the first time. Until now, the Patriot Army had little or no capacity to meet the salary expectations of its foreign troops, but since it found about half a million pesos in the Viceroy's treasury, the British were given full pay although the Venezuelan and Colombian troops, who generally did not expect payment, received only half-pay. From this moment on, Bolívar's army was able to pay salaries on a more regular basis.[1]

At this time, Bolívar was busy realizing one of his dreams – the union of Venezuela and Nueva Granada, which he accomplished on 25 December 1819, creating the new Republic of Gran Colombia which included Venezuela, Ecuador and Colombia.[2]

Meanwhile, Vowell and his comrades were able to stay almost three months in Bogotá, training the many new recruits, recuperating from wounds and, as much as possible, enjoying life in the beautiful city during a peaceful time on that side of the Andes. He paints a picture of a joyful Bogotá in August 1819, full of gaiety, with balls, concerts, *tertulias* (soirées), fireworks and parades. He found the local people very hospitable and they enjoyed talking to foreigners, particularly asking questions about Europe, 'about which they have, in general, very confused and indefinite ideas.'[3] He describes the city as sitting at the foot of a very steep hill on whose summit were two chapels accessible by a narrow, winding path with scarcely footing for a goat.

The traveller, whose curiosity may lead him to ascend this mountain, will find himself amply repaid for the difficulty and danger of the undertaking, by the magnificent view from these chapels. The whole of the city, with its numerous churches, monasteries, and private gardens, is below his feet; and the valley of Bogotá, thickly scattered with villages and farms, and so well watered as to appear, in general, as if inundated, is seen in its whole extent, as far as the tableland and town of La Mesa, near Tocayama.

Vowell, *Campaigns and Cruises,* 180

Vowell paid attention to the details of houses and streets, and admired the 'delightful' villa that was Bolívar's refuge to where he '... used to retire from the palace, as often as he could escape from the necessary business of state.'[4] He was interested in the local agriculture, including the type of plough used, the manner of threshing the corn, and the great care taken of mules. And, attentive to the opposite sex, he did not neglect noticing the daily routine and dress codes of the 'fair ladies' of the city with whom he was greatly taken.

The ladies of this city are remarkably lively, and pleasing in their manners. They are in general small in stature, and delicately formed; resembling, in shape and features, the Andalusian women, more perhaps than do any other inhabitants of S. America. The coolness of the climate enables them to take a great deal more exercise than is usual in other large cities; and this gives them a freshness of complexion, rarely to be observed in other parts of this country.

Vowell, *Campaigns and Cruises,* 178

Vowell also enjoyed visiting chapels, churches, convents, and monasteries wherever he went, admiring their artistic merits. Not amiss with his Christian background, he often referred to depictions of Jesus as 'Our Saviour' and considered the Bogotá processions of Holy Week as 'splendid'. However, he was highly critical of the clergy that were corrupt, calling them ignorant and intolerant petty sovereigns in their parishes. He did recognize the worth of the clergy who actually helped others, such as those at the San Juan de Dios Hospital in Bogotá, which he called 'a noble institution', and absolved the friars who ran it 'from charges of gluttony, indolence, and total uselessness, which are imputed, with too great truth, to many of their brethren of other orders.'[5]

Although he hunted, Vowell loathed unnecessary cruelty to animals and this attitude is evident from his mentioning the very deep and rapid waterfall of Salto de Tequedama a few miles outside the city.[6] Here, the aboriginal people of the area would occasionally be paid by visitors to launch an arrow-like tree trunk into the stream, to watch it fall into the abyss, only for it to come back up again, completely shattered to pieces. Vowell denounced Spanish rule under which parties would meet there for the purpose of having a live bullock thrown in, to be swept over the cataract: 'This cruel exhibition, however, as well as that of bull fighting, had been abolished, much to the credit of the Colombian government.'[7] Vowell's observation about the Patriots' disgust of bull fighting is corroborated by Captain Basil Hall of the Royal Navy and commander of *HMS Conway*, which was sailing in South American waters at that time. Hall recorded in his memoirs that,

'In every instance in South America, where the cause of independence has succeeded, two measures have been invariably adopted; one, the abolition of the slave trade, and as far as possible, of slavery; the other, the relinquishment of bull fights.'[8]

The war was not over, by far. The British units were reorganized and Vowell's British Legion, united with the Second Battalion of Rifles, was renamed the 'Albion Battalion' totalling, in all, about 200 Englishmen. With Colonel MacIntosh as its commander, the Albion was given the position of vanguard in the now denominated Army of the South.[9] The Rifles, under Colonel Sandes, were assigned to go with Bolívar to Venezuela where Morillo was now isolated, but as yet undefeated. The Rifles would eventually cover themselves in military glory at the Battle of Carabobo, which finally liberated Venezuela.[10] Vowell was singled out for a particular honour which could have been given only to an upright and scrupulous officer. He was selected to be a member of a permanent court martial panel which was established within each battalion with which to maintain discipline, particularly as desertions of recruits was so common. He was the only European invited to sit at this court. How ironic this honour must have seemed to him in his later life when the tables were turned on him.

Most unfortunately, the competent General Anzoátegui died of an illness in Pamplona on 15 September 1819 and the command of the Army of the South was handed over to the less than competent General Manuel Valdés.[11] Valdés was told not to rely on Bogotá for supplies, so his army would have to forage for food, and was even expected to make its own powder.[12] General José Mirez also was assigned to this army.

The Army of the South left Bogotá on 8 November 1819. Its orders were to march to Quito and, on the way, to deal with Royalist guerrillas scattered throughout the south of Nueva Granada, who were terrorizing the mountainous areas of Popayán, Neiva and Pasto. Vowell graphically depicted the arduous march through the chain of the Andes, across torrential rivers, over precarious cliffs and steep ravines – a difficult and dangerous journey of a thousand miles.

The road, after leaving Santa Fé de Bogotá, passes for a considerable distance along causeways which have been raised in the midst of marshes. After passing the Indian village of Bogotá, from which the capital has received its name, the road is level and good, through Fontabon, as far as La Boca del Monte. Here the escalera [stairs] commences, being a succession of broad stone steps, each a foot in height, cut in the solid rock. By this the army descended, through a deep glen, covered on each side with magnificent forest trees, to a rugged ridge, about a thousand yards below the level of the tableland of Bogotá. It became necessary, of course, to dismount the artillery, and to convey the guns and their carriages to the bottom on mules. The confusion was very great among the baggage animals, several of which fell under their loads, and rolled over each other, to the great embarrassment of the peons.

Vowell, *Campaigns and Cruises*, 196-197

On 23 April 1820, the Albion Battalion made a successful surprise attack on a large Royalist party a few miles from Neiva in La Plata, with few losses being suffered by the Patriot Army. Vowell reported that, 'The Royalist army lost several killed and wounded, and retreated precipitately over the mountains, leaving behind them their baggage and stores.'[13]

According to Vowell, from Neiva, there were two ways to cross the *Páramo*. Ordinary travellers used a shorter route of about fifteen days and Vowell gives an account of this unbelievably difficult and dangerous road through swampy forest, with its narrow shelters called *tambos*, which were no more than ruinous huts full of scorpions, mosquitoes, and vermin of all types. This route necessarily required the employ of Indian carriers, called *Chasqui*, without whose help it would be impossible to cross, and who would convey goods and passengers on their backs across deep gullies.

They carry their load on a pad which rests on their shoulders, in the same manner as that used by the porters in London… With the assistance of a garrote or stout staff, which they find essentially necessary for steadying them in the perilous, slippery descents, they carry with apparent ease from six to eight arrobas (that is, from a hundred and fifty to two under pounds) at a kind of trotting pace, and can persevere in this hard work for a month together, travelling eight or nine hours a day… When they carry passengers, they have a small chair, with elbows, strapped to their shoulders. In this, each traveller secures himself firmly, so as to avoid, as much as possible, any motion which might shake the bearer, and probably throw him off his balance.

Vowell, *Campaigns and Cruises*, 200-201

It is clear from his detailed descriptions that Vowell had taken this route at some point. However, it was not a route that any army could take. The Patriots chose a much longer, winding track through the mountains that would take them a month to traverse. It is possible that Vowell did not leave Bogotá with the army, but followed days later, taking the shorter route until he caught up with them. That would account for him being familiar with both routes.

> *The road, winding through rocky defiles, was frequently obstructed by torrents, across most of which bamboo bridges were thrown. These had, in general, been greatly damaged by the enemy in their retreat, but were readily repaired by our soldiers, as material was to be found in plenty, and the construction was very simple. The road wound along the edges of torrents, meeting occasionally small villages and tambos, with patches of barley, potatoes, and aracacha. Notwithstanding the weather being comparatively fine, when we passed this Páramo, we lost nearly as many men as at the former one. A short time previous to our arrival, the Padre Cura (parish priest) of a neighbouring village died here, on the top of the pass, together with all his attendants, from the inclemency of the weather.*
>
> Vowell, *Campaigns and Cruises*, 203

A number of aboriginal people were employed to carry baggage and powder, as even mules found it impossible to cross the *Páramo*. One of these, a chief named Lorenzo, confided in Vowell that he was such a bitter enemy of the Spaniards that while acting as a guide, he had a decoyed a few of them off the road to their deaths – such was the deep animosity which the Spanish powers had fostered among the aboriginal peoples.[14]

On 6 June 1820, the Albion vanguard finally reached the town of Pitayo at the foot of the mountain range. By now, after more than six months of travel, the Battalion was in a weakened condition, depicted by Vowell as severely fatigued, half-starved, having had no rations for two days, in ragged clothes and with weapons in bad order for lack of time and shelter to clean them. Unfortunately, the unit found no provisions of any kind in the vicinity, and while they were wandering around looking for foodstuffs, suddenly the Spanish launched an attack on the English. A three-hour battle ensued in which the enemy had all the advantage of surprise and the deployment of fresh, rested, well-fed troops.

> *Every man knew, however, that the case was desperate, for it was out of the question to think of retreating over the Páramo they had just passed. They, therefore, vigorously attacked the Spaniards, who were advancing down the heights into the town; and in spite of a heavy fire, drove them, at the point of bayonet, back again up the hill and into the woods that surrounded the town. The enemy fled in confusion to Guambía, leaving the road for about three leagues strewed with arms, accoutrements, and baggage. They lost, also many killed, wounded, and prisoners; these last were subsequently shot, by order of Valdéz.*
>
> Vowell, *Campaigns and Cruises*, 205

As one historian has noted, 'For saving the day at Pitayo much credit was due to Lt Col MacIntosh and his 200 Englishmen.'[15] But, as well, the creole Neiva Battalion demonstrated great bravery at the battle of Pitayo. The historical record shows that the toll on the Patriots was 30 dead, and 62 wounded, including 3 from the Albion Battalion, while the Royalists lost 4 officers, 130 dead, and 80 wounded. The Patriots took 150 prisoners, who, according to Vowell, Valdés had shot.[16] For the British officers this would have been a sore issue, and one which cast misgivings on Valdés' leadership.

The defeated and now dispirited Spanish army retreated to Popayán, leaving the road that led to the valley of Cauca open to the Patriots, but this road was wretched. Encumbered as the Patriots were with the wounded, not having enough mules to carry them, their baggage or powder, they had to traverse a rutted and muddy road where often the mules would be stuck up to their middles, or would collapse with exhaustion. The troops themselves were exhausted for lack of food. Despite all this, Vowell, as always, was able to note the beauty of the Cauca valley through which they were passing.

> *The view of the valley of Cauca is exceedingly beautiful, as it first opens on the sight, from a steep hill over the little city of Caloto, which is the first habitable place to be seen, on emerging from the gloomy woods that cover the mountains… The valley forms an extensive amphitheatre, and is perfectly level, to the very feet of the lofty mountains by which it is surrounded on every side, particularly toward the sea coast. The River Cauca, from which the valley takes its name, smooth in its course through the low country, winds along the valley in a serpentine direction, and may be traced in all its fertilizing wanderings from this eminence.*
>
> Vowell, *Campaigns and Cruises*, 207

The city of Cali, Vowell viewed as large, clean, with a mountain stream running through it, well-stocked gardens and overall, a place where sickness was hardly known. In contrast, and unfortunately, the Patriots were not in Cali, but had to remain in the town of Quilichao, which they reached on 1 July 1820. Vowell recounts that the war had put an end to extensive gold mining operations in the area since the slave labourers and hired peons had been pressed into one army or another during the conflict. They encountered desolately poor women and children '… cowering and dejectedly, from their miserable hovels.'[17] They stayed for a few weeks in this depressing town, training the recruits they had been gathering from the towns through which they had travelled. They withstood severe thunderstorms, which killed one soldier, as well as several earthquakes 'remarkable for their violence and duration.'[18] More significantly, they suffered from lack of medical provisions. The men of the Albion were particularly incensed because some of their number had died due to the army's lack of appropriate medical instruments for amputations, and there was no money available with which to obtain them. There was much sickness and desertion among the recruits.[19] In early July, they finally reached the city of Popayán after only a small skirmish with the enemy.

Vowell's narrative bears witness to the misconduct of the army's commanding officer. General Valdés did not allow the troops into the city, but instead he ordered them to camp outside it and for three days allowed only he and his staff to enter Popayán where '… he filled his coffers with plate and contributions – funds voluntarily given by the inhabitants in support of the Patriot Army – and indulged, without scruple, in every species of excess.' This infuriated Colonel MacIntosh, who was already disgusted by Valdés' general behaviour; Valdés had ordered that the body of an English officer, who had died of a fever, was to be buried in the sand by the River Cauca. Furthermore, his addiction to gambling led him to embezzle army funds to pay his gambling debts while in Cali. So displeased was MacIntosh with this state of affairs, that he threatened Valdés with marching his Albion Battalion back to Bolívar; in this, he was supported by Colonel Carvajal. Vowell revealed that when Valdés finally accepted that MacIntosh was serious about leaving, '… he became as abject as he had been before insolent and overbearing. Conscious that his conduct would not bear investigation, and dreading Bolívar's uncompromising rigour, he wept like a child'.[20] It was left to General Mirez to dissuade Colonel MacIntosh from leaving.

Valdés seemed largely indifferent to the needs of his troops, and made no attempt to keep up their morale. Another British volunteer wrote of Valdés:

'General Valdéz is a tyrannical, despotic, bloodthirsty monster, whose ferocious deeds have since caused his suspension by Congress.'[21]

With leadership such as this, it is no wonder that recruits were deserting so often; military experts believe that successful outcomes for armies lie in the bond between leaders and followers, and it is upon the behaviour of officers that the men depend.[22] It is evident that Sucre became aware of Valdés' limitations as he wrote to Bolívar in 1823, discussing Valdés' aptitude to carry on a particular siege:

'Valdés would die before giving up, but I fear that due to his nature he will not have all that is needed to withstand a siege, where there are so many details to attend to: the economy of the provisions, care of the soldiers amid scarcity, the health of the troops in a crowded and small venue, policing, repair of fortifications damaged by the enemy, the constant vigilance, scrutiny and boring espionage, and in all, so many details that a siege needs. I am sure Valdés has all the capacity, but you know his nature is to tire soon and my fear is that he will get bored in a few months of this tiresome work.'[23]

Vowell did not criticize Patriot leaders in a gratuitous manner; it is characteristic of him that if he was critical, it was not because of race, colour, or class, but because of behaviour as a leader of men. In contrast to Vowell, General Florencio O'Leary, Bolívar's aide-de-camp, who left very lengthy memoirs of the revolutionary war, showed racial and class bias when he systematically rated all the Patriot leaders in very narrow categories, with comments such as: 'mulatto', 'a man of colour', 'a son of a mason', 'a bastard', 'of obscure parents and very poor', 'of decent origin', 'mulatto, ferocious and sanguinary', 'of good family', '…his mother was a coloured woman', '…his parents miserably poor'.[24]

The Albion stayed in Popyán for about a month, giving Vowell time to explore medicinal plants and the wild animals of the area, and even to discover that a local mountain – El Trapiche – was purported, at the time, to be the source of the Orinoco, Magdalena and Cauca Rivers.[25]

Popayán is a venerable ancient city, situated on the banks of the river Cauca, in a fertile and well cultivated plain. In the neighbourhood is the extinguished volcano of Purazé, from which snow is constantly brought down on mules to the city, for the purpose of cooling water and making ices. We felt the wind that blows from this mountain very chilling… The city contains several handsome public buildings… The inhabitants of this city were, generally speaking, very wealthy previous to the war, but have been reduced to comparative poverty by the repeated exactions and contributions imposed by both parties, as they alternately gained possession of the city.

Vowell, *Campaigns and Cruises,* 216

Even in Vowell's time, graffiti was an outlet for public protest, as he discloses:

'So frequent were the changes of masters, about this time, that the walls in the Plaza were placarded by the soldiers of the two hostile armies in large letters, each party, as it was, obliged in turn to retreat, leaving some memento of its hatred to the other.'[26]

Vowell was not as Eurocentric as could have been expected, and one indication is that he appreciated the relics of ancient aboriginal societies, many of which could still be found in and around Popayán. Apparently, two local families had carefully saved many gold ornaments depicting grasshoppers, beetles, fruits and flowers, of which Vowell comments with admiration, 'These were interesting proof of the ingenuity exerted by the ancient possessors of the land; and were invaluable in the eyes of an antiquary.'[27] He faults the Spaniards' gold lust, evident since they arrived in the New World, for melting down such precious articles and he adds this further condemnation:

'Well may the Spaniards be called throughout South America, *Los Godos* – the Goths! A name which they have richly merited, by this, and innumerable similar instances of ignorance, rapacity, and devastation, that have disgraced them in that part of the world.'[28] [29]

It is remarkable that Vowell recognized the cultural plundering of the indigenous societies by the Spanish. These harsh words towards the Spanish Empire may very well have come back to haunt Vowell in his later life, when he experienced first hand the ignorance, rapacity and devastation caused by another empire – the British Empire – on its own people and those of another continent.

Furthermore, in including in his book an anecdote about a tribe of fierce aboriginal people, supposedly cannibals, hostile to strangers, Vowell displays again his open attitude towards different cultures. The tribe traded with an old Franciscan padre, for many years a resident of a village close to it, who would place on the ground the articles his parishioners had for sale, and promptly retire to a distance. Then, the men of the tribe would come forth and leave on the ground the amount of gold grain they thought each article was worth. Vowell concludes, 'Not a word passed between the parties concerned; but the dealings were conducted by these uncivilized beings with the most scrupulous honesty.'[30]

The Patriot Army of the South was suffering from sicknesses and lack of medical resources; they were ill-equipped, had no soap or shoes, little clothing and only beef for food. In November, the Patriots received some reinforcements of arms and supplies, which had come from the British merchant, Benjamin Halton.[31] Finally, on 2 January 1821, they left Popayán, heading towards Quito, but first they had to pass through Pasto, the home of '… a nation of civilized Indians who have been always inveterate enemies to the Patriots.'[32] During this rough passage, they were attacked constantly by Pasto guerrillas. The Patriots ran into a large force of Royalists near the Mayo River, but fortunately they did not put up much of a fight, although the roads became muddier and marshier. After crossing the formidable Juananbú River, particularly dangerous because of its great depth, rapidity, and its tendency towards sudden floods, Vowell recorded a remarkable natural, yet ominous, occurrence.

> On a mountain, near the village of Tambo Pintado, where we bivouacked the day after passing the River Juanambú, we saw very distinctly, at sun rise, gigantic shadows of ourselves, which were thrown by the sun on the clouds, as they slowly ascended out of the vallies beneath. It was observed, at the same time, that each individual saw his own shadow only, and not that of any other. This phenomenon, which our Indian comrades could by no means comprehend, and had always been taught to consider as an actual vision of the Vulto, or evil genius of the Cordillera, made a great and unfavourable impression on their minds, as to the result of the battle, which we all knew was impending. They were, unfortunately, confirmed in their superstitious forebodings, by the total defeat we so shortly after experienced.
>
> Vowell, *Campaigns and Cruises*, 227

On 2 February 1821, they encountered the enemy trying to take the city of Pasto. The Patriots were physically weak and strained by constant skirmishing. The Royalists were positioned on a small field of maize known to the Indians as 'The Plain of Blood', and to get to the enemy the Patriots had to pass through a narrow, winding defile scarcely admitting two abreast. According to Vowell, inexplicably, as the infantry was about to attack, Valdés ordered the cavalry to the front – a serious tactical mistake, as it blocked the Patriot infantry – and since, inevitably, the cavalry encountered heavy fire, it had to quickly retreat, with dire consequences, jamming the narrow ravine. The Royalists had held on to Pasto, the important gateway to Quito from the north.

> *After losing many of their number, and among the rest, that staunch friend of the English, Colonel Carvajal, of the Guias, they retreated over the infantry, which was thus thrown into confusion, and the day was irrecoverably lost. Valdez, who was one of the first to leave the ground, conducted the retreat with such shameful precipitation as to lose the whole of the baggage and powder. The following day, though not pursued, except by a few parties of Indians, blowing conch-shells and cows' horns along the hills, he re-crossed the Juanambú, and scarcely halted in his panic flight, until he reached the river Mayo.*
>
> Vowell, *Campaigns and Cruises*, 229

Relief came at the Mayo River in the person of General Antonio José de Sucre[33] who met the Army of the South next day, on 6 February 1821, to take over command from Valdés. Bolívar had sent Sucre, his most able general, as quickly as he could to his troubled army. It was indeed unfortunate that Valdés was relieved of his command only after he had lost more than half of his men and had not even managed to reach Quito.[34] Sucre promptly wrote to Santander stating that he found the army so completely demoralized that the steady stream of desertions was understandable because '… there was *nothing, nothing, nothing* for the subsistence of the troops… It is a dying corps that *will* die if it is not revived by government help.'[35] He found the hospital full of sick and wounded men, with no medicine; soldiers, beggar-like, with only one article of clothing, while officers were practically naked, having lost all their baggage, and there was no money with which to pay them. Comparing Vowell's account of the travails of the army with that of Sucre, we observe that if anything, Vowell's account was circumspect.

Sucre came bearing welcome news that an armistice of six months had just been declared.[36] Vowell and Sucre, both of the same age, soon got to know each other, and the former described the latter. Sucre went on to become the second most important man in the war after Bolívar, as his Marshall and most beloved officer. Later he became the first president of Ecuador.

> *General Sucre, who was a native of Guayana, was much of Bolívar's size and make. In his face, which was lightly pitted with the smallpox, he was much fairer, and he did not, then, wear mustachios. His features were pleasing, and his manners were mild, but in the early part of his military career, at least, there was nothing striking in his appearance; nothing that pointed him out as the future victor of Ayacucho. However, in this retreat, which was his coup d'essai,*

he manoeuvred with considerable skill, and conducted us in safety to Popayán, through a country where provisions were scarce, and which was occupied by several strong guerrillas, commanded by Godo caudillos, who paid no respect to the armistice.

Vowell, *Campaigns and Cruises*, 229

The exacting O'Leary had some fine praise for the four most important Patriot leaders and saved the best for Sucre; according to him, Bolívar was the greatest man of the revolution, Páez the most extraordinary, Santander the most fortunate, and Sucre was the most perfect by far.[37]

Alas, Vowell was not to enjoy the company of Sucre for long.

CHAPTER TWELVE

The Sea Wolf

'Wouldst thou'– so the helmsman answered, – 'Learn the secret of the sea?
Only those who brave its dangers
Comprehend its mystery.'

Henry Wadsworth Longfellow

THE city of Guayaquil[1] had successfully revolted against the Spanish and hoisted the flag of liberty on 9 October 1820. Bolívar, keen to obtain from Guayaquil its recognition of the government of Gran Colombia and its help in liberating Quito, asked General Sucre to go there to lead the Quito campaign with a new corps of black recruits which had been formed in Cali. Colonel MacIntosh and Major Vowell were among the four key British officers who were assigned by Sucre to go with him to Cali to train this new corps which was to be known as the Santander Battalion.[2] This appointment is an indication of the regard his superiors had of Vowell's skills as an officer and his reliability. Therefore, at Popayán, on 2 March 1821, General Sucre handed over command of the defeated Army of the South to General Pedro León Torres and left for Cali with Vowell, MacIntosh, and the other two officers.

In Cali, Vowell began training well-fed and well-equipped men, since Sucre had secured funds for the army from Benjamin Halton, a British merchant and strong supporter of the Patriots, who had lent 10,000 pesos to cover the costs of clothing and arming the Patriot troops. Sucre praised Vowell and his fellow officers when he said of the Santander Battalion: 'They have good officers and you know that these are the soul of the corps.'[3]

On 22 March 1821 Vowell and about 400-600 men left Cali with General Sucre headed for the port of San Buenaventura from where they would sail for Quito.[4] The thought of a sea voyage filled the mountain-born recruits with horror, such that many tried to desert, and to the extent that Vowell recorded seasoned soldiers had to be posted into each company with orders to shoot anyone attempting to escape. It was yet another wretched road they had to traverse: narrow, with thick underwood. They marched several days through a dense forest that had never seen the footprint of men, cutting their way through with machetes. Sporadically, they came to steep hills.

These were nearly perpendicular, particularly one called La Vivora (The Viper), and could only be surmounted by climbing from tree to tree, assisted by the roots and hanging bejucos, each man handing his musket to another before raising himself. This tedious and laborious way of proceeding was, occasionally, varied by deep morasses, through which we were obliged to scramble, and by wading the torrent repeatedly from point to point. It was necessary, on these occasions, to form a double chain of the troops, who held fast by each other's hands. Without this precaution, the least stumble would have proved fatal to men so fatigued with marching as to be incapable of the exertion necessary for recovering themselves.

Vowell, *Campaigns and Cruises,* 234

These hills, Vowell relates, were infested with snakes which darted upon them, as well as a myriad of mosquitoes, scorpions and swarming black, biting ants: 'As we were all under the necessity of proceeding barefoot, it being impossible to wear either boots or shoes through the mud and water, we were exposed, not only to the attacks of these insects, but also to thorns and splinters, which lamed many of the men.'[5] The marshy ground was so damp that they could not even make, and sit around, a fire, but had to sleep leaning against trees, shivering from the cold mountain breeze. Always looking at the bright side, Vowell wrote: 'We had, however, the advantage of being in some degree protected from the mosquitoes, from the smoke that rose from the half-kindled wood.'[6]

Along the way, Vowell managed to observe and describe local aboriginal tribes, as well as many wilderness denizens such as the dangerous wild hog or *pecari*, multiple types of monkeys, sloths, anteaters, panthers, and capybaras. They finally reached San Buenaventura, which they found to be a very small and rustic place, with no natural provisions for the troops. But, demonstrating sound leadership, even now in his first important command, General Sucre had the foresight to anticipate this situation, and had sufficient rations for the troops sent there beforehand until they sailed. In a rare display of emotion, Vowell wrote of their first glimpse of the sea:

'We enjoyed, from this place, the first view of the Pacific Ocean, after our tedious march over the broadest part of the continent. The sight of the sea gladdened us foreigners, like the face of a long lost friend, having been for such a length of time inland travellers. It even made us forget, for the moment, how many weary leagues of its blue surface lay between us and England.'[7]

They sailed to Guayaquil on 4 April 1821, in the *Emperor Alexander,* a small British merchant corvette. It was a tedious journey of one month with many lulls in the winds, which depleted their water supply. This particularly distressed the new recruits whom Vowell realized had never experienced water rationing before. Furthermore, with the need to eat salted food, their thirst had increased. One of the men attempted to obtain more water by concealing the death of a comrade to get his ration 'until the shockingly offensive smell betrayed his secret.'[8] They finally landed at the bay of Santa Helena 'to the great joy of all of us.'[9]

The army was confined for a while in Santa Helena, a native village a few miles outside Guayaquil, due to the suspicions of the Guayaquil government towards the arrival of these unsolicited Gran Colombian troops. They were finally allowed to enter, by using catamarans to move down the Guayaquil River, an excerise which Vowell described:

> They also bring down the river abundance of pine-apples, musk and water melons, cocoa-nuts, plantains, etc, and among other tropical fruits, the best sweet oranges in South America, the rinds of which are scarcely thicker than a card. The profusion of fruit is indeed surprising, and the river, for many leagues above Guayaquil, meanders though orange groves and flourishing plants of every description. The fruits are exposed for sale in heaps, along the streets, at a very cheap rate, and form a sight that charms a stranger on his first arrival. There are likewise to be seen in the same place, yellow parrots from Chocó, loros (parrot), tucans, and other scarce birds of the most brilliant plumage, besides every variety of monkeys, among which the bearded capuchin is pre-eminent in ugliness.
>
> Vowell, *Campaigns and Cruises*, 244

Guayaquil itself did not favourably impress Vowell: he described the city of about 20–30,000 people as hot, muddy, filthy, and and ridden with fever. It was prone to earthquakes and including a violent one on 27 June 1821. Despite such surroundings, as ever, he remained attentive to the opposite sex, particularly amused by the bathing customs of the ladies of the city.

> Women of all classes in Guayaquil are excellent swimmers; and regularly bathe in a crowd, about day-break, and towards evening, without any shelter, and most of them without any covering. They swim about, perfectly at their ease, although the public thoroughfare is along the bank, and the merchant vessels lie at anchor close to the shore. There cannot, in fact, be a more exposed place for bathing than that which the Guayaquileñas have selected; but the ladies allege, as an excuse, that there are so many females in the water at the same moment as to make it impossible to recognize, with certainty, any individual.
>
> Vowell, *Campaigns and Cruises*, 247

Unfortunately, Vowell fell ill from the fever which swept Guayaquil, and he was left behind with the other sick and wounded when General Sucre left the city and headed for Quito on 29 June 1821. It was here in Guayaquil that Vowell added another episode to his adventurous life – the task of defending the city and thwarting a counter-coup.

According to Vowell, the president of the newly established Republic of Guayaquil committed the double folly of believing the conversion to the Patriot cause of a former Royalist commander, Colonel López, and giving him command of one of the new Patriot regiments. López persuaded the captains and crews of the six large, former Spanish gunboats moored in Guayaquil harbour to conspire with him. He told them to take possession of two armed brigs and then to threaten the city. Foolishly, López paid the men beforehand; they promptly got drunk and started the 'rebellion' by shooting and plundering haphazardly, even before López had time to ride out to his troops who were stationed outside the city. Vowell describes a city in panic fearing full-scale plundering. There was also a real fear that any foreigners in the city would be massacred. As such, 'under the direction of a few sick officers', one of whom was very likely to have been Vowell, all the English and American sailors, clerks and porters who happened to be in the city at the time, were assembled to set up guns, while the civilian foreigners, together with the sick and infirm, gathered in the shelter of a large private house. The ad-hoc military force opened a 'well directed' fire on the gunboats, which, pursued by a group of vessels under the command of a captain of the Chilean navy, fled, ran aground, and was captured.

Soon after this gunboat incident took place, another such event occurred on 25 October 1821, when a British naval hero, Lord Thomas Cochrane, now an Admiral, and head of the Chilean Naval Squadron, astounded the population of Guayaquil by sailing the Squadron's six warships, up the Guayaquil River – hitherto considered not navigable to such great ships.[10] He was welcomed with great enthusiasm and his arrival would be a turning point in Vowell's life.[11]

Lord Cochrane was, after Nelson, the most renowned hero of the British Royal Navy for his skill, as well as for his audacity, which prompted Napoleon to call him 'Le Loup des Mers.'[12] During the Napoleonic Wars, Cochrane's outstanding exploits as a frigate captain so inspired C.S. Forester that he modelled his fictional naval hero, Horatio Hornblower, on him. An eccentric son of an eccentric Scottish lord, Cochrane was admired by his crews because he made sure his ships carried good food, drink, and other necessary supplies, and also, not the least, because his record of capturing enemy ships meant monetary prizes for all on board. As one of his biographers has stated:

'Cochrane's care and concern for his men was one of his noblest characteristics, earning him personal loyalty and their confidence in his fighting abilities.'[13]

A progressive and upright man, despite many idiosyncrasies – such as not bearing fools lightly and possessing a quick temper – he relentlessly denounced the administrative corruption within the British Admiralty that saw ships and men endangered because of faulty shipbuilding and unsafe supplies. He was a leading figure in the Radical Movement and was, in short, a thorn in the side of the Admiralty.

In 1818, due to Cochrane's impressive sailing abilities and his outspoken dedication to liberty, in an inspired stroke of genius, the new Republic of Chile, asked him to command a naval squadron, which it had created in October 1817, to rid it of the continued presence of Spanish ships and garrisons.[14] The idea belonged to the Chilean, Bernardo O'Higgins, who faced the prospect of having to establish a naval squadron without ships, able seamen, or money.[15] José de San Martin,[16] the Argentinian Patriot, was aware that Chile's liberation could only be obtained by directly attacking the Viceroyalty of Perú:

> 'But for this plan to succeed, he needed a naval squadron that could dominate the south-eastern Pacific and could carry an army to the coast of Perú. The squadron also had to be strong enough to keep sea lanes communication during the whole campaign.'[17]

The British Naval establishment no doubt rested easy when Cochrane accepted to head just such a naval enterprise far from Britain, but in this way Chile and Brazil gained a champion who went on to contribute significantly to their liberation from the Spanish and Portuguese empires.[18] As one Chilean historian has stated:

> 'To control the Pacific there was no more effective way than to get English officers, and among them, to command the squadron, there was no one who could equal Cochrane, who by the way, was considered the best British seaman.'[19]

Cochrane shared the command of the Chilean Squadron as Vice-Admiral with Rear-Admiral Manuel Blanco Encalada, a young man who had been an ensign in the Spanish navy for four years, and thus had more naval experience than any other Patriot officer.[20]

Chile's liberty had been won the year before through the combined efforts of Bernardo O'Higgins and San Martin, but the Spanish ships were a constant threat. Ships were very expensive and Patriot forces were rarely able to buy them, and they relied mostly on capturing them from the enemy. At that time, the Spanish still held garrisons at Lima and in Callao, which were maintained easily by ships, and not via difficult inland roads.[21]

Guayaquil had the only shipbuilding yard with a dry dock in the Pacific and it was to here that Cochrane sailed in order to carry out vital repairs to his ships, which were all in poor condition.[22] By this time, Lima had been liberated and the Spanish garrison at Callao had surrendered after a long siege by Cochrane. However, the two last remaining Spanish frigates in the Pacific, the *Prueba* and *Venganza*, were still sailing free, headed for Acapulco, with Cochrane in hot pursuit. Cochrane, however, was in dire need of good officers for his ships.

Meanwhile, Vowell was suffering from 'a severe attack of rheumatism, of which there was no prospect of amendment in this climate.'[23] He obtained leave of absence from General Sucre and was trying to return to Europe, when he and a fellow officer, Lieutenant George Noyes, were recruited by Cochrane. Vowell subsequently gave up

The Vowell family home at 19 New King Street, Bath. Currently it is the Herschel Museum of Astronomy, established in honour of astronomers, William and Caroline Herschel, who lived there before the Vowell family. (Peter Victor)

The home of Susan
(née Vowell) and
Rev. Michael Becher,
Mallow, Cork,
Ireland. (Peter Victor)

Above: The banner under which Simón Bolívar
led the Patriot forces during the liberation of
the Americas was adorned with the slogan
Libertad o Muerte – Liberty or Death.

A portrait from 1819 by M.N. Bates
of Simón Bolívar aged 36. Vowell met
Bolívar when he was about this age.
Bolívar is known as 'The Liberator'
as he freed Venezuela, Colombia,
Ecuador, Bolivia and Perú from the
Spanish Empire.

Right: José Antonio Páez. Undisputed
leader of the Venezuelan plainsmen, or
Llaneros, he was Bolívar's chief cavalry
commander. Later in his illustrious career,
Páez was thrice president of Venezuela.

The vast, lush expanse of the Venezuelan *llanos*, or savannas, stretch from the Orinoco Delta to the foot of the Andes, then south to Colombia. It was the scene of intense battles between the Patriots and the Spanish. Vowell wrote an outstanding description of the social life of the *llanos* in 1818-19.

Flamingos and egrets scatter in alarm above capybaras in the Venezuelan *llanos*, where the abundant biodiversity includes over 350 species of birds and over 50 species of mammals.

Grand Marshal Sucre defeated the Spanish at the Battle of Ayacucho, securing the independence of Perú and giving a death blow to Spanish rule in the Americas.
He was Bolívar's most trusted general and closest friend. During his short life he was president of Perú and later Bolivia. Vowell met him before his great victory. (Arturo Michelena. Located at the Congress of Bolivia)

A forensic reconstruction of the face of Simón Bolívar, 'The Liberator', at the time of his death, made possible after his body was exhumed in 2012. (Photography: Prensa Miraflores/Government of the Bolivarian Republic of Venezuela)

Llaneros ride out into the Apure River to capture Spanish gunboats just outside San Fernando. (Gustavo Machado Guzmán, 'Historia Gráfica de la Guerra de Independencia de Venezuela')

Arturo Michelena's depiction of the Battle of Las Queseras del Medio which took place on 2 April 1819. One-hundred and fifty-three patriot lancers were outnumbered by 1,000 Spanish cavalry and attempted to retreat, but General Páez gave the order, '*Vuelvan Caras!*' ('About Face!'), and they won the day.

Simón Bolivar accepts the surrender of General Rodil after the defeat of the Spanish Army at Boyaca in August 1819. (Bettmann/Corbis)

Bernardo O'Higgins by Narciso Desmadryl. O'Higgins was one of Chile's founding fathers who helped free the country from Spanish rule. He founded the 1st Chilean Squadron and the Chilean Navy. (Galería nacional, o, Colección de biografías y retratos de hombres célebres de Chile)

Left: Admiral Lord Thomas Cochrane, 10th Earl of Dundonald, from an engraving by John Cook. After Nelson, Cochrane was Britian's most renowned naval hero, known for his intrepid victories at sea. Chile invited him to command the 1st Chilean Squadron, and he personally recruited Vowell to be Captain of Marines.

Above right: The corvette, *Independencia,* of 28 cannon, was the flagship of the 1st Chilean Squadron in its key naval actions. This model of the *Independencia* is at the Chilean Marine Museum, at Valparaíso, Chile. (Author)

The 1st Chilean Squadron defeated the naval power of the Spanish Empire in the Americas, thus liberating the key ports of Chile and Perú.

Vice-Admiral Manuel Blanco Encalada served under Admiral Lord Thomas Cochrane, commanding the 1st Chilean Squadron. He later became the first president of Chile. A portrait by Nathaniel Hughes.

Left: The Loreto Mission at San José, Baja California, México. It was an indigenous settlement run by priests. The 1st Chilean Squadron visited it to obtain provisions and helped to persuade Baja California to declare its independence from Spain.

A drawing of Lima from the London Illustrated News.

Cox's River Stockade in New South Wales, Australia, was a crude prison that housed gangs of prisoners in irons who were used to build a road north of Sydney. Vowell was employed there as a clerk. (Artist unknown. Permission granted by the State Library of New South Wales. Mitchell Library, State Library of NSW – XV/1)

Part of the ruins of the prison on Norfolk Island, in the Pacific Ocean, 877 miles (1,412 kilometres) east of Australia, stand today as a reminder of its past as an infamous and barbaric penal settlement.

Right: Alexander Maconochie was a Scottish naval officer, geographer and creative penal reformer. He was Governor of Norfolk Island and helped Vowell regain his freedom. (By permission of Michael Maconochie)

Old Casterton Cemetery in Victoria, Australia, contains the graves of the earliest settlers of the area. Among them lies Richard Longfield Vowell, although there is no stone to mark his grave. (Peter Victor)

his plans to return home. He was given the same rank that he had held in the Colombian service, becoming the Captain of Marines, and as such, in charge of the infantry on the ship.[24]

> 'I joined the *Independencia*, Capt. Wilkinson, on the 16th Nov., together with another English officer and some privates, all of whom had marched across the country at the same time with me, and were also invalided.'[25]

Vowell had no notion that more than two hundred years later, this period of his life and the very ship he sailed in, would be referred to in superlative terms by historians:

> 'The combatant seas of a passionate era as was this one, in which the independent destiny of the Americas was being affirmed, echo through the years with names of heroes and anti-heroes, of visionaries and statesmen, of corvettes that fought with legendary emblems, like that of the *Independencia,* under whose cannons the emancipation from Spain was proclaimed.'[26]

Vowell had just joined the naval squadron that would live on in history as the one that eventually vanquished Spanish naval power in the Pacific.

On 3 December 1821 he sailed down the Guayaquil River with Cochrane and the Chilean Squadron and into a new life at sea, with new adventures.

CHAPTER THIRTEEN

Mission to México

*'The magnificent efforts of the Chilean and foreign seamen gave Chile
the firmest foundation upon which naval strength could be rebuilt at any time.'*

Donald E. Worcester, *Sea Power and Chilean Independence*, 1962

AFTER about two months in Guayaquil, Vowell left with the Chilean Squadron headed towards Acapulco to search for two elusive Spanish frigates, the *Prueba* and *Venganza* and, as much as possible, to liaise with Mexican Patriots.[1]

'During these fifty days the squadron was also necessarily kept in inaction, having achieved nothing beyond the capture of a few merchantmen along the coast, and a fruitless chase of two Spanish frigates, the Prueba and Venganza.'[2]

These were Cochrane's recollections. Vowell, however, had many more memories to put to pen concerning these days.

At this time, the seven ships of the Chilean Squadron consisted of three frigates, a corvette, two brigs, and a schooner.[3] Its crews were mostly rural Chileans, with a good measure of Perúvians, Guayaquileños, and men from the Pacific islands.[4] When the Squadron was established in 1813, its officers were mostly British with some Americans, as this was the most effective way for Chile to quickly procure experienced officers.[5] By 1822-1825, there were 20 British officers and 19 Chilean officers, and the seamen and marine infantry were all Chileans.[6]

Vowell's duties as commander of the marine infantry consisted of training and exercising the men for battle, making them understand orders, and maintaining rigid standards of cleanliness and discipline.[7] He had ample experience in these matters, having trained so many men for the Venezuelan and Colombian armies. An important part of his duties would have been to regularly drill the men in loading, priming, sponging, running back the guns, carrying balls, handling powder, and musket practice. Organization and discipline on a warship took on an even greater importance than that of an army on the ground. The 19th century cannons in a sea battle ploughed through men and the ship's wood, blasting deadly splinters everywhere, tearing men from limb to limb, breaking masts and timber, pulling down sails and rigging, tangling lines; in short, creating havoc which could sink the ship altogether. There was always danger from fire and from the stores of gunpowder on board. Therefore, the seamen and the infantry had to know exactly what their duties were during these chaotic events and carry these out regardless.[8]

The Spanish Viceroy of Perú – José Fernando de Abascal y Sousa – kept the Chilean coast blockaded via his privateers who attacked foreign ships bound for Chile. The Spanish Empire had two major centres of power in the New World – México City and Lima – therefore neither Chileans nor any other South Americans would ever be free until the Spanish power in Lima was broken.[9] With the formation of the Squadron, Chile became the sole Patriot country that was challenging Spanish naval power in the Pacific. This was not an easy task since Chile had neither local naval expertise nor maritime commerce because the Spanish had placed Chilean commerce into the hands of Perúvian ship owners and therefore seasoned hands were not really available. When it obtained seamen, these all had to be trained from the very beginning. The navy had a chronic and severe lack of funds and there were crucial organizational difficulties such as lack of rules, signals and battle plans and, sadly, many personal rivalries for command. However, with the skill and dedication of two key men – Manuel Blanco Encalada in charge of the navy and Lord Cochrane commanding the ships – this small Squadron became a disciplined and effective fighting force which Spain had to reckon with.[10]

On 11 December 1821 the Squadron arrived at Cocos Island, a very small island south-west of Costa Rica and, due to its isolation, a favourite place for pirates and corsairs to stop for water. Its idyllic landscape was not lost on Vowell.

> This island is high, and of a conical shape. It has a beautiful appearance, standing alone in the middle of this vast ocean, and being constantly covered with verdure. Water is to be had here in abundance... there are numerous clear cascades, rushing down, in several places, from the craggy cliffs, by which the island is partly surrounded. Innumerable flocks of sea fowl, chiefly consisting of gulls and bobos,[11] breed here. They are apparently but seldom disturbed; for they flew in clouds among the vessels on our approach, alighting fearlessly on the yards and rigging, and deafening us with their clamorous screams.

Vowell, *Campaigns and Cruises*, 256

Vowell's first sea actions occurred off Cocos Island when the Squadron captured a schooner commanded by a pirate called Blair, and when the *Valdivia* chased down a small vessel to discover that the crew had recently turned to piracy and had stolen the ship from the Perúvian government. After these events, Cochrane ordered the schooner *Mercedes* to Panama to search for the Spanish frigates while the fast *Araucano* commanded by Captain Simpson was sent ahead to Acapulco and the rest of the Squadron would follow at its pace.

On 19 December 1821, a strong gale damaged the *O'Higgins* – Cochrane's flagship – forcing it to take refuge in the Gulf of Fonseca in Central America. There was five feet of water in the hold of the *O'Higgins* but Cochrane himself repaired the pumps with his smith's skills – it was quite rare for an officer to carry out such manual work, but Cochrane was that kind of man.[12] The repair, however, was not entirely successful due to faulty equipment. The ships were all in a bad state, the new navy being without funds to properly maintain its ships and, to make matters worse, they were very low on good food supplies, which were pivotal. In a letter of 2 December 1821, Captain Paul Delano, commander of the *Lautaro* wrote of this situation to Cochrane.

> *'The officers as well as the men are dissatisfied, having been a long time on cruise, and at present without any kind of meat or spirits, and without pay, so that they are not able to provide for themselves any longer, though, until starved, they have borne it without a murmur…The last charqui (dried beef) they got was rotten and full of vermin. They are wholly destitute of clothing…'*[13]

Hence, while in these waters they must have warmly welcomed the invitation of the Indian chief of a nearby village to come ashore to buy some of its plentiful fresh food. Ever happy for new experiences, Vowell volunteered to go to the village, along with another officer. They loaded up their canoe with fowls, pigs and vegetables, *'anticipating the thanks of our messmates who had been for some time living on charqui and salt beef'*,[14] but they capsized, losing all their cargo. They were forced to swim a rapid current to an island far off from the mainland where they spent an uncomfortable night and day with their Indian friends, without a drop of water. Fortunately, they were rescued by a passing piragua and barely got back in time before the Squadron was to sail.

Not neglecting his surroundings, Vowell took note of the quantity and quality of turtles, so plentiful that they caught dozens at a time. He certainly enjoyed eating turtle and was amused that the Chileans would not eat them, not even laced with liquor. He noted the volcano of Izalco, which he erroneously referred to as León[15] and several more along the coast displaying their fiery activity.

> *'One of these, in particular, we observed throwing up stones and lava; which could be distinctly seen by day-light, flowing red hot down the sides of the mountain.'*[16]

Cochrane, also impressed by the volcanoes, gave a fuller description:

> *'On the 5th of January 1822, arrived at Tehuantepec,*[17] *a volcano lighting us every night. This was one of the most imposing sights I ever beheld; large streams of molten lava pouring down the sides of the mountain, whilst at intervals, huge masses of solid burning matter were hurled into the air, and rebounding from their fall, ricocheted down the declivity till they found a resting place at its base.'*[18]

The Squadron had another dramatic moment when on 28 February 1822 it arrived in Acapulco where it expected to meet up with the *Araucano*. The political situation in México was ambiguous, with Patriots and Spaniards more or less coexisting.[19] Captain Simpson sailed the *Araucano* out to meet the Squadron before it entered the harbour and encountered the *Mercedes* whose captain informed him that they had failed to find the Spanish frigates in Panama.[20] The rest of the Squadron soon appeared and Captain Simpson was able to alert Cochrane of his Acapulco misadventure. He informed Cochrane that when he had arrived in Acapulco at the end of December 1821, the port was flying the Patriot colours and therefore he went ashore (with imprudent trust, according to Vowell), and was immediately seized and imprisoned. When finally, after much insistence, he managed to get an audience with the governor, Nicolás Basilio de la Gándara, he warned him that Cochrane would arrive soon with the rest of his Squadron and demand satisfaction for this outrage.

'On hearing, however, of the near approach of Lord Cochrane, whose very name brought terror with it wherever he appeared in the Pacific, the governor released Capt. Simpson, with many apologies for the step he had taken.'[21]

After all, this was the intrepid Admiral who had captured the best Spanish warship in the Pacific, the *Esmeralda,* within 15 minutes of a daring raid that saw 150 Spanish killed while he lost only 11 of his own men.[22] He had taken the most secure Spanish port on the Pacific, Valdivia, with such panache that it was undeniably one of the most extraordinary acts of the Wars of Independence.[23]

Despite the release of Captain Simpson, the Squadron could plainly see that the batteries of Acapulco's fort were manned and being made ready to fire. Cochrane, not wanting to unduly antagonize the Mexican Patriots, sent in a flag of truce with assurances to the governor that they only wanted to obtain water and supplies, adding a blunt proviso however that, if offered resistance, they would be compelled to shell not simply the forts, but the town as well. Vowell's interest was such that even while the Squadron was preparing for this action, for which as Captain of the Marine Infantry he must have been getting his men ready, he could still note the beauty of Acapulco.

Immediately after the departure of the flag of truce, the O'Higgins made the general signal to prepare for action; and stood into the harbour, followed by the other ships. The wind being unfavourable, we were obliged to beat in, tacking in succession. On rounding the point of the inner harbour, a beautiful view of the town opened upon us, with its neat white buildings; defended by a strong fort, and several batteries, on which the Mexican flag was flying. As we could plainly discern all the guns to be manned, and the matches burning, we anchored in line abreast of the castle, with springs on our cables, in readiness for action; for we were by no means certain as to what their intentions were respecting us, the flag of truce not having yet returned on board.

Vowell, *Campaigns and Cruises,* 263

The governor saw reason and welcomed the Squadron. Cochrane, surprised at the unfriendly nature of the Méxican encounter, soon learned the reason behind it. Two English officers who had been discharged from service to Chile, had passed themselves off as ambassadors from Chile to México and had spread news that Cochrane had turned pirate and was intent on plundering the coast of México. They were soon shown to be imposters and '... *The reserve, however, immediately wore off, and the most cordial relations were entered into'.*[24] Cochrane's innate charm easily won over not only the governor of Acapulco, but also even the emperor of México, Agustín Iturbide.[25] This was no small achievement for Cochrane who firmly believed in the Patriot cause and therefore wanted Méxican goodwill towards Chile, to which he was firmly loyal. At one point, Cochrane had been offered many benefits to leave the service of Chile for Perú, but he answered that he was a Chilean seaman and he would not betray his country nor the vows he had made to it.[26] Cochrane had also expressed great pride in his Chilean crew, stating:

> '*I have never seen a greater display of bravery than that of my comrades. The best crew of a British boat would not have improved the perfect way in which orders were carried out.*'[27]

Vowell then sailed with the *Independencia* to Baja California and the *Araucano*, to obtain the much needed food provisions for the Squadron. They planned later to meet up with the Squadron at Guayaquil and also were ordered to keep an eye out for a large Spanish ship expected out of San Blas, supposedly carrying a million-and-a-half dollars. The *Araucano* went to the Loreto Mission and the *Independencia* to the San José Mission.

Vowell's next adventure involved leading his men to board and take an enemy ship. It occurred on 17 February 1822, when they reached the bay of San José and found an anchored sixteen-gun Spanish brig there. Captain Wilkinson disguised the *Independencia* to look like an English merchantman, camouflaging its guns, and in this manner surprised and captured the Spanish ship with its valuable cargo of wares. According to Vowell, the brig's deck was crowded with aboriginals who were helping to replace the rudder, and upon seeing the *Independencia* running out its cannons, they jumped overboard, even though they were two miles from shore.

> '*Our boats soon picked them up, and brought them on board; for we did not wish the arrival of a Patriot man-of-war to be yet made known at the town.*'[28]

The mission in San José, like the rest of California, was still aligned with Spain rather than the Méxican Patriot government and it was giving sanctuary to two Spanish officials who were waiting for a ship to return them to Spain. Vowell was in charge of their capture.

Capt. Wilkinson, considering it expedient to have sufficient hostages for the delivery of the cattle he proposed to purchase, ordered a party of marines on shore in the middle of the night, with orders to surprise the two Spanish officers, and bring them on board. This was put in execution with the greatest ease; for they had not the least idea that the ship they had seen anchor in the roads was an enemy, and were taken while playing cards in the Sala de la Misión. The next morning they were liberated, on pledging themselves to have cattle brought in from the country for sale.

Vowell, *Campaigns and Cruises*, 269

The cordial situation with Spain in México was such that one of these Spanish officials, Don José Antonio Quartara, ex-governor of San Blas, became very friendly and useful to the Squadron while it was in Acapulco.

Another eventful foray on shore was less successful. According to Vowell's account, an American lieutenant named Campbell was sent ashore with some marines and seamen to scuttle a small Spanish schooner lying in the neighbouring harbour because it might warn the port of San Blas about the presence of the *Independencia*. The lieutenant succeeded in his task without any opposition from the local indigenous people, but imprudently he later went back to check that the boat was not being raised again and took with him only one companion, at which point, seeing that they were unprotected by the marines, the natives killed them both. A further disaster was to unfold.

The men of the detachment which had halted in the village were enjoying themselves in the mean time, having been provided with a plentiful breakfast of fish, eggs, and aguardiente [hard liquor]. They had no suspicion whatever of treachery until they suddenly received a volley from their own arms, which they had carelessly left in a corner of the room, and which some Indians, who had entered unperceived, had seized. Several were killed and wounded and the survivors, having their hands tied to horses' tails, were marched in that manner to the silver mines of El Real de San Antonio, where they were put in irons.

Vowell, *Campaigns and Cruises*, 270

Captain Wilkinson was able to obtain the marines' release when the president/priest of the missions of South California arrived soon after. Vowell states that the presence of the Chilean Squadron persuaded the president of the mission that the cause of the Royalists was hopeless in the Pacific and that his persisting loyalty to Spain would only bring about the calamities of war to the area. The role of the Chilean Squadron was instrumental therefore to this conversion of Baja California to the Patriots' cause.

Vowell was eyewitness at the historic moment of the declaration of the independence of Baja California, following the example of México. The Squadron was invited to be present at this event, which took place on 17 February 1822, a colourful occasion that Vowell sketched with detail and humour. Fifteen hundred Indians were present, armed with lances and Spanish rifles. The Californians, excellent horsemen, rode fine horses and both riders and horses wore deerskin dress and flaps, which protected them from the cactus and thorny undergrowth of the area.

'These were always ornamented, being stamped with various figures of flowers, birds, and beasts, much in the style of those designed by the Chinese.'[29]

On Capt. Wilkinson's arrival, with a few of his officers, the Indians formed a semicircle round the Padre Presidente, who stood on a flight of steps in front of the Mission, and asked them whether they would swear to maintain the independence of the country. To this they unanimously assented; as they would have done, with equal readiness, to any other proposition of the missionary's making. To their great surprise and delight, the Independencia fired a salute on a signal that had been preconcerted. They answered with an irregular feu de joie – loading with ball cartridge – which certainly had more the appearance of a skirmish than a rejoicing. A barrel of Pisco aguardiente, sent them from on board, completed their joy.

Vowell, *Campaigns and Cruises*, 272

The whole affair ended in a strained, Keystone Kops kind of way. After a veritable feast of turtle, salmon and venison that was beyond any feast they had ever seen, and which very much pleased Vowell's discerning palate, the president, who spoke not a word of English, invited the officers to ride around the mission vineyards and sugar cane fields with him. Captain Wilkinson decided to send one of his men to the party of seamen who were gathering water for the *Independencia* with orders for them to board ship, to head off any possible quarrelling with the indigenous people. The Padre President fancifully thought that the seaman was plotting to kidnap him onto the ship and he took off at full gallop over hedge and ditch towards the mission. The Captain, Vowell and all the officers, having no idea why the Padre had fled, followed him at the same pace.

'This served to increase the poor friar's terror to the utmost, and caused the greatest alarm in the village, through which he rode, ventre á terre, with his habits streaming in the wind, and pursued, as the Indians naturally supposed, by the English heretics.'[30]

It took some effort to convince him and the entire mission of their innocence; notwithstanding, fearing an ambush, they took a different route back, which turned out to be a wise idea.

Once again, Vowell's sense of adventure came to the fore, this time volunteering for an especially dangerous task. Captain Wilkinson, having seen no sign of the *Araucano*, became increasingly worried upon hearing rumours from the Indians that strangers had been seen in and around Loreto Mission. He proposed to send one of his officers overland to reconnoitre and bring back any men from the missing ship he might encounter. Don Quartara, the Spanish prisoner, and the President of the mission strongly opposed this plan as extremely dangerous to the officer who would have to pass through the wilds of California filled with jaguars and panthers, and *'Indians who would murder any European for the sake of his clothes especially one belonging to a ship, which they all knew had arrived in rather a hostile manner'*.[31] This did not deter Vowell. Perhaps it was his ease with the Spanish language or perhaps it was his quest for new experiences, but either way he volunteered, heedless of the risk. Chilean historian, López Urrutia, refers to Vowell's courage and to his excellent description of the country he traversed during this mission.[32]

The road between San José and San Antonio after ascending gradually for a few miles from the level of the sea shore, suddenly climbs, by a precipitous ascent, to an elevated table land. This extends, on the right, to the borders of the gulph, where it sinks abruptly down to the beach, as if undermined and blown up; on the left, it reaches to the feet of a lofty range of mountains, whose summits, moulded in fantastic cones and pyramids, we discovered when at sea, the evening before we made the low land. A very remarkable rent appears on the brow of the loftiest of these; and the solid rock has been laid bare, in nearly a straight line, from the summit to the base, where a very deep and broad ravine begins, which has cleft the table land throughout, as far as its termination near San José. This quebrada (ravine) is about a hundred yards in width, and from fifty to eighty in depth. We descended into it repeatedly, in the course of our journey.

Vowell, *Campaigns and Cruises*, 275

It is typical of Vowell's style that he avoids the personal pronoun and refers to himself as the commander of the marines when relating the event,[33] with total lack of self-promotion. Even though avoiding the personal pronoun was a common authorial voice of the era, in comparison with the writings of the others, Vowell was particularly circumspect about his role. He rode disguised in deerskins and slept every night in the woods avoiding contact with people, rode through difficult terrain, past coyotes and rattlesnakes so numerous that at one time Vowell killed eighteen or twenty. Finally, he found one of the *Araucano* marines who informed him that the foreign seamen of the ship had mutinied and run off with the vessel.[34] Vowell and his companion officer both turned back to San José with the disconcerting news. Meanwhile, Captain Simpson arrived at San José in an open boat, to report that most of his crew had mutinied and taken his ship and that the rest of his crew was still at the Loreto Mission. This was bad news indeed. The *Araucano*, perhaps the fastest of all the ships in the small Chilean

Squadron, was lost. The *Independencia* immediately set sail for Loreto to pick up these men, arriving on 4 March 1822. Unfortunately, had they stayed at San José they would have been able to intercept the Spanish ship leaving San Blas with a small fortune on board. As Vowell bemoaned, this was no small mortification for them.

They made one stop at the small harbour of Guaymas for provisions and Vowell commented on the climate, grapes, and wine of the region.

> *The climate of California is temperate and pleasant. Although the air is rather cold in the mornings, in consequence of a breeze from the ocean, that sets in about day break, the weather is warm enough in summer to ripen grapes, and bring sugar cane and tobacco to perfection. The inhabitants rarely make anything but a coarse syrup, and an ardent sprit from the cane; but from the grape they get a very pleasant light wine, much resembling champagne. Provisions of every kind are remarkably cheap, and the soil is in general very fertile.*
>
> Vowell, *Campaigns and Cruises,* 278

Vowell and the *Independencia* sailed for Guayaquil and when they arrived, they had a further disappointment for they learned that the Spanish frigates they hunted had surrendered to the Patriots at Guayaquil on 15 February 1822, and were now under Perúvian control. But, all in all, the *Independencia* could have very well boasted of its voyage to California, as one historian has done: '*This was a most successful venture, as the Chileans attacked Royalist forces all along the coast, captured a brig and even proclaimed the Independence of California.* '[35]

Not finding the rest of the Squadron in Guayaquil as expected, the *Independencia* proceeded to Coquimbo, Chile where further adventures awaited Vowell, and yet another brush with death.

CHAPTER FOURTEEN

Life in Chile

'The ... years spent in uniform had cast over them the spell of an entirely different world from that they were set on entering. The spell was, in part, one of experience – of strange places, of unfamiliar responsibility, of excitement and even of danger.'

John Keegan, *A History of Warfare*, 1994

T HE *Independencia* finally rejoined the rest of the Squadron when it entered Valparaíso in June 1822. Maria Graham, widow of a British captain and also a friend of Cochrane, who resided in Chile, wrote insightful letters and a diary of her time there. She recorded the Squadron's return to Chile on 22 May and referred to Lord Cochrane's difficult voyage to Acapulco during which he chased the two last remaining Spanish ships that, in the end, surrendered at a Patriot port.

'May 22. The Chilean Squadron, under Lord Cochrane, has returned to Callao, from its dangerous and difficult voyage to Acapulco, after chasing the two last remaining Spanish ships into Patriot ports, where they have been forced to surrender.'[1]

The view that Vowell saw as he approached Chile was described in an unusually lyrical way by another seaman, Captain Amasa Delano in 1800:

'The country in the kingdom of Chile is remarkable for its mountains... They lie nearly parallel to the shore, from fifty, to a hundred and fifty miles inland. They appear magnificent beyond description when viewed from a ship's deck eight or ten miles off shore, particularly when the sun is setting and the atmosphere clear. It then shines on their westerly side next the sea, in some places beautifully shaded where one mountain stands a little in front of another, making the most interesting and splendid appearance that can be conceived of.'[2]

Most military/naval narrators would have been content with a few lines about a place or view – however inspiring – such as those above, but not Vowell, who went beyond the primary impressions, and proceeded to find out and describe as much as he could about this new land he was fighting for. Considering that Valparaíso, with its brown grass and stunted bushes, by no means corresponded with its name, he offers a detailed description of the city in which nothing seemed to escape his notice, not even the washerwomen who lived in the many ravines that traversed the town.

> *The hills rise so abruptly from the sea shore, that there is only room for one street... The hills retire a few hundred yards from the sea, at this spot, giving room for a very pleasant part of the suburbs, called El Almendral, or the almond grove. In this there is one very long and broad street, and numerous country houses, with gardens, and peach orchards... The ranchos, or cottages of the smallest description scattered over the face of the different hills, are innumerable. They are built, wherever it is possible on a level patch of ground, four or five yards square; although the path leading to it would hardly be attempted by a goat. Most of these ranchos have a retamo, or large broom tree, growing in front, the bright yellow flowers of which have a lively appearance.*
>
> Vowell, *Campaigns and Cruises*, 282-280

As for the Chileans in general, Vowell considered them a very cheerful and hospitable people, fond of the society of foreigners, especially the English '... for whose country and national character they profess great esteem, and speak always with the greatest respect and gratitude of *el gran Canning* (the great Canning).'[3] Vowell refers thus to George Canning who was British Prime Minister in 1827.

This is echoed also in the journal of Maria Graham:

> 'English tailors, shoemakers, saddlers, and innkeepers, have out their signs in every street, and the preponderance of the English language over every other spoken in the chief street would make one fancy Valparaíso a coast town in Britain.'[4]

On 19 November 1822, a major earthquake shook Valparaíso along with the entire coast of Chile. A fierce first shock was followed by a series of lesser ones that heaved the earth and made the sea rise and then recede. Maria Graham wrote to a friend of the earthquake:

> 'I found the ancient bed of the sea laid bare and dry, with beds of oysters, mussels, and other shells adhering to the rocks on which they grew, the fish all being dead, and exhaling the most offensive effluvia.'[5]

The effects of the earthquake were so severe that the coast of Valparaíso was raised a full three feet, but inland the elevation was as much as six or seven feet.[6] It nearly destroyed the town.

During this 'awful convulsion of nature', as Vowell called it, his extraordinary luck once more helped him escape certain death. The night of the earthquake Vowell was to have slept in the home of a Mr. Ford, but was unexpectedly ordered to duty on board the *Independencia*. Had he stayed ashore he certainly would have perished with Mr. Ford, his wife and children, who were all buried in the rubble of their house. On board, Vowell felt that the vessels '…were shaken as roughly as if they had been grazing over a rocky shoal.'[7] He described a night of terror, as he and his marines rushed into the devastated city to help with public order.

> *Many of the inhabitants were killed at once, in their beds. Others, who had escaped into the open air, were knocked down by the falling tiles and crushed to death under walls, in attempting to fly through the narrow streets. The confusion was dreadful; every open space being crowded with fugitives, distracted by terror, mostly half naked… They continued to run about without any settled object, beating their breasts and praying aloud; most of them enquiring, in agonies of fear, for their parents and children… A brilliant meteor passed over Chile during the night, and greatly augmented the alarm of the terrified inhabitants. Day light at length came; but it was to disclose the melancholy spectacle of a ruined and deserted city. The people were seen, in disconsolate groups on the hills, without shelter, without food, and many without sufficient clothing; and, as the trembling motion of the earth scarcely ceased for a moment, it was highly dangerous to venture among the tottering houses in quest of anything. Many, however, braved the danger, and continued to dig in the ruins for the mangled bodies of their friends who had perished.*
>
> Vowell, *Campaigns and Cruises*, 292-296

The seven years that Vowell spent in the service of Chile allowed him to feed his keen curiosity about the country and its people. The Chilean translator of *Campaigns and Cruises*, José Toribio Medina, commented that he was a diligent narrator and observer, not only of transcendent military and political events, but also that he had delved deeply into Chilean national customs of the time, including popular dances and tunes.[8] Just as he had immersed himself in the *Llanero* culture, so Vowell immersed himself in Chile where everything seemed to interest him: the Chileans' weapons and dress, their gambling, their horses and horse races, their mules and cattle round-ups, falconry and hunting practices. Nor did he neglect their music, stories, quarrels, religion and superstitions. Chile's vineyards could not have escaped Vowell's attention, for he wrote knowingly, 'The climate of Chile is too temperate for the sugar cane, or cacao; and very little tobacco is grown in the country. Vines are very extensively cultivated, and a very good wine and brandy is made from the grapes.'[9] He was captivated by Chile's beautiful rivers and topography, and its flora and fauna. He painted a delightful picture of the road from Valparaíso to Santiago in 1822.

> *The high road from Valparaíso to the capital passes over two very steep and high mountains, called Cuestas… On reaching the top of the Cuesta del Prado, one of the most magnificent*

*views, probably to be seen in the world, suddenly opens on the traveller. The level and highly
cultivated plain of Santiago lies below his feet, covered with plantations, and watered by the
rivers Maypu, Mapocho, and other mountain streams… At the farthest end is seen the city itself,
conspicuous, at the distance of thirty miles, for the number of its white steeples and towers, and
surrounded by small villages and Quintas [villas]. The background of this lovely scene, is formed
by the mighty Andes, rising in all their majesty, in an immense semi-circle, and reducing into
comparative insignificance, the ridges of high mountains that arise between them and the
valley… This is by far the finest view of the Andes that can be had in Chile.*

Vowell, *Campaigns and Cruises*, 323

Vowell was also taken by the capital, Santiago, and commented on its handsome
churches, convents and monasteries, its schools and government houses, its cafés and
festivals. Even the homeless dogs in the streets of the capital warranted a mention.

*The streets, on entering Santiago, are mean and ill-paved, but improve very much on advancing
into the centre of the city. There they are flagged on both sides, with red porphyry from San
Cristoval, and most of the houses are handsome. The Plaza Mayor is spacious and kept very
clean… A rocky eminence rises abruptly near the river, in the outskirts of the city, on which
stands a fort called Santa Lucia… The view from the hill of Santa Lucia is extensive and
beautiful.*

Vowell, *Campaigns and Cruises*, 325-342

The *Huasos* (which Vowell spelled '*Huazos*'), Chile's mountain horsemen, whom he
recounted, so disliked dismounting from their horses that they would eat their meals
and transact business while on horseback, Vowell believed, actually, made by far the best
seamen of any part of South America.[10] But, ever attentive to the opposite sex, he much
preferred the company of the women.

*The Huazas are much fairer in complexion, and smaller in stature, than the men of the same
race. They are a cheerful set of women, mild and pleasing in their manners, and very hospitable
and attentive to strangers. They form a pleasing contrast to their boisterous, quarrelsome husbands
and brothers; not partaking of any of their amusements, except the fandango, of which they are
extremely fond.*

Vowell, *Campaigns and Cruises*, 309-310

Of the Chilean ladies in general, he wrote,

'The *Chilena* ladies appear to be particularly pleased by the foreigners always joining the party at the *estrado*, listening to their singing and entering into conversation with them… In truth, the society and conversation of the females, in every part of South America, is far preferable to that of the men.'[11] [12]

He admired the Chilean ladies' attire, and especially their hair:

'The *Chilenas* dress, at present, much like the English ladies; except that they will, on no occasion, wear a bonnet, and merely cover their heads with a shawl when they go out of doors. They very justly consider their raven locks a far more becoming ornament than any artificial covering; and, even the very poorest females take the greatest pains in plaiting and adorning their hair; they take a decent pride in letting it be seen.'[13]

Vowell's sensitive view of women made him despise any abuse against them, so much so, that he felt compelled to include in his book several stories in which women had been unjustly treated – stories that one would not expect to find in other military narrations of the times. He writes of a Chilean nobleman who, in a jealous rage, murdered an innocent woman on a Santiago hillside using his sword no less – an affront to a soldier such as Vowell – as well as the story of a Spanish mayor who humiliated a young Patriot woman by cutting off her hair and marching her around the plaza; '… the indignity was too great for her to bear; she sunk under it, and died in a decline, shortly after the Patriots regained possession of their city.'[14] Vowell was not witness to these events, and yet he thought it important enough to retell them. And in his historical fiction, he denounces the fact that women were used for the ambitions of their fathers, either by marrying them off to wealthy men, or by disposing of them in nunneries.

He included in his narrative a dramatic moment he witnessed, in 1823, from the deck of the *Independencia* – an act of daring by an Englishwoman during a fierce gale in which eighteen vessels were lost in twenty-four hours. The woman, a captain's wife aboard a sinking ship, wrapped her infant child into a trunk, and when she was sure people on the relatively near shoreline were watching, hurled it into the sea, where it drifted towards the shore; the Chileans managed to lasso the trunk and rescue the baby. The Englishwoman then threw herself in to the '… tremendous sea that was running, and as her courage and presence of mind deserved' [15] was also rescued by the *Huasos* on shore.

As well, Vowell also took pity on women during the public penance ceremonies of Holy Week, which he witnessed and considered completely fanatical:

'As for the females, it is painful to behold the weak, nervous state, to which they are reduced by fasting and penance, and by the appalling sermons they hear, from the friars who attend for this purpose. Their friends always find it necessary to provide carriages of some description, to convey them home, for they generally come out fainting and in hysterics.'[16]

He had, nonetheless, no such sympathy for male weaknesses of the same ilk:

'But it is absolutely ridiculous to see two or three hundred stout men, literally roaring and blubbering like children, and falling on their knees in the street to every acquaintance they meet, to beg their pardon for any offence they may have given them.'[17]

Even crime in the city was of interest to Vowell, who believed that robberies and murders were common because there were hardly any executions, except in cases of peculiar atrocity and – foreboding his own future – '… where the criminals have no friends to interest themselves in their behalf.'[18] Criminals were simply banished from the city or sent into the navy for a few years. However, his sensibility towards women, clearly, did not extend to female criminals, whom he stated invariably went unpunished, even for murder, because the convent nuns would claim them as penitents.

When the *Independencia* anchored in Callao, the major port of Perú, Vowell had the opportunity to see Lima, riding there to accompany Captain Wilkinson. Of Lima, Vowell wrote,

'The number of churches, convents, and other religious buildings is incredible; there is scarcely a single street, where there is not at least one to be seen. This gives Lima a magnificent appearance, when viewed from the harbour, or from any place in the neighbourhood; but, on a nearer approach, the stranger is struck with the mean aspect of the dwelling houses; few having any windows towards the street, although they are spacious and handsome within.'[19]

Although Vowell did not appear to stay in Lima for any great length of time, he did manage to give his attention to the women of Lima. According to Vowell, the *Limeñas* wore a close fitting dark dress that impeded them from taking long or quick steps, and a black silk mantilla that covered their faces except for one eye. Not surprisingly, this he did not think as charming as the traditional dress of the ladies of Bogotá.

The Limeñas are led thither (to the public market) by their love of flowers… All the females of South America are remarkably fond of flowers, especially the clavel, or carnation, for which they give exorbitant prices… The ladies of Lima, in common with most of the South American females, pique themselves on the neatness of their shoes, and the small size of their feet. The Quiteñas, on the contrary, invariably wear shoes too large for them. These they stuff out with wool or cotton, for the purpose of resembling Europeans, for they consider a small foot the most certain mark of Indian descent.

Vowell, *Campaigns and Cruises,* 376–377

It is clear that while in the service of Chile, Vowell had a full social life, interacting with local men and women, which gave him insights to their way of life.

Vowell earned yet another Patriot medal when, in 1822, Bernardo O'Higgins awarded all the members of the Chilean Squadron a medal in honour of their splendid service to the country. Unfortunately, the cash-strapped government never actually minted it.[20]

CHAPTER FIFTEEN

The Last Spanish Flag

'Destroy their settlements in America, and Spain falls.'[1]

Admiral Sir Edward Vernon, MP

THE Squadron was in a bad way. Cochrane considered only the *Independencia* to be seaworthy. Most of the ship's companies had left the Squadron in 1822 and every day the navy acutely felt the financial neglect visited upon it by an impecunious Chilean government.[2] There was still scope and need for the Squadron, nonetheless, as the war in Perú was by no means over, and the Spaniards still had Chiloé.

The Archipelago of Chiloé, at the southern tip of Chile, was the Spanish Empire's last fortified port on the Pacific. The *Independencia,* completely repaired after its California voyage, was urgently sent to blockade Chiloé and so stop a United States ship that was expected to arrive, bearing officers, arms and money for Antonio de Quintanilla, the Spanish governor there. Vowell admits that although they raced from Valparaíso to Chiloé in a record eighty hours, they were unfortunately too late to intercept the ship. Nevertheless, they were ordered to stay in that very cold, rainy, and isolated spot on blockade duty, of which he wrote:

> *'A blockade is at all times, and under all circumstances, an unpleasant, harassing service to perform; but it becomes doubly so, off a rocky dangerous coast, where bad weather, and heavy gales of wind, may be constantly expected. The western coast of Chiloé, off which we were stationed, does not contain a single harbour, being chiefly guarded by inaccessible rock.'*[3]

True to form, Vowell fought the blockade boredom by paying attention to the topography of the archipelago and its other natural features such as the red cedar, diminutive ponies and large herds of swine, sea otters, seals, and seafowl that abound in those islands. This is the very land that nine years later would equally fascinate – and exasperate – Charles Darwin. During his voyage on *The Beagle,* he had the opportunity to examine Chiloé's topography, sea, volcanoes, and impenetrable forests. Interestingly, he found it detestable due to the rain and throughout his long journey around the world, with all the uncomfortable situations he would have encountered, it was the weather in Chiloé that Darwin complained about.[4]

After spending what Vowell referred to as tedious months, the *Independencia* headed to Valdivia for much needed repairs as the inclement weather had taken its toll on the ship. Valdivia, a port north of Chiloé, had been one of the most fortified cities in the colonies of the Spanish Empire, a veritable military stronghold, until Cochrane took it in a spectacular manner in 1819.[5] To Vowell, Valdivia seemed a gloomy, uninviting, wretched looking place but the Valdivians he considered: '... *Remarkable for their cheerful manners, and healthful rosy complexions, in which they resemble the peasantry of Somerset and Devonshire. The Chilenos have long remarked that the officers of their regiments, when sent to garrison Valdivia, rarely remain bachelors ...*',[6] and the same applied to many Englishmen who were attracted by the resemblance the Valdivianas bore to their own countrywomen.

At Valdivia harbour they encountered the schooner *Mercedes* just having arrived from Valparaíso and through its commander, Captain Barragan, Vowell and his fellow officers learned that Chile was in the throes of political upheaval. The information they received was that the prime minister, Rodríguez, stood accused of financial wrongdoing, the army in Concepción commanded by Ramón Freyre was in revolt for want of pay and clothing and sided against the president Bernardo O'Higgins[7] who backed Rodríguez. Then, the commander of the 8th Regiment of Foot garrisoned in Valdivia, requisitioned the *Independencia* to take the troops to join Freyre, and threatened to sink her if Captain Wilkinson did not comply.

'There was however, no necessity for taking this precaution, the Chileno navy having to the full as much reason to complain of the conduct of the minister towards them as the army.'[8]

Captain Wilkinson assembled his officers to ask their opinion, and they were unanimous in siding with Freyre.

Vowell also learned that on 18 January 1823, Cochrane had resigned his command and had gone to fight for Brazil. Cochrane had had enough of San Martin who, to his mind at least, had become an oppressive dictator of Perú, had antagonized him, and undermined the Chilean Squadron. To add to the political turmoil, there was a battle for power going on between O'Higgins and Freyre. Cochrane believed that as a foreigner he should not take part in these internecine struggles.[9] He said farewell to Chile with these words:

'Chilenos – My Fellow Countrymen – You know that independence is purchased at the point of the bayonet. Know also that liberty is founded on good faith, and on the laws of honour, and that those who infringe upon these, are your only enemies, amongst whom you will never find, COCHRANE.'[10]

The troops boarded the *Independencia* and sailed to Talcahuano, a port north of Concepción, where with the help of three requisitioned merchant vessels, they picked up the rest of Freyre's soldiers and sailed to Valparaíso, a twenty-four hour voyage. Arriving with this force, Vowell was not only witness to, but also participant in, the deposing of O'Higgins and the taking of power by Freyre.

No news whatever had reached O'Higgins of the arrival of the Independencia with the 8th Regiment, at Talcahuano; nor could the signal posts on the coast convey any intelligence to the port, on account of the fog. But when the sea breeze set in, and cleared it away, the vessels were seen entering the harbour, full of troops, which were landed before any measures could be adopted to prevent it. No resistance was offered, either by the forts, or the Lautaro and Galvarino, both which vessels were manned and armed, although the rest of the squadron was paid off and dismantled… The inhabitants of Valparaíso received the troops with great demonstrations of joy; many even of the ladies hurrying to the beach, with baskets of melons, and other refreshments for the soldiers.

Vowell, *Campaigns and Cruises,* 362

On 5 April 1823, Bernardo O'Higgins finally resigned and Ramón Freyre became the president of Chile.

Sometime after, the *Independencia* was ordered to sail an ambassador of Freyre's government to Callao, Perú and upon reaching the port discovered that the Spanish army, under General José de Cantarac, had recently, in February 1824, overpowered the Patriot Colombian troops under Generals de Sucre and Valdéz, and temporarily retaken Lima. The port was teeming with the Colombian troops and one wonders what feelings Vowell had, seeing there the army to which he had given so much, and if he encountered any of his old comrades. If he did, he did not say in his narratives.

In Callao, described by Vowell as an ill-built place, excessively dirty with offal of slaughtered cattle rotting in the streets, he took a close look at a frightening place – the dungeons of the main castle, El Real Felipe, an infamous prison where Patriots had been incarcerated. His language betrays a horror of what the prisoners must have gone through, and this foreboding passage may give us an inkling of what his own feelings towards prison would be in his later life.

Under the bastions are the Casas-Matas, a series of gloomy dungeons, where hundreds of Patriot prisoners were confined by the Royalists. Scarce a ray of light could penetrate into these subterranean cells, for the only small grated window that was allowed to each, did not open into the castle ditch, but into deep narrow trenches dug for that purpose in the works; so that not the least glimpse of the sky, nor of any human being, could be enjoyed from them. The total privation of a proper circulation of air was so severely felt in these crowded receptacles of misery, that the soldiers, who were on guard on the prisoners, have been known to faint away on entering them.

Vowell, *Campaigns and Cruises,* 368

Vowell commented on the cruelty often perpetuated on the prisoners by their guards, who would take their only provision, one real and a half – about nine pence – which was their very inadequate daily allowance:

'To whom were they then to complain of this cruel robbery? To their jailors, who were eager for their death, and would willingly have accelerated it, to escape the trouble of attending to their wants.'

As Vowell rode to Lima with Captain Wilkinson, they encountered on the road many Limeños who had fled in great numbers to Callao but were now returning to their homes. On arrival, they saw the lawless confusion reigning there, consequence of the brief Spanish foray.

In the capital, the streets looked desolate; scarcely a shop was open, and the different squares showed the traces of the enemy's bivouacs and watch-fires. The few inhabitants who ventured to let themselves be seen, appeared to wander about, as if the aspect of the place was new to them; looking cautiously round them, at every turning, in expectation of the sudden return of the Spanish forces. The churches were open, and though still very splendid, had all been plundered more or less of their rich ornaments.

Vowell, *Campaigns and Cruises*, 371

The Patriots, however, would soon prevail in a decisive manner. On 6 August 1824, Simón Bolívar, having marched his army across the Andes again, defeated General Canterac at Junín, a defeat that greatly demoralized the Spanish troops. Four months later, on 8 December 1824, on the plains of Ayacucho, Field Marshal José Antonio de Sucre demolished the Spanish army and Spanish power in Perú, taking even the viceroy, José de la Serna, prisoner. Thus, with these two battles Bolívar and Sucre put an end to Spanish rule in the Americas – there was only one Royalist stronghold left: Chiloé. The Spanish Governor of the Archipelago of Chiloé, Antonio de Quintanilla, was very active attacking Patriot ships as he could depend on two armed privateers to do so.[11]

President Freyre was determined to take Chiloé and after the three-month return voyage to Valparaíso, Vowell and the *Independencia* were sent to Talcahuano to receive recruits for this expedition. To Vowell's dismay the 'recruits' were:

'... Deserters, criminals from jails, and vagabonds of every description ... The greater part of them were nearly naked, and all of them half-starved and sickly ... In the whole, about four hundred of these passengers were embarked all of them in as filthy a condition as was to be expected from men just out of a South American calabozo (jail).'[12]

There were even a dozen or so orphans among the 'recruits'. It is obvious that Vowell did not care for the company of the criminal kind. He reports that despite taking every precaution, disease broke out, fever and smallpox, and consequently several died, a great many were sent to the hospital and, in Vowell's words, *'much to our sorrow'*[13] the *Independencia* lost its commander as Captain Wilkinson became ill on arrival at Valparaíso and died within thirty-six hours.

Vowell's new commanding officer on the *Independencia* was Captain Paul Delano, a captain from Massachusetts who had been in Chile's service since 1819. Vowell was now the senior officer of the Squadron marine infantry and he wrote with a sense of pride, on 18 February 1824,[14] that he *'... was exchanged by the commander-in-chief's orders, to the Lautaro, where the President's flag was flying at the main'.*[15] With Captain Bell commanding the *Lautaro,*[16] they sailed to headquarters in Talcahuano to rendezvous with the rest of Freyre's army.[17] The Squadron, now under the command of Captain Robert Forster, at this time consisted of the *Independencia* (corvette), *Lautaro* (frigate), *Voltaire* (corvette), *Chacabuco* (corvette), and the *Galvarino* (brig). They picked up more troops in Valdivia in readiness to attack Chiloé. It was spring of 1824.

There is a document dated 1 October 1824, signed by O'Higgins and by the Squadron accountant Francisco Monroy, certifying that Richard 'Longeville' Vowell served on board the *Independencia* as Captain of Marines from 13 November 1821 to 18 February 1824, the day on which he was transferred to the *Lautaro*, and that *'... in all that time he has not been absent even one day from this service, always present at every review.'* It is interesting to note that in all the naval documents relating to the Squadron, Vowell's name and those of all the officers are preceded by the title 'Don', which indicates the status of a gentleman.[18]

Aboard the *Lautaro*, crowded with men of different corps, horses, and even bullocks, confusion reigned. Vowell explains that for most of the army men this was the first time on board a ship and their officers did not keep naval discipline. The *Lautaro* was hit with foul winds which, as it had a tendency to roll heavily, increased the difficulties of those on board. But to Vowell the greatest discomfort was the noise, which he amusingly refers to:

> *While lying close to each other, near Fort Corral, we had the music of no less than five military bands, accompanying the expedition, which continued to play from morning to night, with scarcely any intermission, to the great delight of the criole officers and soldiers. But, as almost all the musicians composing the bands were, in the strictest sense of the word, learners, their constant practising was not among the least of the minor 'Miseries of the Expedition'. Those who have been accustomed to the quiet and comfort of a British man-of-war, can form no idea of the confusion, and total absence of both, in the gun-room of a Patriot frigate carrying troops.*
>
> Vowell, *Campaign and Cruises,* 397

It seemed to Vowell that most South Americans had a natural talent for music, and that so long as instruments were to be had, it was easy to set up a regimental band.

However, he added wryly: *'It was usual for a colonel to select from the ranks some of the best-looking young crioles for musicians, without any previous enquiry being made whether they had any ear or taste for music; that being always taken for granted.'*[19] Hence the cacophony. Interestingly, Napoleon himself shared the same opinion as Vowell about the British navy, as he is reported to have said to the *Bellerophon's* Captain Fredrick Maitland to whom he capitulated on 15 July 1815, *'What I admire most in your ship is the extreme silence and orderly conduct of your men; on board a French ship everyone calls and gives orders, and they gabble like so many geese.'*[20]

On board the *Lautaro*, there was definitely a clash between army and navy. In a warship, men were brought together for months at a time in close quarters and the only way to maintain harmony – apart from discipline – was by a good dose of forbearance and reciprocal consideration. Vowell criticizes these army officers on board as being almost all illiterate and ill-bred, having no idea of mutual accommodation, of crowding at meals and being intolerant of any discomfort. The army troops nearly blew up the *Lautaro* by the *'... criminal carelessness of the troops, who would pay no attention whatever to the established rules of the service'.*[21] Impatient for their rations to be cooked, they built a separate fire of their own without anyone from the ship's crew noticing, and set fire to part of the deck that was immediately over the powder magazine. Then, their panic was such that they became completely ungovernable, even trying to jump ship. And, in an uncharacteristic generalization, Vowell chides: *'Beside, as all South Americans are inveterate gamblers, and by no means patient and philosophic on experiencing a reverse of fortune, there was a constant succession of cards, dice, and quarrels, during the whole passage.'*[22] This was probably a fair and legitimate reflection of his experience and observations at that time.

Freyre called a council of war, in which Vowell as marine commander and the senior Squadron officer, would have taken part. Vowell faults Freyre for being indecisive and following the advice of inexperienced officers since he decided not to enter the harbour of San Carlos and headed for the harbour of Chacao. Obviously, Vowell had advised an attack on San Carlos but his advice was not taken. Vowell called this irresolute conduct and attributes it to the failure of the expeditions because it was later ascertained that had they attacked San Carlos, Governor Quintanilla would have been taken completely by surprise since most of his militia were out helping with the harvest, and would have, therefore, promptly capitulated.

They remained inactive in Chacao for some time. This inexplicable delay frustrated Vowell, as he believed that it gave Quintanilla time to fortify his points of defence. The Squadron then suffered a misfortune: the loss of the *Voltaire* which was driven out to sea, the crew barely escaping with their lives. Vowell narrates that Freyre's army twice tried to march overland to San Carlos but its lack of knowledge of the terrain and the severe attacks by militia and indigenous warriors impeded it. Freyre, who could not decide what to do, delayed the expedition longer in the port of Remolinos, and then another stroke of bad luck hit them. One of the transport brigs entangled itself so badly on the *Lautaro* that to avoid sinking they had to cut its cables, thereby losing the anchors and forcing the *Lautaro* to turn back to Valparaíso, leaving the President and all his entourage – Vowell included – to join the other smaller ships. Thus, the expedition ended unsuccessfully with an uncomfortably crowded passage back to Valparaíso.

The future of the Squadron was bleak. Since Field Marshal de Sucre's triumph at Ayacucho on 9 December 1824, Spanish power in Perú and in the Americas had come to an end. Consequently, the Chilean Senate considered it had no more need of a Squadron since surely Governor Quintanilla in Chiloé would peacefully capitulate. Short-sightedly, they ordered the complete disarmament of the Squadron on 11 July 1825.[23] This was a serious blow to the Squadron officers and men, and Vowell had the added sorrow at this time of the death of one who had been his companion since he arrived in Venezuela. Even though in his narrative Vowell tried not to be personal, he made a point of mentioning the death of Lieutenant George Noyes in 1825 on board the *Lautaro*, in Valparaiso Bay and was precise as to his burial: '… *he was buried by his countrymen in Fort San Antonio'.*[24]

Meanwhile, Simón Bolívar was determined to get rid of the last Spanish stronghold in Chiloé and was pressing Chile to reorganize its Squadron to do so.[25] In a letter Bolívar stated:

> '*I have also written to the Perúvian Council of Government suggesting the advisability of their urging the government of Chile to hasten its expedition against Chiloé and warning that this Island might come into the hands of some foreign power that could do us harm. England herself would not refuse it, as Chiloé, being the first port of call for those who round the Cape could make England's commerce preponderant in the Pacific.*[26]

According to Vowell, Bolívar himself was making plans for an attack with his Colombian troops but the jealous Chilean government wanted Chiloé to be freed by Chile. This was not far from the truth as, aware of misrepresentation and sensibilities, Bolívar suspended an expedition he had planned with 3,000 Colombians and Perúvian troops to take Chiloé in order to give Chile a chance to act.[27] A more convincing prod for Chile may have been the musings of the Perúvian Congress to take Chiloé and incorporate it into their country.[28] This would have certainly moved Chile to get ahead of the game. In any case, the decree of the Chilean Senate to disband the Squadron was cast aside and a second naval expedition to Chiloé was hastily organized. It had five warships and four transport ships and this time Vowell was aboard a brig recently taken from Spain – the 20-gun *Aquíles,* which was the flagship of Admiral Manuel Blanco Encalada, commander of the Squadron. They reached Chiloé in January 1825.

On 10 January a vanguard army detachment was landed on Puerto Inglés in the Archipelago of Chiloé with orders to silence the guns of the Balacacura batteries. Early next morning, under heavy rain, the bulk of the army landed there. Then the Squadron – the *Aquíles, Independencia, Chacabuco* and *Galvarino* – without troops on board as they had been landed, forced its way into the harbour of San Carlo – a daring manoeuvre considered improbable by Royalists – and defied the blazing guns of Agui Castle, the batteries of San Antonio, Campo Santo and Muelle, and Puquillahue, as well as the gunboats, and headed toward fort Balacacura. The crossing took place in complete order and it greatly boosted Chilean morale. As the men–of–war directed their fire on the batteries and the gunboats that patrolled the beach, Chilean army detachments overpowered and spiked battery guns and the rest of the troops were landed. It has been referred to as a *'heroic crossing of the Squadron under intense heavy artillery fire that lasted about half an hour.'*[29] The firing was heavy but there was no serious damage to the ships, even though Vowell's ship, the *Aquíles*, being Admiral Encalada's flagship, was the most hit and damaged.

The remaining gun boats sought refuge within the breakwater of the San Carlos fort, protected by four batteries and more than two hundred infantry on the beach. Before a boarding party could be sent on the dangerous mission to cut out the gunboats, Vowell narrates that:

> '*The boats of the squadron, however, got nearly alongside of them undiscovered before day-break; and we succeeded in cutting out six gun-boats, under an incessant and very heavy fire. One, only, made its escape through the morning mist, up the Estero de Pudeto, where it was scuttled.*

It turned out to be a clear and fine day and, visible to all, one of Chile's great volcanoes, (which Vowell believed to be Pico de Villarica, but most likely was Calbuco which is closer) began spouting smoke, to the delight of the Chileans who considered this a good omen.

> *The Huazos, on board the Aquíles, repeatedly pointed to it during the battle, exclaiming that 'Tahita Cordillera' (Father Mountain) was umpire between his children and the Godos; and calling the long line of black smoke, that was issuing from the crater, and drifting with the trade-wind to the northward, his signal to renew, for the last time, the fatal "guerra a la muerte" (war to the death).*
>
> Vowell, *Campaigns and Cruises*, 411

After the Squadron's successful attack on the gunboats, it was then up to the army, led by Freyre himself, to defeat the Spanish infantry. Even during such battle, there was a part of Vowell that could admire the deadly scene.

> *Every manoeuvre of both armies could be distinctly seen from the men-of-war, whose tops and rigging were crowded with spectators (who had already played their part) as if they had been represented in a panorama. The firing of the forts, too, answered by the fleet of Patriot gun-boats, which exultingly displayed the ensign of Chile over that of Spain, assisted to fill up a most beautiful, as well as highly interesting moving picture.*
>
> Vowell, *Campaigns and Cruises*, 411

Two days after this battle, on 12 January 1826, Governor Quintanilla surrendered the Archipelago of Chiloé and the Chilean Squadron had the honour of finally liberating Chile from Spain and vanquishing the last stronghold of the Spanish Empire in South America. Vowell wrote – with emphasis – about the symbolic moment when Spain's last remaining New World colony was no more: *'The following day, Agui*[30] *hauled down* **the last Spanish flag,** *then flying between California and Cape Horn, and hoisted the Chileno colours in its stead.'*[31] This was an exhilarating experience for Vowell and those around him as they witnessed what neither Bolívar nor Sucre were able to see: the final moments of the Spanish Empire in the Americas.

CHAPTER SIXTEEN

Home Again

*'God and a soldier all people adore in time of war,
but not before. And when war is over
and all things are righted, God is neglected
and an old soldier slighted.'*

Anonymous

FOR Vowell and his fellow officers, the end of the War of Independence was bittersweet, as it was also the end of the Chilean Squadron. The ships' companies, with the exception of the *Aquiles*, were either laid off or put on half-pay. The ships were dismantled or sold to Argentina, and the *Independencia*, Vowell's first ship, after almost sinking as she sailed off, was declared not seaworthy, while the *O'Higgins* tragically disappeared at sea with about six hundred men on board. It was an unfitting end to the ships of the Chilean Squadron.

Vowell, however, continued in Chile's service, even though the Squadron had been reduced to the *Aquiles* brig only. Being the commander of the Squadron marines, the highest ranking officer in the marine infantry, probably made a difference to him and may have been the reason that he stayed in the Squadron instead of leaving, and he may also have felt the pull of his valued friends and fellow officers.

Taking advantage of some leave, he and some of his friends decided to travel to parts of the interior of Chile they had not seen before. They bought horses: *'We sallied forth on our land cruise, early on a fine summer morning toward the end of November'*.[1] Vowell and his companions headed toward the Valley of Aconcagua on a circular path starting from Valparaíso, past what he called the pretty village of Viña del Mar, then north-east and finally south to end up in Santiago. They travelled through an area that is today the National Park of La Campana and saw Mount Aconcagua, the highest point in South America. Along the way they indulged in a common male pastime of that era, shooting game, which included flamingos, cranes, duck, foxes and even, sadly, a wild swan.

Not all Vowell's leisure time was taken up with hunting, as he also delighted in taking detailed note of the many wild berries and shrubs and their uses, and noted the numerous different types of trees, beautiful flowers and brilliant butterflies. He saw polecats, condors, ostriches, pumas, and he marvelled at the richness of the soil in the valley of Limache.

The soil in this part of Chile, close under the lofty Bell mountain, or Campana de Quillota, is extremely fertile: and the abundance and variety of fruit which grows here with little or no cultivation, astonishes an European traveller. On one single plantation he may gather, in the highest state of perfection, apples, pears, and quinces; oranges, lemons and citrons; peaches, apricots, and nectarines; cherries, plums, and strawberries; figs, grapes, and pomegranates; olives, chestnuts, walnuts, and almonds, with which he is already acquainted; besides the indigenous lúcuma, melocotónes (peaches), sweet citrons, and above all, the luscious chirimóya, called here, and in Perú, 'the Queen of Fruit'.

Vowell, *Campaigns and Cruises*, 422

Upon their return to their hotel in Santiago, they found orders waiting for them to join the *Aquíles* without delay *'as she was hastily fitting for sea, destination, as usual, unknown.'*[2]

Vowell and the *Aquíles* were bound for Chiloé to restore the legitimate government of Governor Col. José Santiago Aldunate who had been overthrown in May 1826 by an adventurer, a Sergeant Major Fuentes. Fuentes had been emboldened, states Vowell, by the knowledge that Chile now had only one brig in its squadron and therefore believed himself impregnable in Chiloé. With a transport carrying 200 to 300 men, they sailed into the archipelago, flying Perúvian colours to deceive Fuentes. The deposed governor was aboard the *Aquíles* and when his presence was known the native and Chilean troops rallied round him. At this point, Vowell and the *Aquíles* had a close brush with disaster.

On passing through the Remolinos, the brig had a very narrow escape from being lost with all on board; for, the wind being light, she was swept by the eddies, from which this channel takes its name, among the rocks, where she had barely depth to lie at anchor without touching, in a rapid eddying current. Had she touched, she must inevitably have upset; and the nearest land to us was a perpendicular cliff, where there would have been no chance of saving a single man. After losing an anchor and chain, as well as a kedge and hawser, we escaped this danger, and came to an anchor in our old berth near Barcacúra.

Vowell, *Campaigns and Cruises*, 439

It all ended well as Fuentes was forced to capitulate and was taken prisoner on 19 July 1826.

Another unusual task awaited the *Aquíles*. The Chilean Governor Pinto decided to remove the mint from Santiago where the unproductive silver mines made the metal scarce, and transport it to Coquimbo where silver was plentiful. Vowell points out that this was an unpopular political move in Santiago but a popular one in Coquimbo. It was a very difficult task to remove the cumbersome machinery and great granite slabs onto the ship without benefit of wharf or cranes in Valparaíso, which they had to oversee. In the end, the task was done and Vowell described the rejoicing, with music band and all, in Coquimbo once the *Aquíles* arrived.

From there, Vowell and the *Aquíles* sailed with a special government envoy to Callao, Perú. This bears mentioning because on the way Vowell describes a most unusual view of the Andes range that he saw from the ship's deck.

> As we ran along the coast with a fair wind, we frequently saw the Cordillera, covered with perpetual snows; an object which never fails to attract the attention even of the natives, who are constantly in the habit of gazing on them. The highest and most distant peaks were never to be discerned, except, for a very short time, before and after sun-rise and sun-set. In many instances, we could observe the well-defined outline of some very remote peak, on the sun's disk, as it rose; but the mountain appeared immediately to melt into air, and became invisible to us, from its extreme distance. We observed the same singular appearance at the rising of the moon, and in a far more beautiful manner; for no other mountains whatever were to be seen at the moment, except the single peak interposed between us and that planet.
>
> Vowell, *Campaigns and Cruises*, 443

It was clear to Vowell that the cessation of the war did not bring civil peace: '... *The different parties in Chile had leisure to quarrel more openly among themselves; as is usual in such cases in most new republics.* '[3] He describes some of the political woes of Chile as a time of bitter and constant disputes between the two main parties – the Pelucones (Whigs) and Liberals. There were rounds of conspiracies, violence, and impunity for those who conspired. The troops were easily corrupted by offers of funds and anarchy seemed to hover over the land. As elections were called, frequent and violent quarrels erupted at voting stations. And with enormous political sagacity, Vowell placed a great deal of the blame on the elites who sought power with their wealth, talents, and influence, and used every intrigue to secure power. His insight was so astute that it could have been applied forward into Latin America's future for the following one hundred and seventy years.

> The conspiracies against Pinto began once more to be serious and insurrections were of frequent occurrence in Santiago, being principally headed by Col. Infante, Don N. Urriola, and other demagogues. These were men of desperate fortunes, but allied to good families in Chile, either by birth or marriage. The interest of their relatives was powerful enough with Government to save them from those consequences, which often fell severely on the subordinate agents in these

> conspiracies. *The principals, meanwhile, merely retiring to their friends' estancias (country homes) for a few days, until justice had been satisfied by a few severe examples, appeared afterwards boldly in public, ready to seize on another opportunity of disturbing the peace of the country afresh.*
>
> Vowell, *Campaigns and Cruises*, 444

It is at this point that Vowell understood it was time for him to leave Chile, which must have caused him some sadness. He notes that most of the foreigners had already left the Chilean Squadron '*… but nearly all those who remain are married in the country, and are, of course, settled there.*' Obviously, Vowell was not one of these, despite having had many opportunities to settle in Chile, as had so many of the foreign Squadron officers who left the service. There is no record that Vowell married in Chile and we may only speculate that his restless spirit did not crave a domestic life and he had not yet spent his desire for change, adventure, and risk. He does give, however, a clear political explanation of his decision to leave the service of Chile, similar to that of Lord Cochrane.

> *When a country is thus agitated by civil war, prudence appears to dictate to all foreigners that propriety of retiring from the struggle; more especially if they have entered the service of that country at a time when it was united to oppose a common enemy, and with an expressed or implied understanding, that they were to serve against him alone. In civil war, as in family quarrels, faults are usually to be found on both sides; and the stranger, in either case, who imprudently interposes, will assuredly find himself considered de trop, when a reconciliation takes place. If he has been active and zealous in the cause he has adopted, he will be hated by both parties as an incendiary; and, if he has recommended moderation by precept or example, he will be despised and suspected, by friends as well as foes, as a time-server and spy.*
>
> Vowell, *Campaigns and Cruises*, 457-458

Vowell demanded and obtained a leave of absence to go to Europe in November 1829. The only difficulty he had was to ascertain who had the authority to give it as there were two who claimed to be president of Chile.

'After a very good passage of about four months… I landed at Portsmouth in the spring of 1830, after 13 years absence.'[4]

It would not be the end of his adventures.

CHAPTER SEVENTEEN

Facing Another Empire

'Graviora manent.

(The worst is yet to come.)

THE historical record states that Richard Longfield Vowell died in Bath in 1837. This is not the case. Having returned to Bath, Vowell dedicated himself to turning the copious notes he had taken throughout his thirteen years in South America into a book. His mass of material was so great '... that he feared, were he to embody it all in his narrative, he might be accused of plagiarism, or of the still less venial offence against many readers – the "bestowing all his tediousness upon them".'[1] He must have been continuously writing down his impressions as he lived out his adventures, and this may be one of the reasons the *Llaneros* referred to him as 'the student'.

During the War of Independence, the army's life was not one of continuous battle or training. There were times of tedious waiting, as there are in any war, and it is evident that Vowell used that time to write. My search for his original manuscripts in libraries, archives, and in historical societies across three continents, and among his living relatives, proved fruitless. Perhaps, in the future, someone may yet find his original notes.

Within a few months Vowell finished his book and then discovered there were numerous others in circulation and written by British volunteers who had fought in South America. He may well have considered these incomplete, or even unfaithful accounts of the South American patriot wars, written by those who had spent scant time there compared to himself. In a statement given to the press the day *Campaigns and Cruises* was launched, Vowell explained:

'But may not one, who was among the earliest volunteers that assisted to clear the land with their personal exertion, be allowed to glean after the harvest has been gathered in? Especially as no single individual, as far as he is aware, has traversed the country to such an extent, nor resided in it for so long a period, and in such eventful times.'[2]

It was not unusual at that time for authors to omit their names, and in fact, a number of volunteers also published books without their names on them. One can perhaps speculate that the reason Vowell did not have his name printed on his book was because he did not want to compromise any standing he might still have had with the Chilean Navy. However, his anonymity was not so strict since he openly gave statements to the Bath press as being the author of the book.

Having finished writing his book, inaction must have sat ill on Vowell after leading a very active military life. His future must have loomed heavily before him. He was then thirty-five years old, an experienced army and navy officer, but with no British recognition or contacts, and little or no prospects of any kind for a similar career in England. Conceivably, Vowell could have begun the life of a writer, but his restless spirit seemed to reject sedate living. His relationship with his sisters could not have been easy after such a long absence. It is not known if, upon his return to Bath, his unmarried sisters were still in the city or if they had already gone to live with Susan and her husband in their comfortable home in Mallow, as they did in later life.[3]

A review of wills indicates that all of them had funds with which to live by and did not need Vowell to support them. In what manner, with what purpose or function, could he have inserted himself into their daily life, whether in Bath or in Mallow? He had very little money, most of his inheritance having long been spent while fighting with Bolívar's army. Chile could not have given him much, and he was not a man to be comfortable living at the expense of his sisters. Home life once again failed to keep him at home. Leaving behind the family he would never see again and the comforts of life in England, he once more left for an unknown land – this time, Australia.[4]

In November 1832, Vowell emigrated to Australia on the *Prince Regent*, arriving in Sydney on 19 February 1833. At this time, more British people were moving to Australia, as it was no longer seen exclusively as a repository for criminals, but also as a place of opportunities, where immigrants would be welcomed. It is conceivable that Vowell also sought a warmer climate as his bouts of rheumatism had prompted him to leave Bolívar's army.

During the voyage, Vowell made himself useful to *Prince Regent's* Master, Captain John Aiken, particularly as all passengers and crew were quarantined on arrival for a month due to an outbreak of smallpox.[5] Vowell obtained an excellent letter of reference from the captain, which he would use to obtain employment in Australia:

Sydney, March 21, 1833.

This is to certify that the Bearer, Richard Vowell, came as passenger in the Ship Prince Regent, under my Command, and during the said passage, he conducted himself with great sobriety and was always willing to aid and assist whatever laid in his power, and from appearance seems to be a hard working man and worthy of a situation, and capable of being trusted to anything that may be put in his power under them who may employ him.

I am Y. O. S, John Aiken

Vowell had two other letters of reference with him. One was from Colonel Wilson – the same Wilson who had left Bolívar's army under dark circumstances, and with whom Vowell must have met up on his return to England. In his letter Wilson states,

I certify that Mr. Richard Longfield Vowell served under my command as a Captain in the year 1818. I considered him a highly honourable and enterprising Officer in whom I could place the fullest confidence. He is the son of Major Richard Vowell, formerly of the 66th Regiment.

The mention of Vowell's father suggests that Wilson or his family had been acquainted with Vowell senior.

The third letter of reference was from Basil Kendall, a fellow officer from Chile, living in Australia, who wrote:

Barkers Steam Engine, March 25, 1833.

Thereby certify that the Bearer, Rd. Longfield Vowell was Captain of Marines in the Chili State service, being myself as brother officer with him upwards of three years on board the Achilles (the Aquíles), *ship of war in the above Service, and that I also knew him to be for a length of time Major of Brigade, in the Service of the Liberator Simon Bolivar. He was always in active service, and was a trustworthy and honourable officer.*

Basil Kendall. [6]

Basil Kendall would go on to become the father of Henry Kendall, the first Australian poet to draw inspiration from the Australian land and its traditions.

Vowell found employment. He was hired on 15 April 1833 as a clerk at the 2nd Cox's River Stockade, a remote convict camp where prisoners were digging a road through solid rock and thick forest.[7] And it was here that the most bizarre episode of Vowell's life occurred.

In England, from the mid-16th century to the turn of the 17th century, criminal prisoners were executed very frequently, for minor offences. This was considered as a barbarity and a scandal among thoughtful people.[8] Having executed their 'worst' criminal offenders, the English transported the rest of their 'undesirables' to Australia.[9] By 1775 to 1790, there was a convict crisis in England as endemic diseases spread in overcrowded jails. Transportation to Australia was then conceived as an alternative and, undoubtedly, it was cheaper than building and maintaining jails in England.[10] During the later years of the 1820/30s there were significant legal reforms, but transportation continued its pace and between 1831 and 1840, with an average of more than 5,000 convicts per year sent to Australia.[11]

There were several types and levels of incarceration in Australia which included terrible jails and convict road gangs. But there was also a semi-free existence for those convicts assigned to work for settlers, as well as 'open prisons' made up those allowed to live independently and earn a living, having been given a 'Ticket of Leave', but not permitted to leave the country.[12] If a convict finished a sentence of a fixed number of years, he could obtain a Certificate of Freedom and could return to England or Ireland, although apparently few chose to return. A 'Ticket of Leave' was a sort of release on parole, usually given for good behaviour, whereby the convict could live and work independently but had to report regularly to authorities. It was the means of obtaining later a Conditional Pardon, which meant the convict was free but could not leave the Colony. Only with an Absolute Pardon could he leave, though these were rarely given.[13]

Able convicts, working in gangs, were used as free labour – some might say, slave labour – to build public works.[14] There were, in 1835, about sixteen iron gangs in New South Wales. Each gang had a military guard, and a convict overseer. The overseers were generally thoroughly brutalized men. Dressed in uniforms of grey and yellow, iron gang convicts worked with iron collars around each ankle joined by a chain, which weighed between six and nine pounds.[15] As one historian points out:

> 'Road parties were the worst punishment. A convict was worked from sunrise to sunset, was fed with the coarsest food and subject to the most rigid discipline, watched over by a capricious and tyrannical ex-convict as overseer. The parties were herded from one place to another, and either lodged overnight in movable huts on wheels or kept penned into stockade like animals.'[16]

The 2nd Cox's River Stockade, located close to the Blue Mountains, north of Sydney, near the present town of Lithgow, housed road gangs who were digging a road planned by Thomas Mitchell, Surveyor General of New South Wales, to cross the Blue Mountains to the town of Bathurst. It was a difficult terrain. With no machinery, the gangs cut down trees, hauled and split rocks. They, literally, carved out a road, using their hands, shovels, pickaxes, iron bars, hatchets and explosives.[17]

Operations had started as recently as 1832 and, indeed, the 2nd Cox's was the first Stockade erected for the use of iron gangs in building roads.[18] Sue Rosen and Michael Pearson, historians of the Stockade, describe it as square in shape and surrounded by a high fence. The convicts' huts were within the fence and the auxiliary buildings housing a hospital, the military and superintendents, lay outside it. There were approximately 500 to 800 convicts.

There were severe penalties, and virtually no hope of escaping detection. Crimes of violence at the Stockade against and between gang members were a feature of life.[19] Surrounded by the Cox's River on three sides, the Stockade was far from any town or settlement, the river and the thick forest forming a formidable barrier to any escape. One writer at the time described its isolation clearly:

> 'High, steep forest-ridges, stony, and but thinly clad with verdure, encircled the spot, and crowned like the gigantic walls of a prison all around. Moreover, the place was very solitary, unfrequented by travellers, and perfectly out of the way.'[20]

In 2004, I visited the place where the 2nd Cox's River Stockade once stood, accompanied by local historian, Ollie Leckbandt,[21] who has saved for posterity hundreds of artefacts from the site. One could still appreciate the rugged environment, and the relative isolation of the place, which must have been overwhelming over two hundred years ago.

One of the Stockade's inmates, convict Thomas Cook, who left a passionate and indignant record of the abuses and cruelties suffered by prisoners, described it as a hellish place, a 'Den of Infamy' where soldiers marched prisoners at the point of bayonets, punished them with cat-o'-nine-tails, where there was habitual violence among the prisoners and widespread homosexuality was used as a tool for humiliation and abuse:

> 'The inclemency of the weather, the haggard countenances of the men, the severity of the cold and the want of a second blanket to save half the frozen men from perishing, the cruelty of the overseers who robbed us of our rations, a sheet of bark for my head, the half of a thread-bare blanket for my covering; many a tear did I shed when contemplating my hard fare, and this slight offence for which I had been doomed.'[22]

In 1838, some prisoners tried to escape from the Stockade and in their subsequent defence, they complained of the treatment they had received, stating that they would rather be shot than remain there. Their wish was granted.[23]

Vowell's job as clerk meant he was in charge of the Stockade documents, as his letter of application demonstrates.

Sydney, March 25th 1833.

Sir, In compliance with your commands, I have the honour to hand you the certificate of character given me by the Master of the Prince Regent; and beg leave to refer you to Col. Wilson for further particulars. I am not a professed clerk, but shall endeavour, by diligent application, to render myself worthy of your protection.

I have the honour to be, Sir, very respectfully, your obedt. Servant,
Richard Longfield Vowell

Most British people were unaware of the 'distant realities' of Australia.[24] Vowell also must have totally misjudged the kind of situation he would be encountering. Instead of a quiet writing job, his functions would encompass those of a jailer since at times his position was referred to as that of 'clerk and constable'.[25] It is clear, however, that he was not an overseer of the gangs since these were positions given to convicts. He may have known also from his few acquaintances there '… that only a minority of free men were prepared to accept the debasing task of policemen, overseers of convicts, gaolers, flagellators, so that most of these occupations were mostly filled by men still under bond.'[26]

He could not have foreseen the brutality of the establishment into which he entered, nor would he be the first to be misled by the penal system in Australia. It affected even Alexander Moconochie, Governor of Norfolk Island, who wrote that he '…was shocked, as any perceptive visitor from Britain might be, at the difference between what he had thought was going on in Australia and the reality.'[27]

Vowell reported to W. Foster, the Superintendent of Convicts at Cox's River, an elderly former military man who was described by Bishop William Ullathorne[28] as '…addicted to intemperance, indulged in prolonged fits of insobriety, the effect of which had been to impair his health and render him unfit to discharge his duties.'[29]

What happened next to Vowell has to be pieced together by analysing the paper trail of official documents and public notices. The record shows that two years after being hired, on 15 May 1835, a reward of 25 pounds was posted for Vowell, who was charged with '*Surreptitious alteration and Forgery of Warrants of Sentences of Prisoners to work in Irons at that place, and has absconded.*'[30] This refers to forging the time left to convicts' sentences which a clerk could be bribed to reduce. We know that monetary gain was not something that had ever motivated Vowell.

Three days later, on 18 May, W. Foster informed the Colonial Secretary, who was the head of the administration of the colony,[31] that Vowell had voluntarily returned and that he had reinstated him as clerk in charge of the books and papers of the Stockade.[32] Vowell must have given Foster a believable account as to why he was supposedly missing for a day, and have credibly defended himself from suspicion of forgery. Foster, while accepting Vowell's explanations, did not write them down because it is quite likely that they would not have reflected well on Foster's administrative capacity. The Colonial Secretary's notes show that he had doubts about Foster's abilities as superintendent.

> '*Mr. Foster may not be brought away from the Stockade at Cox's River, until further notices, and if it shall be found necessary, that you will provide for the temporary discharge of the duty of Superintendent…*'[33]

In any case, five days later, on 23 May, the Colonial Secretary instructed Foster to discharge Vowell and find another clerk. There is no mention of arresting him. It is clear the authorities did not believe that Vowell had forged any documents. This letter from the Colonial Secretary arrived in Foster's hand on 27 May.[34]

On 25 May 1835 the Stockade was rocked by the news of the escape of five convicts, four soldiers and – most surprising – the clerk, Richard Longfield Vowell.[35] Foster's version of events is that on 25 May he had to go to the post office, seven miles away, and therefore, he gave his watch to the clerk, Vowell, so that he could record the time of anything that may occur in his absence. On his return, he found that Vowell was gone along with his watch.[36] Thomas Cook refers to this incident stating that:

> '*It so happened that Mr. Foster's Clerk, an Emigrant, had been bribed by two men in Irons, named Grimes and Jimmins… to alter the Books and Warrants, in reference to their Sentences, from 12 to 9 months…*'[37]

Cook, another Stockade clerk, had also been suspected of bribery and it was in his interest that those suspicions be cast elsewhere, especially once Vowell had gone missing. Cook himself records that '...the clerk having absented himself from his employ and joined a number of soldiers and prisoners belonging to the Stockade in taking arms.'[38] However, Cook's narrative is not entirely reliable as certain passages are clearly self-serving and contain falsehoods.[39] Cook had a dubious character as well as a criminal past, but he wrote a good account of the awful penal situations he endured.

Captain McCummings, of the 4th Kings Own Regiment stationed at the Stockade, recognized that Vowell was a free man and therefore, he could not accuse Vowell of escaping. Neither was Vowell being accused of forgery. Therefore, McCummings charged Vowell with stealing Foster's watch and a blanket that was missing.[40]

Captain McCummings suspected that the leaders of the convicts were two men named McCann and Bryant, and since one of them had been a midshipman, the Captain surmised that they would head to a nearby bay to seize a whale boat.[41]

A posting for Vowell's arrest was issued and it contains the only description that we have of him as '... about 5'9', slender make, lost front tooth in upper jaw, emaciated.'[42] This begs the question, why was Vowell emaciated? One can only surmise that living conditions at Cox's River Stockade must have been so bad that even the administrative staff was affected.

The most puzzling issue is that Vowell would 'escape' with these men. Why would he flee? The only punishment for Vowell that the Colonial Secretary contemplated was the loss of his job. Vowell did not know that he had been fired because the Colonial Secretary's letter ordering his dismissal reached Foster on 27 May, two days after Vowell had 'escaped'. So Vowell left his job at the Stockade a free man, under no cloud of being accused of forgery, yet in company of soldiers who were deserting their post and convicts who were escaping.

Vowell could have walked away from the Stockade at any time. But, why would he help soldiers desert from their duty? Vowell was the same man who in South America felt revulsion at soldiers deserting or being derelict of their duties, which he viewed as '... an unpardonable breach of discipline.'[43] He had been a diligent member of the court martial panel of Bolívar's Army of the South whose function had been to deal with deserters. He thus knew very well how serious the military offence of desertion was. In his Savannas of Varinas, he wrote of one of the heroes of his story, '... for, although determined to leave the service, he shrunk from the idea of adding to desertion the more atrocious military offence, of abandoning a post that had been solemnly confided to him.'

Considering his character and past experiences, it would have been more understandable that Vowell would side with escaping convicts, but highly unlikely that he would side with deserting soldiers. Although he would not have condoned desertion, it is most likely that, at the same time, he would have been repulsed by the dire situation in which soldiers on stockade duty found themselves. He would have considered those situations beneath the standards of normal military functions.

One writer at the time described the arduous and demoralizing duties of the soldiers guarding iron gangs:

'The duties of the troops are most harassing; there is no relief of sentries; they are posted all day with their loaded firelocks, and constantly on the qui vive. I venture to say that the regiments in New South Wales are the least soldier-like, and the worst conducted of any her Majesty possesses. But the truth is, the soldier has little encouragement to behave well; his home indulgences of billet and marching pay are put an end to; the proper custom of a two-hours' sentry only is utterly disregarded; his barracks, bedding, and general accommodation are wretched...'[44]

A broadsheet, published in Manchester in 1835, described the conditions in Australian iron gangs. The author could well have been describing exactly 2nd Cox's River Stockade. There is a good chance that this article was, in fact, written by Vowell himself. Observing the language, style of writing, spelling and punctuation of a writer, the following tract on iron gangs reveals startling similarities to Vowell's style of writing.[45] In the original, emphasis relating to the extraordinary punitive sentencing is conveyed using italics, exactly as Vowell used in his original work:

Nothing is more dreaded by the men than Iron Gangs, as when their sentence is expired they have *all that time spent in irons to serve again,* as every sentence is now in addition to the original sentence. If a man is nearly due for his ticket of leave, and is flogged, he is put back for a certain time, unless for theft, and then he forfeits every indulgence. If an iron gang man has served any number of years in the country, he must begin again; he is the same as a new hand; he has to wait the whole term of years before he receives any indulgence... The delinquents are employed in forming new roads, by cutting through mountains, blasting rocks, cutting the trees up by the roots, felling and burning off. They are attended by a Military Guard, night and day, to prevent escape; wear Irons upon both legs, and at night are locked up in small wooden houses, containing about a dozen sleeping places; escape is impossible; otherwise they live in huts surrounded by high paling, called stockades; they are never allowed, after labour, to come without the stockade under penalty of being shot; so complete is the confinement, that not half-a-dozen have escaped within the last two or three years; they labour from one hour after sunrise until eleven o'clock, then two hours to dinner and work until night; no supper. The triangles are constantly at hand to tie up any man neglecting work, or insolent... Not one day of liberty will he ever enjoy: *he will have all his sentences in addition to his original sentence to serve again.* Picture to yourself this hot climate, the labour, and the ration, and judge for yourself if there is laxity of discipline. It is to places such as I have described that the Judges now sentence men from the English bar – poor wretches! Did they know their fate, be assured, respected Sir, it had been well for them had they never been born.

State of Convicts in New South Wales, 1835, Manchester 1835.[46]

There is no doubt, however, over Vowell's thoughts about the punishment the Spanish gave prisoners during the South American War of Independence, which he articulated clearly in *The Savannas of Varinas*. His own words must have haunted him at the Stockade as he saw the same treatment meted out by, and to, Englishmen.

> *Don Estevan was then barely seventeen… He was publicly flogged at each corner of the Plaza, together with several other young and distinguished patriots of the same age, who, in addition to undergoing this barbarous punishment, were compelled to witness the execution of their relations and friends, which took place immediately after… When the execution was over, the surviving prisoners were marched back to their dungeon; and from thence were sent to work in chains on the fortifications of Mompox. The severe labour at which they were obliged to slave, with scarcely any intermission, from daybreak to night, the scanty sustenance allowed them by Government, and the unwholesome damps of the* casas matas (dungeons) *into which they were crowded by night, without even straw to keep their wearied limbs from the moist pavement, speedily released the greater number from their bondage.*
>
> Vowell, *Savannas of Varinas*, 176

Vowell and the escaped men wandered around the forest looking for sustenance and failed to make it to the coast. If they had a plan, it was not a sound one. Nineteen days later, on 13 June 1835, Vowell, the soldiers, and the escaped convicts were captured. They were sent to Parramatta, the seat of the New South Wales government, and two months later , on 10 August, were taken for trial to Sydney, where the Supreme Court sat. There was rarely bail for these offences and one can only imagine the distress Vowell must have felt during his months of imprisonment. Did he feel remorse for taking a foolish risk, or did he feel anger at being falsely accused? Did he remember the words he wrote describing the waiting for a military court in *The Earthquake of Caracas*?

> The prisoners were then called in, and made acquainted with their sentences. It was listened to, by some of them, with the indifference natural to those who have no families to leave; and by others with exultation, for it relieved them from the dreadful apprehensions under which they had laboured during their trial. A military court, indeed, had been associated, and not without reason, in their terrified imaginations, with ideas of scaffolds and executioners; disagreeable objects, which they had often gazed at with indifference, when the fate of others was concerned, but which now haunted them in all their most horrid colours.

The Supreme Court records indicate that Vowell and the others were accused of robbing one man[47] of a musket, a pistol and one blanket for a total worth of 60 shillings, and another man[48] of two watches, two guns, two knives and gunpowder for a total of 98 shillings.

The Court records throw up yet another puzzle. Referring to him by his full name, Richard Longfield Vowell, he is described as a 'Labourer'. In British culture, speech and intonation are sure labels of class and status, most especially at that time. The minute Vowell opened his mouth to speak, his education and class would have been evident; he could never have been confused with a labourer. Furthermore, why would someone working as a clerk, a position that entailed a higher level of education and good writing skills, be referred to as a labourer? This is an indication that the authorities were set beforehand on not giving Vowell any chance of deferment or leniency.

The trial itself presents concerns. Our modern notion of a fair trial is by no means what it was in 1835. British law did not yet operate under the principle that a person is considered innocent until proven guilty. [49] Trials were quick and lawyers were rarely present. They were not about presenting evidence, but constructing a case against the defendant with the word of the prosecutor pitted against the – mostly defenceless – defendant. [50] The full statements of the defendants rarely appeared in official writing, and, in this case, we have no record of what Vowell might have said in his own defence since the official record of that trial is missing. [51]

The judge hearing their trial was Sir William Westbrooke Burton, a man of Vowell's age, who was generally considered an upright and capable judge. He was, however, a strict disciplinarian. The year before, he had presided at the trial of the leaders of a rebellion on Norfolk Island – Australia's most infamous prison – which ended in the execution of fourteen men. This rebellion and trial had a marked influence upon the judge. A few years later, upon taking up his position as Governor of Norfolk Island, Alexander Maconochie, a man of enlightened ideas on the penal system, discovered that there was a disproportionate number of prisoners who had been tried in 1835 and who had been sent, unjustly, to Norfolk Island. [52]

Judge Burton, in trying to explain away the many capital convictions of the years 1833–35, expressed the very controversial opinion that the reason for such a state of affairs was due to an overwhelming lack of religious principles on the part of the convicted men. Furthermore, he was biased against Roman Catholics and refused to allow them to make the Sign of the Cross when being sworn in. [53]

Judge Burton left a notebook in which he took informal notes during his trials. His handwriting is hard to discern, being only words and phrases jotted down. He wrote down the offences of the convicts and soldiers accused with Vowell, but he only had this to write about Vowell's offences, sections of which are illegible. What follows are the sentences that are readable in the judge's notebook, which is difficult to read:

> '*By Vowell: no threatening language… was just standing at the door drinking milk which the woman gave over. Yes the milk was in a bucket, but he drank it out of a fruit pot. By Vowell – he said nothing to any one – no threats… Vowell's defence shews his (breakfast) but says he was (without?) and only went for…*' [54]

This indicates that Vowell was not threatening anyone; that he simply asked the woman for some milk, which she gave him.

There was no evidence given that Vowell carried arms, that he threatened or was violent to anyone, and at most, what could be said is that he 'retained' Foster's watch, which the Superintendent himself had placed into his hands; today it would not be robbery, but perhaps theft or petty crime (i.e., without violence). Vowell however, was singled out by a convict, James Monds, as the one who put ideas into the men's heads about freedom and escape to South America. Monds, in a convoluted, self-serving letter to the authorities alleging his complete innocence, accused Vowell of being *the principal promoter and conductor* who persuaded him *with his romantic views towards a meditated escape to South America.*[55] It might have been true that Vowell, whom we know was a good storyteller, may have inspired them, but that is no proof that he conspired with them. Another interpretation of the facts is that, inspired by Vowell's tales, the men compelled him to accompany them in the escape so that he would help them reach South America. Surely Vowell did not need to escape, but could have simply walked freely out of the Stockade. This could very well have been a more sinister repeat of his adventure in Barinas when he was forced to accompany Vicentico Hurtado and his bandits. Of that episode Vowell wrote: *Although I was obliged to accompany them, wherever they went, and to be an unwilling spectator of their lawless proceedings, they never urged me to assist them in any way.*[56]

In any case, Judge Burton found them all guilty. In November, one of the convicts, John Fisher, was tried separately, accused of threatening violence, and executed. The soldiers received support from the army and were given lenient sentences. Vowell was convicted on slim evidence, the word of a drunken and unreliable boss, self-interested convicts, and no proper defence. Along with the convicts, Vowell, with no contacts or friends of any note to speak up for him, was condemned to death, but the sentence was commuted to life imprisonment in Norfolk Island. Many would have preferred death.

Chronology of the 2nd Cox's River Stockade Escape

27 March 1833
The Colonial Secretary recommends the appointment of Richard L. Vowell as clerk and constable of the 2nd Cox's River Stockade.

15 April 1833
The Colonial Secretary approves hiring Vowell as clerk and constable with a salary of two shillings and three pence per diem.

15 May 1835
A reward of 25 pounds is posted for Vowell, charged with forging of warrants of sentences of prisoners to work in irons, and for absconding.

18 May 1835

Superintendent Foster writes to the Colonial Secretary informing him that Vowell, suspected of forging warrants of sentences, absconded but had returned, and was reinstated as clerk 'again placed in charge of the books and papers of the Stockade.'

23 May 1835

The Colonial Secretary instructs Foster to discharge Vowell and find another clerk.

25 May 1835

Convicts James Shawn, William Shaw, James Monds, John McCann, four military soldiers of the 4th Regiment (among them Samuel Powell and William Marsden) and a clerk, Richard L. Vowell, escape the Stockade.

13 June 1835

James Shawn, William Shaw and Richard L. Vowell are captured and accused of robbing Richard Keefe at Monkeydillow, robbing a musket (40 shillings), a pistol (10 shillings) and one blanket (10 shillings), a total of 60 shillings worth of goods.

19 August 1835

In Sydney, Vowell is sentenced to death for robbery, but his sentence is commuted to hard labour in irons on Norfolk Island.

21 September 1835

The Sheriff's list of 70 prisoners to be sent to Norfolk Island includes Vowell.

1839

Vowell appears as clerk/constable at Norfolk Island.

CHAPTER EIGHTEEN

I Will Fear No Evil...

'The greater the power, the more dangerous the abuse.'

Edmund Burke, Speech on the Middlesex Election, 1771

ORFOLK ISLAND. The very name inspired terror, it being Britain's most punitive prison of the 19th century and perhaps of all of its history. Located 1,500 miles east of the Australian coast in watery isolation, surrounded by cliffs up to 300 feet high, it was described by French explorer, La Perouse, as a place fit only for angels and eagles. He should have said fallen angels. Its exceptional natural beauty – pine woods, gentle hills, superb coastline and abundant birdlife – became a place of unbelievable human cruelty systematically legitimized by state policy and carried out by brutalized, often sadistic, men.

In 1825, the British Empire designated Norfolk Island as a convict settlement for the maximum punishment of recalcitrant convicts numbering anywhere between 1500 to 2000 convicts. The governor of NSW, Sir Thomas Brisbane, believed that at the island he would deter crime by sheer terror, monstrously saying it would be the *'ne plus ultra of convict degradation.'*[1] Brisbane even proposed that the island be ruled by martial law, thus avoiding the *'complicated machinery'* of civil courts and trials.[2] As pointed out sagely by Shakespeare, the first step towards tyranny is to eliminate lawyers and law courts. The next NSW governor, Sir Ralph Darling, followed in this vein, declaring: *'My object was to hold out that settlement as a place of the extremist punishment, short of death.'*[3] The men unfortunate enough to be sent to Norfolk Island were not to be given false hope, or hope of any kind – as Brisbane declared: *'I could wish it to be understood that the felon who is sent there is forever excluded from hope of return.'*[4]

Severe punishment was to be handed out to convicts who were doubly convicted, having committed further crimes since arriving in the country; but it was also the place where many English political dissidents and Irish patriots of the 1798 rebellion ended up.[5] Vowell was not a convict, but a free man. If he had committed a crime, it would have been a first offence only and not one to send him to a prison that was supposedly for convicts of multiple crimes. However, his harsh punishment was most likely due to the fact that the Court had been led to believe that Vowell's stories of liberation in South America had spurred the convicts and soldiers of the 2nd Cox's River Stockade to escape. Therefore, Vowell became *de facto*, a political prisoner and hence was sent to Norfolk Island, where Irish political prisoners also ended up.

Vowell's arrival at Norfolk Island in mid-September 1835[6] would have been the same as that described by Thomas Cook, who after serving at the 2nd Cox's River Stockade, was also sent there:

> '... *the place of horror Norfolk Island... My feeling on landing here, no pen or language can correctly describe. In a state of nudity we were ranked up on the Beach, and after undergoing a minute and most indelicate inspection, our miserable rags were huddled on, and we were marched to the Police Office, and from thence to the Barrack Yard. From this instant all my hope of happiness was to cease.*'[7]

Dressed in long, yellow, cutaway loose frock coats, a straw hat and, in winter, a coarse woollen jacket, the convicts carried out hard, incessant work from dawn until 4.30 in the afternoon.[8] The work was punitive, not productive. There was an expectation that the settlement crops would have some results, but in fact the convicts' labour was principally to punish them. The work consisted of tasks such as breaking ground, felling timber, lime burning, erecting buildings, making roads, boat tender duties, or working a crank mill for corn.[9]

One hour was allowed for a midday meal but the prisoners had no breakfast or dinner. In 1826, every afternoon, convicts were given 1 lb of flour, 1 oz of sugar and ½ lb of salt, 1 lb of raw beef or 10 oz of raw pork. They had to find a way to cook it themselves. By 1844, they were being given breakfast and supper of hominy, salt junk for dinner and maize bread. The deficiency of this diet brought about many deaths and endemic dysentery.[10] Vowell, who always enjoyed good food, would have suffered, but his experience in the long arduous campaigns of the *llanos* when he survived days on end on only unsalted beef would have helped him to cope.

From the journal kept by Reverend T. Sharp who visited Norfolk Island in 1839, we know two things about Vowell's time there: that he obtained a position of responsibility as a clerk and that he had not lost his faith. Vowell was spared the worst of the hard labour because he was an educated man and his skills were needed; it was a standard practice that educated convicts were set to the relatively easy paperwork of record keeping for the convict administration.[11] Reverend Sharpe made a list of thirty-two men who received Holy Communion from him. The very first entry on his list reads: '*Overseer R.L. Vowell, Supt. of Conv. Clerk*'[12] meaning that Vowell was an overseer supervisor of clerical work relating to documents rather than in charge of outdoors physical labour. On the reverend's list there was one other overseer and a constable but all the others listed were simply prisoners. Although the reverend conducted the service for all prisoners, only those listed came forward after the service, to a separate room, to receive Holy Communion. He thought it important enough to write their names down in his book. Reverend Sharpe's journal further reveals that prisoners who conducted themselves with propriety were allowed to have gardens, that the overseers were given privileges, were better clothed and fed than others and had a portion of their time, perhaps two years, of transportation remitted. We can assume safely that these small mercies were extended to Vowell. Rev. Sharpe noted:

> 'Many of these have been communicants before and have conducted themselves generally with prudence and discretion and with some of them I am much pleased. I think they are really desirous of being true Christians. In this Island, those who are anxious to serve God truly have many difficulties to struggles against. They have no place where they can go to for private prayer and meditation, when at work they must see and hear many things which cannot but be very grievous to a tender conscience, to a mind enlightened, to a heart wishful that all should serve God...'

The good reverend greatly understated the difficulties.

One difficulty was rampant homosexuality, which Thomas Cook denounced both at the 2nd Cox's River Stockade and at Norfolk Island. Most British people considered homosexuality an abomination at the time and, indeed, it was illegal. It was certainly in existence, including in schools and the armed forces, but in a covert way because it was not socially acceptable and was legally punishable. However, the homosexuality that took place in this context was not related to affectionate relationships, but to sadistic humiliation and rape in which sex was merely the instrument of violence, power and domination.[13] Norfolk Island was a veritable Sodom, produced by the oppression of 'an authority whose own capricious brutality could offer no road back from their abasement'.[14] Vowell also would have been as revolted as Cook. He could not have been a homosexual and live to tell the tale in the masculine dominated culture of Latin America, particularly in the military where he would have been at least shunned and, most probably, the Llaneros would have killed him. If a person's character is reflected in what they write, then in Vowell's writing we can detect his heterosexual attitude towards women but, more to the point, his attitude about the proper conduct toward prisoners, toward unnecessary cruelty to man or beast, toward the dishonour of misused authority, all of which indicate that this sort of abuse would have been abhorrent to him.

Another difficulty was the type of men who governed the island. It was fortunate for Vowell that, when he arrived, the commander of Norfolk Island was Major Joseph Anderson, a Scot of the 50th Regiment and veteran of the Peninsular Wars.[15] The previous two governors, Major Joseph Foveaux and James Morisset, had been unrestrained sadists who took pleasure in the excruciating punishments they meted out and in the atmosphere of terror they created through the intrigues of their informants. Anderson was an improvement; he was only a stern disciplinarian and a flogger who once gave five men 1,500 lashes before breakfast.[16] Records of some of the punishments include up to 200 lashes, and three to eight months' solitary confinement on the chain. He and his officers led a pleasant life on the island, shooting, riding, and living in oblivion to the suffering of the convicts around them.[17] Anderson left Norfolk

Island in February 1839 to be succeeded by two governors who, most fortunately, were more lenient and governed for about six months each.[18]

Vowell's luck turned for the better on 6 March 1840, when Captain Alexander Maconochie arrived to be governor of Norfolk Island. Indeed, his arrival was lucky for the entire island. Maconochie has been called *'a prophetic reformer, a noble anomaly in the theatre of antipodean terror and punishment.'*[19] Maconochie believed that criminals were not destined by fate or nature to be bad. He believed that criminals could be reformed but that the unusual cruelty of the convict system, instead of reforming people, succeeded in degrading them. Despite enormous political pressures against him, Maconochie introduced at Norfolk Island a mark system whereby prisoners would be paid marks for their good work and behaviour but have marks deducted for bad conduct. In the end, after obtaining a certain number of marks, the prisoner could obtain a Ticket of Leave. This was nothing short of revolutionary in a British culture imbued with belief in punishment and sceptical of reformation of the supposed 'criminal class'. Going against prevailing opinion, Maconochie believed that prisoners should be punished for the past and trained for the future and that by their behaviour they should be able to influence and reduce the length of their sentences.[20]

Upon his arrival, Maconochie realized that there were many prisoners who should never have been sent there at all and that a disproportionate number of those had been tried in 1835. He attributed this to an overreaction of the courts to the convict rebellion that had occurred in 1834 at Norfolk Island. In that year, the convicts were driven to their limits by the sadistic floggings of Morisset, a veritable monster, to the point that it became common for convicts to agree to kill each other in a macabre sort of lottery. It was the only mass convict uprising in the history of Australian transportation, and it failed. Judge William Westbroke Burton presided over a trial of 55 men charged with mutiny – as if this was a military affair. Burton's conscience was moved by the circumstances of this trial, by the honesty of the rebels – most of whom wanted to die – and furthermore he did not think the informers were trustworthy. Nevertheless, there was no pity – let alone justice; out of 55 accused, he sentenced fourteen to hang.[21] In a dispatch to the Colonial Secretary, Machonochie complained of the erratic nature of the sentencing to Norfolk Island and the influence of the 1834 rebellion on sentencing the following year,

> '… *that the number of second convictions to this Island had never borne any relation at all to the severity practiced on it. They vary from year to year according to some totally different law and remarkably enough <u>very much</u>* (Maconochie's underline) *the greatest number in any one year was in 1835 immediately subsequent to the awful examples made in 1834.'* [22]

To implement his mark system, Maconochie relied on convict overseers. Being an overseer, Vowell would therefore have had the opportunity to speak with him and state his case. They surely would have discovered that they had a few things in common: both Maconochie and Vowell were former naval officers, both spoke Spanish as well, and each had served under a Cochrane – Vowell as Captain of Marines in the Chilean

Squadron under Lord Admiral Thomas Cochrane, and Machonochie as lieutenant aboard the *Ethalion* under a cousin of Lord Cochrane, Captain Thomas Cochrane, the son of his uncle, Admiral Alexander Cochrane.[23] It is no wonder that in the very year of Maconochie's arrival, 1840, Vowell was allowed to write a letter to the Colonial Secretary asking for mitigation of his sentence,[24] and a few months later, on 27 January 1841, the Colonial Secretary confirmed that Vowell's life sentence was commuted to seven years.

It is not known exactly what year Vowell left Norfolk Island; a sentence of seven years would have ended in 1842, but since he would have been eligible to have time subtracted for good behaviour according to the mark system, it is most likely that he left in 1841.

Maconochie's innovative and creative reform approach elicited fierce political opposition and he remained in Norfolk Island only until 1843. Back in England, his friends and supporters rallied around his penal reform ideas. Among these he counted Charles Dickens and, by a great coincidence, also George Laval Chesterton, the same who had befriended Vowell in 1818. He was then governor of the Middlesex House of Correction and had become involved in penal reform. Dickens described Chesterton, as '... *a very intelligent and humane gentleman, who has great experience of Criminals, and whom I have frequently consulted in reference to their condition and improvement.*' How sad and astounded Chesterton would have been to know that the adventurous young captain he had met years previously had suffered so unjustly at the hands of another empire – the British Empire.

After he left Norfolk Island, we know only a few facts about Vowell's life. In 1845 he was in Sydney where he acted as a witness to the dissolvement of a partnership of the *Caracas Butchery*, owned by Michael Blakeny and Thomas Speeding.[25] These two must have been friends who, like himself, had served in the Venezuelan Patriot Army. In 1846 he left Sydney on the brig *Essington* for Port Fairy, Victoria, a very busy port at the time with a huge whaling, cattle and wheat trade; Vowell may have gone there seeking employment.

Vowell had correspondence from England in 1847 and 1848; his sisters knew he was alive and were likely to have written to him. Anne and Catherine, who both died in 1854, each left him an annuity of 18 pounds in their wills. He also received a letter in 1858 after their deaths and so another person also wrote to him. These were overseas letters left at the post office for him; it is not known whether he received them.

Ticket of Leave holders such as Vowell were the largest category of 'un-free' labourers in Australia. These single men were important for the labour force and made ideal shepherds, or watchmen in the countryside. It is likely that Vowell obtained a job of this sort at a pastoral run once he had moved to Victoria. There is one important clue to his trail. South of the Grampian Mountains, in the parish of Mirrenatwa, Dundas County is a creek called Vowell's Creek.[26] According to a local historian, the creeks were named simply by giving them the name of the person who was posted there in a pastoral run. Vowell was an unusual name at that place and time and it is most likely that this creek was named after Major Vowell.[27]

Vowell had a very strong constitution – in South America he survived tremendously harsh campaigns on flooded plains and frigid mountains; he survived diseases such as dysentery, yellow fever, and some sort of rheumatism; at Cox's River he was described as emaciated; and he further survived the diet and deprivations of Norfolk Island. But in his forties and fifties, how long could he have led a rough, outdoor life? An entry in the 1868 Bailliers Directory leads us to believe that his education once more may have served him well. It reads: 'R.L. Vowell, Teacher, in Cobden',[28] which indicates that, in all likelihood, he was teaching in his later years.

In the end, Vowell's extraordinary luck held. Against all probabilities, he lived to old age. He did not have property or money to leave in a will, but then he never pursued wealth for itself. He could have returned to England if he had put his mind to it but, his wanderings over, he stayed in Australia for the last 37 years of his life. Perhaps he may have felt stigmatized since he had served time as a convict, but I suspect his innate cheerfulness and resilience overcame past sufferings.

Vowell had a real interest in observing nature and he was also a very perceptive observer of people around him. It is not credible that he would not have found Australia, a unique land that at that time was largely unknown, as fascinating as he had found South America. It is also unbelievable that he would not have continued writing, as he certainly was a compulsive note-taker and fine author. It is to be hoped that in the future some other anonymous narrative or historical fiction will appear about life in Australia in the second half of the 19th century and it will be proven to have been from the pen of Major Richard Longfield Vowell.

After suffering eleven months of paralysis, probably caused by a stroke, on 18 December 1870 Vowell died at the age of 75, at Bruk Bruk, an area outside Casterton, Victoria where he was most probably at one of the several hospitals that local historians say existed in the area.[29] Vowell was not accompanied at his deathbed by relatives, even though he had one nephew, possibly two, living in Victoria at the time.[30] However, he was not alone as those who were with him signed and respectfully recorded on his death certificate his full name and proper title, Major Richard Longfield Vowell, and recorded as well the name and rank of his father.

Major Vowell is buried at the wistful Casterton Old Cemetery. The body of this thoughtful writer and valiant officer who received the highest military award from the hands of Simón Bolívar, who was awarded the medal of the famous First Chilean Squadron, lies there forgotten, without even a stone to mark the place. It is to be hoped that the countries he helped to liberate – Venezuela, Colombia, Ecuador and Chile – may yet still honour his memory.

> *'Two things have altered not*
>
> *Since first the world began.*
>
> *The beauty of the wild green earth*
>
> *And the bravery of man'*

T. Wilson[31]

A Personal Note

T HIS is not a history book per se, but a biography: a story of one man who lived through, and took part in, events of historical importance. I have not only been interested in Major Vowell's military life, but also in the social and natural environments that he encountered and wrote about during his life. However, my modest effort cannot begin to do justice to the many tales of heroism, of sadness, pain, and also of successes and achievements that occurred during the quest for freedom from colonialism of the peoples of Latin America and the Caribbean, as well as the peoples of Australia, which so many learned historians have written about.

As I wrote this book, I discovered that across time, Vowell's life and mine coincided in peculiar ways. Firstly, Major Vowell served with three of my ancestors: General José Antonio Páez, to whom I am related through my father; also with General Jacinto Lara, and General Pedro León Torres, to whom I am related on my mother's side.

Secondly, there is one of Major Vowell's anecdotes that solved a family mystery. He observed that among the many medicinal and poisonous plants that grow along the Orinoco there is a type of *bejuco*, or liana, which the Indigenous people use for protection against snake bites. It is ground up into a paste and is then applied to the upper arms should they have been scratched. According to Vowell, 'This species of inoculation is repeated at certain intervals; the juice of the bruised plant diluted with water, being also occasionally drank.'[1] Major Vowell, greatly interested in the natural environment around him, revealed that as he travelled through the Venezuelan *llanos* with the troops of General Cedeño, some of the men, having received this treatment, were immune to snake bites. They could take refuge in abandoned, snake-infested huts along the way, which Vowell and his other companions would not dare to enter. Nonetheless, these *Llaneros* could bring the snakes out with their bare hands and not be bitten. This anecdote explained something that had always puzzled me. Often having heard from my mother that her father had been immune to snake bites due to a 'cure' given to him by an old hacienda Indigenous man when he was very young, I had dismissed this as a family fable or a superstition, but it troubled me because my mother was scientifically inclined, and not a superstitious woman at all. Vowell's account however, indicates that it was no such thing, but rather the application of an ancient knowledge of native plants was at play. This would have been the reason why my grandfather, Numa Pompilio Osuna Sáez, was also protected from snake bites.

And the last coincidence is that today there is also a type of 'South American mania' occurring that is attracting world attention to the sub-continent as its countries experience a further political awakening. If, in the 19th century, it could be said by Torrente that, 'The capital of Venezuela has been the principal forge of the American insurrection'[2] so too it could be said of present times when a modern day *Llanero* from Barinas, President Hugo Chávez Frías, took up Bolívar's standard for the integration of South America.

Synopsis of the Military and Naval Career of Major Richard Longfield Vowell

---

Military and Naval Actions
Battle of Calabozo
Battle of El Sombrero
Battle of El Semen, La Puerta
Battle of Los Cerritos
Battle of Cantaura
Battle of San Fernando
Battle of Pantano de Vargas
Battle of Boyacá
Battle of Pitayo
Military engagement at Paypa
Military engagement at Tunja
Military engagement at Neiva
Military engagement at Popayán
Military engagement at Mayo River
Military engagement at Pasto
Defence of Guayaquil
Naval action: capture of pirate *Blair*
Naval actions along the Pacific coast of México
Siege of Chiloé
Liberation of Chiloé

Vowell's Commanding Officers
Colonel Donald MacDonald
General Manuel Cedeño
General José Antonio Páez
General Simón Bolívar
Colonel James Rooke (British Legion)
Major John MacIntosh (British Legion, Albion Batallion)
General José Antonio Anzoátegui
General Manuel Valdés
General Antonio José de Sucre
Admiral Lord Thomas Cochrane (Commander Chilean Naval Squadron)
Captain Robert Forster (Commander Chilean Naval Squadron)
Admiral Manuel Blanco Encalada (Commander Chilean Naval Squadron)

Military and Naval Units
First Venezuelan Lancers
Bolívar's Guard of Honour
Paéz's Guard of Honour
First Venezuelan Hussars
Lancers of Victoria
Rifles of Oriente
Bolívar's Dragoon Guards
British Legion
Albion Battalion
First Chilean Naval Squadron

Ranks Attained
Lieutenant: First Venezuelan Lancers
Captain: Bolivar's Guard of Honour
Major of Brigade: Lancers of Victoria, Rifles of Oriente,
Bolivar's Dragoon Guards, British Legion, Albion Batallion
Captain of Marines: Chilean Squadron
Captain and Commander of all marines in the Chilean Squadron

Ships in which Vowell served
Independencia (1821–1824)
Captain William Wilkinson
Captain Paul Delano
Lautaro (1824–1825)
Captain Bell
Aquíles (1825–29)
Captain Robert Simpson

Distinctions Received
Star of the Liberators
(Given by Simón Bolívar – certainly in April 1819, and probably again in July 1819)
Only European officer member of the court martial panel, Albion Batallion (1819)
Medal of Honour of the First Chilean Squadron
(awarded by Bernardo O'Higgins, 1822)

ENDNOTES

Prologue

[1] The full title was: *Campaigns and Cruises, in Venezuela and New Grenada, and in the Pacific Ocean; from 1817 to 1830: with the Narrative of a March from the River Orinoco to San Buenaventura on the Coast of Chocó; and Sketches of the West Coast of South America from the Gulf of California to the Archipelago of Chiloé. Also, Tales of Venezuela: illustrative of revolutionary men, manners, and incidents. In three volumes.* London: Longman & Co., 1831

[2] Vowell took part in the Battles of Calabozo, El Sombrero, El Semen, Los Cerritos, Cataura, San Fernando, Pantano de Vargas, Boyacá, Pitayo. He also took part in actions in Paypa, Tunja, Neiva, Popayán, Mayo River, Pasto and in the defence of Guayaquil. His naval actions included the capture of pirate and Spanish ships, a siege of Chiloé and later, the liberation of Chiloé. See Appendix: 'Synopsis of the Military and Naval Career of Major Richard Longfield Vowell.'

[3] Juán Uslar Pietri, Prologue to *Campañas y Cruceros*, Richard Vowell, Cultura Venezolana, 1952,

[4] A.R.V., *El Terremoto de Caracas por un Oficial de la Legion Britanica*, Banco Central de Venezuela, Caracas, 1974

[5] Vowell, Richard, *Las Sabanas de Barinas*, Biblioteca de la Academia Nacional de la Historia, Caracas, 1973, p XIX, XX

[6] Juan Uslar Pietri, *Prologue*, XXIX

[7] Banco Central de Venezuela, *El Terremoto de Caracas, por Un Oficial de la Legión Británica,* Nota Preliminar del Traductor (A.R.V), 1974, 10

[8] Jose Toribio Medina states that the French translator of Vowell's work observed that '...when the book was published in London, the most accredited newspapers unanimously gave it brilliant praise.' See *Viajes Relativos a Chile*, Fondo Histórico y Bibliográfico Jose Toribio Medina, Santiago, 1962; Jose Toribio Medina, *Memorias de un oficial inglés al servicio de Chile*, (partial translation of *Campaigns and Cruises)* 1968, Prológo, xii. Vowell's work also received excellent reviews from the *Gentlemen's Magazine*, Vol. 101 (II), July–December, 1831; and from the *Bath Chronicle*, numbers 6 and 20, October, 1831.

[9] *Campagnes et Croisieres Dans Les Etats De Venezuela et de la Nouvelle-Grenade; Par Un Officier du 1er Regiment de Lanciers Venezueliens.* Translated by Alphonse Viollet, Paris, 1837

[10] A recent article focusing on the travels of Richard Longfield Vowell is Matthew Brown's *Richard Vowell's Not-So-Imperial Eyes: Travel Writing and Adventure in 19th Century Hispanic America*, Journal of Latin American Studies, 38, 95-122, Cambridge University Press, 2006. This article also describes Vowell as a person who did not fall into many of the harsh 'imperial' prejudices common at the time about colonialism and indigenous peoples.

[11] In 1919 Luis Romero Zuluoga identified Vowell as the author of *Campaigns and Cruises* in the article *Quién fué el autor de Campaigns and Cruises in Venezuela?* El Universal, 19 August 1919; José Toribio Medina, translator of part of Richard Longfield Vowell's book, also confirmed his authorship in 1924.

[12] Carlos Sunyer, *El autor de la obra Campañas y Cruceros en Venezuela – Richard Longfield Vowell*, Revista Chilena de Historia y Geografía, julio–diciembre No. 120, Imprenta Universitaria, Santiago, 1952, 120.

[13] Among the Latin American writers who praise Vowell are Rufino Blanco Fombona, Juan Uslar Pietri, José Toribio Medina, Carlos Sunyer, Luis Romero Zuluaga, Edgardo Mondolfi Gudat, as well as innumerable others who cite Vowell's writing, sometimes even without acknowledging his name.

[14] Romero Zuloaga, quoted in Vowell, Richard, *Las Sabanas de Barinas*, footnote 22.

[15] Rufino Blanco Fombona, in Richard Longfield Vowell, *Campaigns and Cruises* translation by Luis Terán, *Memorias de un Oficial de la Legión Británica*, 1916, Prólogo.

[16] López Urrutia, *Los Insurgentes del Sur*, see www.bbslaguna.com.mx/CarlosLopez/introduccion.htm

[17] Carlos Sunyer, *El autor.*

[18] López Urrutia, *La Escuadra Chilena en México 1822,* Chile: Editorial Francisco de Aguirre, 1971, Prólogo, xvii.

[19] López Urrutia, *La Escuadra,* 69.

[20] Manuel Segundo Sánchez, *Bibliografía Venezolana,* ed. 1965, p. 42 quoted in the Introduction of *Campaigns and Cruises,* Venezuelan Ministry of Defence, Caracas, 1973.

[21] Juán Uslar Pietri, in Richard Longfield Vowell, *Las Sabanas de Barinas,* Caracas: Biblioteca de la Academia Nacional de la Historia, 1952, Introducción, XXVI.

[22] 'It is well known that parallel to this song of the traditional written music at the level of a symphonic chorale, there existed another, product of the day-to-day life on the military campaign as it is demonstrated by Captain Vowell – a British Legionnaire who fought in the front lines of our Independence – in his book *The Savannas of Barinas.'* CD, *'Testimonios sonoros de La Libertad- Canciones Patrióticas del siglo XIX'* edited by the government of the Bolivarian Republic of Venezuela, PDVSA La Estancia, Correo del Orinoco, 2010.

[23] Eric Lambert, *Voluntarios Británicos e Irlandeses en la Gesta Bolivariana,* III: 388, Caracas, 1993

[24] Luis Terán translated the section of *Campaigns and Cruises* that relates to Venezuela, *Memorias de un oficial de la Legión Británica,* Editorial América, 1916; republished in 1973 by the Library of the Venezuelan National Academy of History. José Toribio Medina translated the section of *Campaigns and Cruises* that relates to Chile, *Campañas y cruceros en el Océano Pacífico,* Buenos Aires-Santiago de Chile: Editorial Francisco de Aguirre, 1968

[25] There were many volunteers in the wars of South America who wrote memoirs; among the best known are, D.F. O'Leary, G. Hippisley, W. Miller, A. Alexander, G.L. Chesterton, and J. Hackett. There are alo several anonymous narratives.

[26] George Laval Chesterton, *A Narrative of proceedings in Venezuela in South America, in the years 1819 & 1820; with general observations of the country and people; the character of the republican government, and its leading members, etc. also a description of the country of Caracas, of the force of General Morillo, the state of the Royalists; and the spirit of the people under their jurisdiction.* London: John and Arthur Arch, Cornhill, 1820, v,vi

[27] Author unknown, *Recollections of a Three Year's Service during the War of Extermination in the Republic of Venezuela and Colombia by an Officer of the Colombian Navy, London:* Hunt and Clarke, 1828, 155

[28] John Roberton, surgeon of Bolívar's Army, quoted by Jose Rafael Fortique, *John Roberton, Cirujano del Ejército de Bolívar,* 1972, 43

[29] A.R.V. *El Terremoto,* 1974

[30] *Bath Chronicle,* 6 October 1831

[31] To my knowledge, there are original copies of Major Vowell's book at the Venezuelan National Library, the Bodleian Library in Oxford, and at the Library of Congress and the Harvard Library in the USA. WorldCat indicates that there are 23 original copies in several countries and in different translations. It was available for sale on the Internet as a rare travel book for thousands of dollars and more recently, part one of *Campaigns and Cruises* has been available for download at Google Books.

[32] In 2010, Biblio Bazaar re-published Vowell's books, *Campaigns and Cruise, Tales of Venezuela,* and *The Earthquake of Caracas.*

[33] George Laval Chesterton was a British volunteer, but he stayed only one year in Venezuela, leaving in disgust over the Patriot Army. Having been captured by the Spanish, he then favoured their side in the war.

Chapter One

[1] He died of TB, penniless, betrayed, and heartbroken at the age of 47 on 17 December 1830. He is buried in the National Pantheon in Caracas, alongside many of those who fought with him for independence.

[2]   Hasbrouk, *Foreign Legionaries*, 18

[3]   J.H. Parry, *The Spanish Seaborne Empire*, Hutchinson of London, 1966, 355

[4]   Since 1998, 3,000 books have been published on President Hugo Chávez, including books written in Japanese, Chinese, African, and in Indigenous languages. In the USA alone, 150 books have been written related to him. See Rafael Ramón Castellanos' *Hugo Chávez and the Bolivarian Revolution*, El Perro y la Rana Publishers, September 2010. A site count on Google reveals that there are more sites on Venezuela than almost all other Latin American countries, and sites on President Chávez far outstrip those for any other Latin American leader. These are indicators of renewed public interest.

[5]   Don Francisco de Miranda was a captain in the Spanish army, fought in the US Revolutionary War and was a General in the French Revolution. His name is carved in the Arc de Triomphe in Paris.

[6]   *Bell's Weekly Messenger*, Jan. 18, 1818, in Hasbrouck, *Foreign Legionaries*, 63

[7]   R.H. Humphreys, *British Consular reports on the Trade and Politics of Latin America*, Vol. LXII, London: Office of the Royal Historical Society, 1940

[8]   Between 1503 and 1660, Spain obtained 185,000 kgs of gold and 16 million kgs of silver. See Eduardo Galeano, *The Open Veins of Latin America*, Monthly Review Press, 1973, 23

[9]   E. Galeano, *The Open Veins*, 22-27

[10]   'The modern age opened… with the accumulation of capital which began in the 16th century… which resulted from the treasure of gold and silver which Spain brought from the New World into the Old… I trace the beginnings of British foreign investment to the treasure which Drake stole from Spain in 1580.' John Maynard Keynes, *Essays in Persuasion*, W.W. Norton, 1963, 361-362

[11]   This occurred under the Asiento Treaty (1713-50).

[12]   John Lynch, *The Spanish-American Revolutions,* NY: W.W. Norton & Co, 1973, 39; Alfred Hasbrouck, *Foreign Legionaries in the Liberation of Spanish South America*, NY: Columbia University Press, 1928, 43

[13]   Robert Steward, 2nd Marquis of Londonderry and Viscount Castlereagh, was at the heart of British politics for roughly 25 years. See C.J. Bartlett, *Castlereagh*, MacMillan, 1966.

[14]   C.J. Bartlett, *Castlereagh*, MacMillan 1966, 70-71

[15]   Humphrey Milford, *Britain and the Independence of Latin America,* 1912-1830, Oxford: University Press, 1944, 14

[16]   George Canning (1770-1827) served as Foreign Secretary and later briefly as Prime Minister

[17]   Hasbrouck, *Foreign Legionaries,* 42-43

[18]   William W. Kaufmann, *British Policy and the Independence of Latin America 1804-1828*, Archon Books, 1967, 121

[19]   Milford, *Britain and the Independence*, 4-5

[20]   Vicente Lecuna, *Expedición de Los Cayos*, Caracas: Litografía y Tipografía Mercantil 1928, 1937; 2 vols, Fundación Polar, Historia de Venezuela www.simon-bolivar.org/bolivar/exp_de_los_cayos.html#inicio; Venezuelatuya.com

[21]   Drusilla Scott, *Mary English, A Friend of Bolívar,* England: The Book Guild, 1991, 29

[22]   Edgardo Mondolfi Gudat, *Páez Visto por Los Ingleses*, Fuentes Para la Historia Republicana de Venezuela, 2005, 69

[23]   On 19 March 1817, Castlereagh declared Great Britain neutral; any backing of the Patriots would be against the treaties signed with Spain on 5 July 1814.

[24]   Hasbrouck, *Foreign Legionaries*, 40

[25]   *Narrative of a Voyage to the Spanish Main in the Ship Two Friends*, Author unknown, London 1819, 1

[26]   By 1814, the Duke of Wellington had finally driven the French out of the Iberian Peninsula.

[27]   Milford, *Britain and the Independence*, 11

[28]   Arthur Herman, *To Rule The Waves – How the British Navy Shaped the Modern World.*' Harper-Perennial, 2004, 250

29 The main merchants were Powles and Hurry, Herring Barclay and Richardson. See Drusilla Scott, *Mary English*, 29

30 Vicente Lecuna, *Selected Writings of Simón Bolívar*, The Colonial Press, 1951, I, 196; también: www.geocities.com/Athens/Acropolis/7609/bolivar/angostura.html

31 The British blind eye was short lived; on 17 November 1817, British subjects were forbidden to take part in the conflict between Spain and her colonies. This measure, however, turned out to be unenforceable.

32 John Keegan, *A History of Warfare*, Vintage Canada, 1993, 9

33 Hasbrouck, *Foreign Legionaries*, 29

34 www.venezuelatuya.com/biografias/morillo.htm

Chapter Two

1 Despite the fact that England had a military academy (Sandhurst, founded in 1799), the majority of English officers acquired their military education in the field. The army had a purchase system whereby commissions, or officer entry ranks, were bought by men from the upper classes in order to join the army. In practice, the art of war was not as complex as to necessarily demand a formal education. However, France, Austria, Prussia and Russia did rely on their military academies to train their officers. See John Brewer, *The Sinews of Power: War, Money and the English State 1688-1783*, Routledge, 1989

2 Chesterton, *Peace,* 141-50

3 The family name Vowell was also spelled Fowell in the 16th century.

4 Victor Bonham-Carter in *Elinor with the Pleading Eyes* by Estelle Holloway, Preface, Williton Printers, Somerset, (undated)

5 Holloway, *Elinor*, 72

6 Personal conversation between author and Mrs Estelle Holloway in Bath, September 2001. Mrs Holloway is the author of *Elinore with the Pleading Eyes* and *Christopher of the Blackwater*, both histories of the Vowell family.

7 J.C. Beckett, *The Anglo-Irish Tradition*, Ithaca, NY: Cornell University Press, 1976

8 Longford, *Wellington*, 161

9 The index of newspapers for Cork 1750-1827 (CUPM) states that Richard Vowell of the 66th Regiment of Foot married Miss Anne Hamilton, third daughter of the late Joshua Hamilton, Esq, in Youghal, on 29 May 1786. Joshua Hamilton was the son of Henry Hamilton, son of Gustavus Hamilton, Lord Boyne. Anne's mother was Mary Cox, daughter of Sir Richard Cox, Bart of Dunmanway. See Stirnet web page http://www.stirnet.com/HTML/genie/british/hh4aa/hamilton12.htm

10 Beckett, *Anglo-Irish*, 51

11 Oxford University register on Richard L. Vowell, records his father as 'Esquire'.

12 St. James Cathedral is no longer in existence, having been bombed during the Second World War.

13 Mary (c.1787-1835) was the eldest sister, followed by Ann (1789-1854), Catherine (c.1795-1854), (who was Richard L. Vowell's twin), and Susan (1797-1853).

14 Another daughter, Susan, was born later in 1797. Susan Vowell married Rev. Michael Becher on 24 March 1818 at St. Finial's Church, Cork. He was rector at Kilshannig, County Cork, 3 miles SW of Mallow. Their son, Rev. Michael H. Becher immigrated to Australia, married Phillipa Jennings of Melbourne in 1856, and was Rector of St. James (Old) Cathedral from 1876-87. There is no record of him having met up with his uncle, Richard Longfield Vowell in Australia.

15 Britain and France were at war from 1793 to 1814, with only the brief interruption of the Peace Treaty of Amiens (1801-1803).

16 Vowell also received from his father, his gold watch, seals, chain, and silver buttons.

17 Elizabeth Longford, *Wellington – The Years of the Sword*, Panther, 1971, 43

[18] Donald Thomas, *Cochrane, Britannia's Sea Wolf*, Cassell & Co. 1978, 16

[19] Richard Longfield Vowell was at Oxford University from 17 May 1814 to 11 December 1815.

[20] Institute for the Measuring of Worth (www.measuringworth.com)

[21] Estelle Holloway, *Christopher of the Blackwater Side*, 2004, 68

[22] Information from Mr. Lawrence Stone, Registrar-Archivist of Wadham College, Oxford; quoted by Carlos P. Sunyer, *El autor de la obra Campañas y Cruceros en Venezuela: Richard Longfield Vowell*, Santiago: Revista Chilena de Historia y Geografiía, julio-dic. 1952, No. 120, 118

[23] Holloway, *Elinor*, 15-44

[24] Edward Gibbon, *Autobiographies*, (ed.), John Murray, London: John Murray, 1896

[25] M.G. Brock and M.C. Curthoys, *The History of the Universities of Oxford*, Vol. VI, 19th Century, Part I, Clarendon Press, Oxford, 1997; V.H.H. Green, *A History of Oxford University*, London: B.T. Batsford Ltd, 1974

[26] Peter Borsay, *The Image of Georgian Bath 1700-2000*, Oxford, 2000

[27] R.S. Neale, *Bath 1680-1850, A Social History*, Routledge & Kegan Paul

[28] Bolivar's army is also referred to, depending upon the date and the military operations, as the Venezuelan Army, or the Colombian Army, or the Venezuelan-Colombian Army.

[29] Hasbrouck, *Foreign Legionaries*, 55

[30] George Laval Chesterton, *Peace, War and Adventure*, London: Longman, Brown, Green and Longman, 1853, 23

[31] Susan Vowell married Rev. Michael Becher on 24 March 1818 at St. Finbar's. He was prebendary and rector of Kilshannig Church near Mallow, Cork.

[32] Richard Longfield Vowell, *Campaigns and Cruises*, London: Longman, 1831, 69

Chapter Three

[1] *Narrative of a Voyage to the Spanish Maine in the Ship Two Friends*, London: John Miller, Piccadilly, 1819, author unknown.

[2] *Narrative of a Voyage*, 10-11

[3] Alfred Hasbrouck, *Foreign Legionaries* 47; Bartolomé Mitre, *The Emancipation of South America – Being a Condensed Translation by William Pilling of the History of San Martin*. London: Chapman & Hall, *1893, 390*.

[4] Lambert, *Voluntarios*, 1:48; Thomas Rourke, *Simón Bolívar*, London: Michael Joseph Ltd. 1940, 160

[5] Chesterton, *Peace, War*, 23

[6] *Narrative of a Voyage*, 12

[7] J. Hackett, 59

[8] *Narrative of a Voyage*, 29

[9] *Narrative of a Voyage*, 31-32

[10] William White, *Morning Chronicle*, 9 February 1818, in Lambert, *Voluntarios*, 1:101

[11] Vowell, *Campaigns*, 3

[12] Lambert, *Voluntarios*, 1: 66-67

[13] *Narrative of a Voyage*, 27

[14] Gustavus Hippisley was a half-pay lieutenant of the British cavalry; MacDonald was a half-pay lieutenant; Skeene was a retired Lieutenant Colonel of the British cavalry; Wilson was a lieutenant in the Light Dragoons; Hewitt was a sergeant quartermaster. López Méndez gave the rank of colonel to those organizing the regiments, and then chose majors from captains in the British army, captains from cavalry lieutenants, lieutenants from coronets in active service or on half pay, and the junior ranks were chosen from discharged sergeants. See Hasbrouck, *Foreign Legionaries*, 47-48

[15] Margarita Island is a Venezuelan possession, very close to the easternmost coast of Venezuela.

[16] *Narrative of a Voyage*, 42

17 *Narrative of a Voyage,* 45

18 Vowell, *Campaigns,* 4

19 Lambert, *Voluntarios,* 1:92–95

20 Robert Harvey, *Liberators,* Overlook Press, 2000, 154: 'Of the 2,200 in total who went with him, including a hundred women and forty children, only two ever returned – apart from MacGregor himself.'

21 Lino Clemente was Major General of the Patriot Naval Forces; he had a very successful military record. He died at age 67 and is buried in the National Pantheon of Caracas.

22 Carlos Bastidas Padilla, *Los Estados Unidos contra Simón Bolívar,* 4 January 2007, ARGENPRESS, www.argenpress.info

23 The officers were Colonel MacDonald, Major Davies, Captains McMullin and Rottenburg, and Lieutenants Braithwaite, Thomas and Vowell.

24 Vowell, *Campaigns,* 9. '*Un petit pendement bien joli*' – an old French expression for 'dying by being hung on a scaffold'.

25 Vowell, *Campaigns,* 10

26 Vowell, *Campaigns,* 13

27 David Sinclair, *Sir Gregor MacGregor and the Land that Never Was,* Review, 2003, 185, states that Aury was a pirate who held a Mexican letter of marque.

28 Vowell, *Campaigns,* 13

29 Sinclair, *MacGregor,* 186

30 Bastidas Padilla, *Los Estados Unidos*

31 Sinclair, *MacGregor,* 176–184

32 Bastidas Padilla, *Los Estados Unidos*

33 José Félix Blanco and Ramón Azpurúa (eds), *Documents of the Public Life of the Liberator,* Caracas, 1978, cited in Bastidas Padilla, *Los Estados Unidos*

Chapter Four

1 The first European to see the Orinoco was Vicente Yánez Pinzón.

2 A French-Venezuelan scientific expedition headed by Venezuelan, Franz Rísquez Iribarren, discovered the exact origin of the Orinoco on 27 November 1951.

3 Vowell, *Campaigns,* 35

4 *The Morning Chronicle,* London, 24 January 1817

5 *Memorias del General Daniel Florecio O'Leary,* Robert F. McNerney, Jr (ed), University of Texas Press, 1970, 108–109

6 John Lynch, *The Spanish American Revolutions,* W.W. Norton, 1973, 199

7 Lynch, *Spanish American,* 209

8 The correct spelling is Cedeño, but Vowell wrote it as Zedeño.

9 Admiral Luis Brión was Bolívar's friend whose help was indispensable for the conquest of the eastern sea of Venezuela and Angostura. He was a very balanced individual and had a brilliant career. He died of a fever in 1821 at the age of 39. He is buried in the National Pantheon in Caracas.

10 Rufino Blanco Fombona, *El Capitan General Don Domingo Monteverde,* Caracas: Boletín de la Academia Nacional de la Historia, tomo XXXIX, abril-junio, 1956, #154, 123

11 General José Francisco Bermúdez, joined the Patriot cause very early on in 1810 and was the recognized military leader of the eastern part of Venezuela. He was assassinated in 1831 at the age of 49 and is buried in the National Pantheon in Caracas.

12 Simón Bolívar, letter to Fernando Peñalver, exiled citizen in Port-of-Spain, Trinidad, Guayana, 6 August 1817 in *Selected Writings of Bolívar,* (ed) Vicente Lecuna, NY: Colonial Press, 1951, 145

13 The Spanish conquest – which extended to the so-called 'colonial' period – mixed religion with

power, Christianity with usurpation, racism with order. The missionaries' work was part of the effort to make the 'barbarian' Indigenous peoples into 'civilized', obedient, monarchists. Early in 1817, the Patriot general, Manuel Piar, had placed the missions under Patriot control, not Church control.

[14]   Vowell, *Campaigns,* 31

[15]   Vowell, *Earthquake of Caracas*, 65. Unfortunately, the original peoples were victims of terrible diseases and whenever the Europeans made contact with them, the missions themselves unwittingly spread these epidemics. Darcy Ribeiro, a Brazilian anthropologist, estimates that more than half of the aboriginal population of America, Australia, and Oceania died from the contamination of first contact with white men. See: Eduardo Galeano, *Open Veins of Latin America*, 1973, p. 18

[16]   O'Leary, *Memorias*, 110

[17]   Vowell, *Campaigns,* 23

[18]   Vowell, *Campaigns,* 21

[19]   Vowell, *Campaigns,* 23

[20]   Vowell, *Savannas of Varinas*, 296

[21]   También en la conquista de México está bien documentado que indígenas fueron lanzados a los perros para que éstos se los devoraran. Ver: Baez, 2008, 72; ver Bartolome de las Casas, *Brevisima Relacion de la Destruccin de las Indias,*1552

[22]   Vowell, *Savannas of Varinas*, 202

[23]   Fernando Báez, *El saqueo cultural de America Latina*, Debate-Random House, 2008, 85

[24]   Andres Tapia, en J. Diaz, A. De Tapia, B. Vázquez, F. de Aguilar, Edicion de Germán Vázquez Chamorro, *La conquista de Tenochtilán*, Madrid, DASTIN S.L. col. 111, 2002 quoted in Fernando Báez, *El saqueo cultural de America Latina de la Conquista a la globalizacion*, Random House, 2008, 37

[25]   Báez, 2008, 72

[26]   E. Galeano, *Open Veins*, 1973, 12-13

[27]   Daniel Florencio O'Leary was a Catholic Irishman, born in Cork. He arrived in 1818 with Colonel Wilson's regiment, but disgusted with him, he went on to serve under General Soublette, bravely took part in many battles, and became Bolívar's aide-de-camp. He wrote very comprehensive memoirs of the entire War of Independence. He died a general, in Bogotá, in 1854, and is buried in the National Pantheon in Caracas.

[28]   O'Leary, *Memorias*, 49

[29]   Vowell, *Campaigns,* 24

[30]   Typical Venezuelan songs of the interior of the country include this style of verse recitation over and above rhythmic music.

[31]   '*Long Live the Englishmen!*'

[32]   Vowell, *Campaigns,* 26

[33]   The city's full name was Santo Tomás de Angostura, but it was generally referred to simply as Angostura. Vowell, however, refers to it in the plural, as Angosturas, which was likely a usage in his time.

[34]   Angostura is today the modern city of Ciudad Bolívar.

[35]   Vowell, *Campaigns,* 30

[36]   General Santiago Mariño, born in Margarita Island, was the leader of the Patriots in the north-eastern part of the country and belonged to Bolívar's military high command. He and Páez were the principal supporters of the separation of Venezuela from Gran Colombia. He died at age of 66 and is buried in the National Pantheon in Caracas.

[37]   Hasbrouck, *Foreign Legionaries*

[38]   *El Correo del Orinoco* lasted from 1818 to 1822.

[39]   Irene Nicholson, *The Liberators*, London, Faber & Faber 1969, 179-180

40 Extract from *The Bath Chronicle*, 6 October 1831

41 Captain Raymond Edgar was an ex-lieutenant of the 8th Regiment of Foot, who served for eight years in the British Army, and fought in the Peninsular War. He died of yellow fever in Angostura shortly after this incident and was buried with full military honours at the foot of the fort on the hill. See Lambert, *Voluntarios*, 142

42 Lambert, *Voluntarios*, 142

43 General Manuel Piar had been involved in the Patriot cause since the age of 23. A Curacao mulatto, he represented the power of the '*pardos*' or those of mixed race, in contrast to the '*mantuanos*', mostly white elites. He was well-educated and spoke several languages. As a military leader he defended the northern and eastern parts of Venezuela well, and had a key role in taking Guayana for the Patriots. He opposed the leadership of Bolívar and left the army in 1817, but was accused of trying to subvert the military camps to join some sort of '*pardo*' movement.

44 Spanish colonial society was based on a rigid racial system that classified people according to their racial mix. White people were the dominant elite, but even they had to have documents to prove the purity of their Spanish blood to attain certain positions. The rest – mixed people – were called *pardos*. They were classified by racial mix: *mulattos* were white and black; *tercerones* were *mulatto* and white; *cuarterones* were *terceron* and white; *quinteron* were white and *cuarteron*; and *zambo* were indigenous with *mulatto* or black.

45 General Manuel Cedeño joined the Patriot forces very early on and fought so bravely in campaigns across the country that he was called 'Brave among the Brave'. He died of a bullet wound in battle in 1821 at the age of 41, and is buried at the National Pantheon in Caracas. *Diccionario de la Historia de Venezuela*, Fundación Polar.

46 Admiral Brión, General José Anzoátegui, General Carlos Soublette, General Pedro León Torres, Colonel José Ucros, Colonel José María Carreño, Lieutenant Colonel Judas Tadeo Piñado and Francisco Conde; and Piar's defender, Colonel Fernando Galindo.

47 General Rafael Urdaneta was the military leader that had the broadest action across the country. He believed in Bolívar's Gran Colombia, was its last president, and tried to save it. He died at the age of 56 and is buried in the National Pantheon in Caracas.

48 Hasbrouck, *Foreign Legionaries*, 92

49 The Orinoco crocodile, which lives exclusively in the Orinoco River Basin, is one of the rarest reptiles in the world and currently critically endangered.

50 Vowell, *Campaigns*, 57

51 Vowell, *Campaigns*, 47

52 Vowell, *Savannas of Varinas*, 124

Chapter Five

1 In his book, Vowell refers to the Arauca River as 'Arauco'.

2 A league is a measure of distance of about 3 miles; 12 leagues would be about 36 miles.

3 Vowell, *The Savannas of Varinas*, 3. This is part II of *Campaigns and Cruises;* Vowell spells the Venezuelan state of Barinas, with a 'V'.

4 General Daniel Florencio O'Leary, *Memorias*, (ed.) Robert R. McNerney, Jr., 1970, 122; Robert Harvey, *Liberators*, Overlook Press, 200, 159

5 Páez went on to become Venezuela's first president in 1830.

6 Mitre, *Emancipation*, 366

7 Vowell, *Campaigns*, 129;

8 O'Leary, *Memorias*, 108

9 Mitre, *Emancipation*, 367

10 General José Antonio Páez, known as the 'Centaur of the Llanos', was instrumental in the separation of Venezuela from Gran Colombia; he was its first president after this separation and

went on to be president on two more occasions. He died in exile in New York at the age of 83. His body lies in the National Pantheon in Caracas.

[11] Vowell refers to 'Barinas' as 'Varinas'. The sound of the letters 'B' and 'V' in Spanish are symbols of the same sound, distinction depending on position and context. Particularly in the Venezuelan *Llanero* accent, they are indistinguishable, thus explaining therefore Vowell's spelling.

[12] Vowell, *Savannas of Varinas,* 1

[13] Today, Barinas is a state of Venezuela, but its borders are different from those at the time of Vowell.

[14] Sir Walter Scott is considered one of the main creators of the historical fiction genre; his first novel, *Waverley*, was published in 1814 and *Rob Roy* in 1818. Vowell would have had the opportunity to read at least *Waverley*.

[15] See Juán Uslar Pietri, *Las Sabanas de Barinas,* Cultura Venezolana, Introducción, 1952

[16] Even today the rainy season causes floods which at Ciudad Bolivar – formerly Angostura – reach a height of 50 to 60 feet.

[17] Most likely, the Indigenous people Vowell met were from a small group of tribes of the Salivan linguistic stock, now virtually extinct, which in the 18th century lived in the region originating from the Guaviare area in Colombia; or, they could possibly have been from the nomadic Warao, who live nearer to the Orinoco delta.

[18] Vowell, *Campaigns,* 61

[19] Such as C. Brown, G.L. Chesterton, Colonel Hippisley, John Robertson, and the anonymous authors of *Recollection of Three Years Service* and *Two Friends.*

[20] Vowell, *Savannas of Varinas,* 6

[21] The troops from Margarita Island were General Arismendi's forces, but were travelling with General Urdaneta on this trip.

[22] Vowell, *Campaigns,* 65

[23] Robert Cunninghame Graham, *Jose Antonio Páez,* NY: Books for Libraries Press, 1929

[24] Vowell, *Campaigns,* 65

[25] Vowell, *Campaigns,* 67

[26] Vowell, *Campaigns,* 68

[27] O'Leary, *Memorias,* 122

[28] Cunninghame Graham, *José Antonio Páez,* 75

[29] General William Miller, *Memoirs,* London: 1910

[30] Lambert, *Voluntarios,* 166

[31] Vowell, *Savannas of Varinas,* 222

[32] Vowel, *Campaigns,* 74

[33] Francisco Alejandro Vargas, *La Guardia de Honor en La Campaña de los Llanos,* 1975, 57

[34] Colonel James Rooke previously served in the 49th Regiment of Foot, the 8th Regiment of Foot, and the 16th Queen's Light Dragoons. He escaped from a French prison in Verdun, joined Wellington's army, was made aide-de-camp to the Prince of Orange and was wounded at Waterloo. He arrived in Venezuela in September 1817 with his wife, Anna Tucket, of St. Kitts, to fight with Bolívar. In Angostura, he was put in charge of all foreign volunteers. He spoke Spanish.

[35] General José Tadeo Monagas was a fine Patriot and military leader of the north-eastern part of Venezuela. He went on to be president of Venezuela twice and is buried in the National Pantheon in Caracas.

[36] Vowell, *Campaigns,* 71

[37] Vowell, *Campaigns,* 73; Lambert, *Voluntarios,* 167

[38] Vowell, *Campaigns,* 73-74

[39] Vargas, *La Guardia de Honor,* 58

[40] General Carlos Soublette fought in all the major military campaigns of the Wars of Independence. He replaced Docoudray Holstein as Bolívar's chief of staff. He went on to become an able

diplomat and statesman, and was vice-president and then president of Venezuela. He died at the age of 80 and is buried at the National Pantheon in Caracas.

41   Vargas, *La Guardia de Honor,* 58
42   John Keegan, *The Face of Battle*, Pilmico, 1976, 18
43   *The Bath Chronicle*, 6 October 1831
44   At that time, there was no fixed international rule of conduct for war and no Geneva Convention, which started in 1864 under the initiative of the Red Cross, although today's international rules stem from the 1949 Geneva Convention. There was, however, a certain rule of conduct or code attached to the British forces, especially relating to the treatment of the wounded and prisoners.
45   The *Guerra a Muerte* continued until 1820 when Bolívar and Morillo signed an agreement to regulate the war.
46   Vowell, *Campaigns,* 73
47   Vowell, *Campaigns,* 76
48   Vowell, *Campaigns,* 76
49   Vowell, *Campaigns,* 129-130
50   Vowell, *Campaigns,* 77
51   Lambert, *Voluntarios*, 170
52   The town's name is properly spelled 'La Victoria', but Vowell spelled it 'Vitoria', since that is how he would have heard it pronounced in the *Llanero* accent, in which the sound of the 'c' would have been mild or omitted. Vowell spells 'La Guaira' as 'la Guayra', but in Spanish both letters, 'i' and 'y', have the same sound.
53   Slavery was abolished in Britain in 1833, in France in 1848 and in the USA, in 1860. Venezuela ratified Bolívar's abolition in 1854.

Chapter Six

1   General Pedro Zaraza was a brilliant cavalry leader, who had started out as a sergeant. MacGregor handed his own sword to honour to him for his actions in battle. He died in battle in 1825 at the age of 42.
2   Hardy, *Liberators*, 165
3   Vowell, *Campaigns,* 84
4   Vicente Lecuna, *Documentos inéditos para la historia de Bolívar, Campaña de 1818,* Caracas: Boletin de la Academia Nacional de la Historia, tomo XXI, oct–dic, 1938, 343
5   Vowell, *Earthquake of Caracas*, 30, note 10
6   Vowell, *Campaigns,* 86
7   Lambert, *Voluntarios*, 173
8   Colonel Gustavus Hippisley, *Narrative of the Expedition to the River Orinoco and Apure in South America which sailed in Nov. 1817 and joined the Patriot forces in Venezuela and Caracas*, London: John Murray, 1819, 282
9   Lambert, *Voluntarios*, 174
10   Hasbrouck, *Foreign Legionaries*, 28
11   Vowell, *Campaigns,* 87
12   Lambert, *Voluntarios*, 174
13   Vowell, *Campaigns,* 88
14   Vowell, *Campaigns,* 91
15   Vowell, *Campaigns,* 92
16   Properly, his name would be spelled 'Vicente', but Vowell spelled it 'Bicente', as he had heard it pronounced by the *Llaneros*, who would not distinguish the sounds of 'V' and 'B'.
17   Vowell, *Campaigns,* 93
18   Vowell, *Campaigns,* 96

[19] Vowell, *Campaigns,* 96

[20] Vowell, *Campaigns,* 103

[21] Vowell, Campaigns, 105

[22] Vowell, *Campaigns,* 107

[23] In Chesterton's version, Vowell and his party were resting in a natural hollow when they were set upon by Spanish cavalry who killed his companions and left him for dead. It is a shorter version, but essentially, not dissimilar to what Vowell wrote.

[24] Chesterton, *Peace,* 143

Chapter Seven

[1] Vowell, *Campaigns,* 127

[2] General Carlos Soublette was a Patriot leader who had fought under Francisco de Miranda; he helped Bolívar take Guayana and was a member of his high command. He held important political positions in the government of Venezuela. He died at age 81 and is buried in the National Pantheon in Caracas.

[3] T. Rourke, *Simón Bolívar,* 160-191

[4] Gustavus Hippisley, a half-pay lieutenant of the British cavalry, came from a distinguished Somerset family and his wife was Anglo-Irish. He was a fastidious individual who, not finding the Patriot Army to his liking, left Venezuela weeks after his arrival. The book he wrote about his experiences was considered so boring that Lord Byron said he read it in order to fall asleep.

[5] Henry C. Wilson, Anglo-Irish, had been a lieutenant in the British 9th Light Dragoons. He was a complex man, well-educated, with a Masters from Dublin University.

[6] Hasbrouk, *Foreign Legionaries,* 72

[7] Vowell, *Campaigns,* 110.

[8] Calabozo was retaken by the Spanish after Cedeño evacuated it and on 19 May 1818, at Los Cerritos de la Laguna de los Patos, the infantry was defeated. The Patriots lost a very significant part of their arms and munitions. Lambert, *Voluntarios,* p. 199

[9] Vowell, *Campaigns,* 111

[10] Hasbrouk, *Legionaries,* 73

[11] Daniel Florence O'Leary, *Detached Recollections of General D.F. O'Leary,* 20 as cited by Lambert, *Voluntarios,* 207.

[12] Vowell, *Campaigns,* 113

[13] Lambert, *Voluntarios,* 209

[14] Colonel James Rooke, son of Lieutenant General Rooke, had been a Major in the British army and then ADC to the Prince of Orange at Waterloo. He was an experienced and courageous officer who enjoyed the full confidence of Bolívar, whom he joined early in 1817. His bravery and death at the Battle of Pantano de Vargas is the stuff of legends.

[15] Hasbrouk, *Foreign Legionaries,* 82

[16] Venezuelans do not generally drink milk as a beverage, as Europeans do.

[17] Vowell, *Savannas of Varinas,* 39-41

[18] Vowell, *Savannas of Varinas,* 40

[19] Mitre, *Emancipation,* 366

[20] Vowell, *Savannas of Varinas,* 44

[21] Vowell, *Campaigns,* 115

[22] Vowell, *Savannas of Varinas,* 68

[23] Vowell, *Savannas of Varinas,* 68-69

[24] Vowell, *Savannas of Varinas,* 189

[25] Vowell uses the Spanish word 'atahud' meaning funereal bier.

[26] Vowell, *Earthquake of Caracas,* 192

27 Vowell, *Earthquake of Caracas,* 60
28 Vowell, *Earthquake of Caracas,* 225
29 Alexander Alexander, *Life of Alexander Alexander, Written By Himself,* (ed) John Howell, Edinburgh & London: 1830; quoted in Lambert, *Voluntarios,* 155
30 Bashaw is a old term for pasha; Vowell meant that some horses were old herd leaders.
31 Lynch, *Spanish-American,* 213
32 Robert Harvey, *Liberators,* The Overlook Press, 2000, 120
33 Hasbrouck, *Legionnaires,* 17
34 O'Leary, *Memorias,* 60
35 Vowell, *Savannas of Varinas,* 21
36 Vowell, *Campaigns,* 123
37 Lambert, *Voluntarios,* 214
38 The present day city of Barcelona is 160 miles (257 km) from Angostura and about as much from Caracas. In 1818, Barcelona was referred to as a province, a much wider area.
39 Vowell, *Campaigns,* 140
40 Vowell, *Campaigns,* 143

Chapter Eight

1   Hasbrouk, *Foreign Legionaries,* 190
2   Guillermo Morón, *Historia de Venezuela,* Italgrafica Impresores, 6a edicion,1974, 313
3   Morón, *Historia de Venezuela,* 313
4   Lynch, *Spanish-American Revolutions,* 244
5   Vowell, *Campaigns,* 144
6   El Congreso de Angostura proclamó a Simón Bolívar como Presidente de la República el 17 de febrero 1819. Bolívar dió un discurso visionario basado en un tratado brillante de su filosofía política y sus ideales republicanos, que incluían la abolición de la monarquía, los privilegios y la esclavitud.
7   Tomás Polanco Alcántara, *José Antonio Páez, Fundador de la República,* Caracas: Ediciones GE, 2000, 107
8   Lambert, *Voluntarios,* 263
9   Alexander Alexander, *Life of Alexander,* Vol. II, 94–99, citado por Lambert, *Voluntarios,* 288
10 Vowell, *Savannas of Varinas,* 219
11 El chiguire, mamífero de la familia roedor, se encuentra en Suramérica desde Panamá hasta Argentina. Es una criatura mansa, vegetariana, y vive en manadas cerca del agua.
12 Rebecca Earle, '*A Grave for Europeans? Disease, Death, and the Spanish-American Revolutions',* in 'War in History Journal', III, No. 4,1966, 371–83
13 Julio Albi, *Banderas olvidadas: el ejército realista en America,* Madrid: Ediciones de Cultura Hispánica, 1990, 403-5, citado en Earle, *A Grave.*
14 Thomas Rourke, *Simon Bolivar,* London: Michael Joseph Ltd, 1940, 187
15 Robert Pigott, nacido en 1786, fué capitán en el 54th Regiment of Foot inglés durante la Guerra Peninsular y luego del Batallón 1st Garrison; fué retirado a medio pago en 1816.
16 Vowell, *Campaigns,* 151
17 Lambert, *Voluntarios,* 190
18 Captain W.J. Adams, *Journal of Voyages to Margarita, etc.,* Dublin: Pub. R.M. Tims, 1824, 152
19 Vowell, *Campaigns,* 152
20 *The Times,* 21 October 1819, carta desde Angostura del 10 agosto 1819; *The Times,* 23 de octubre 1819, carta de Hamilton, Angostura, 12 de agosto 1819; en Lambert, *Voluntarios, 322-23*
21 Algunos de loe médicos ingleses incluyeron a : Thomas Foley, James H. Robins, Henry George

Maine, Charles Moore, John Roberton (Canadiense), Robert Fry, Alex Acheron, Richard Murphy, Edward Brown, John Stanton, Jacob Ashbury, R.M. Ryding, Michel O'Reilly, William P. Smith, Stephen Mc Davitt. Ver: Carlos García Arrieche, *La Legión Británica en la emancipación de Venezuela y Colombia*, Caracas: Boletín Histórico, Fundación John Boulton, 1971, 369

22   Hasbrouk, *Foreign Legionaries*, 94

23   G. Hippisley, *A Narrative of the Expedition to the rivers Orinoco and Apure, in South America which sailed from England in November 1817, and Joined the Patriotic Forces in Venezuela and Caracas*. London: John Murray, 1819, 383–384

24   Su sirviente fué un criollo francés del las isles del Caribe quien había seguido a MacDonald desde Inglaterra. Ver: Vowell, *Campaigns*, 127

25   W.H. Koebel, *British Exploits in South America*, NY: The Century Co. 1917, 172

26   R. Holmes, *Redcoat*, 249

27   Lambert, *Voluntarios*, 161.

28   R. Holmes, *Redcoat*, 33–36

29   Esta medalla se puede ver en el Museo Bolivariano en Caracas.

30   O'Leary, *Memorias*, 58

31   *Correo del Orinoco, No. 25, 3 April 1819*

Chapter Nine

1   Vowell, *Campaigns*, 163

2   Rufino Blanco Fombona, Prologue, 8, in the Spanish translation of Vowell's *Campaigns and Cruises, Memorias de Un Oficial de la Legión Británica*, Luís de Terán, translator; Bogotá: Biblioteca Banco Popular, 1974

3   Translators' Note No. 16 in, Vowell, *Las Sabanas de Barinas*, Caracas: Ministerio de la Defensa, 1973

4   Luis de Terán, *Memorias de Un Oficial de la Legión Británica*, Richard Vowell, Biblioteca Banco Popular, Vo. 56, Bogotá, 1974, 9

5   Lieutenant Colonel Arthur Sandes was an Irishman from County Kerry who had fought with the British Army at Waterloo. He was an outstanding officer whom Bolívar lauded, saying that the utmost intrepidity could always be expected from him and his men in every engagement in which they took part. Hasbrouk*, Foreign Legionaries*, 318

6   Colonel James T. English was an Irishman from Dublin with a good education who had been a horse dealer, supplying horses to the British Army and later a clerk in the commissariat in Wellington's army. He enlisted, as a Captain, in Hippisley's regiment, the 1st Venezuelan Hussars. Bolívar appreciated his key contribution in bringing in needed English volunteers.

7   John D'Evereux was an Irish adventurer whose military rank of 'general' was dubious. He was an unscrupulous character, who enlisted Irish volunteers, deceiving them with unrealistic promises and he received a sum for each recruit. He failed to make any arrangements for the reception of the troops once they arrived and thus caused them great hardship.

8   George Laval Chesterton, in his *Narrative of Proceedings in Venezuela in South America in the years 1819-1820*, states that English was 'a man too indolent and selfish to trouble himself with seeking the comfort of either his officers or his men', p15. He was even more critical of generals Arismendi, Urdaneta, and Mariño.

9   F.A. Fitzpatrick, *Latin America – A Brief History*, Cambridge University Press 1938, 65

10   Francis Burdett O'Connor was Anglo-Irish from County Cork; his godfather was Sir Francis Burdett, a radical member of the British Parliament. He went on to be chief of staff to General Antonio José de Sucre and Minister of War in Bolivia.

11   Nicholson, 177

12   Terry Hooker & Ron Poulter, *The Armies of Bolívar and San Martín*, Osprey, 1991, 7-9

13   Hooker & Poulter, *Armies of Bolívar*, 9

[14] Casanare is a region of *llanos* named after the Casanare River. At the time covered by this chapter, the area was Nueva Granada; today it is part of the Republic of Colombia.

[15] Fitzpatrick, *Latin America*, 66

[16] A battalion was composed of two infantry units of about three companies per unit.

[17] Hasbrouk, *Foreign Legionaries*, 192

[18] South American Wars of Liberation: http://www.principlesofwar.com

[19] Gen. Jacinto Lara Meléndez was with the Venezuelan Patriot cause since 1810; an honest and capable officer, he took part in all the major battles and was always faithful to Bolívar. Bolívar said of him: 'The men idolize him, and he is the most reliable man in the world.' (Vicente Lecuna, Selected writings, II: 518). He also called him 'The Ulysses of Colombia.' The present Venezuelan state of Lara was named after him. His body lies in the National Pantheon in Caracas.

[20] O'Leary, *Memorias del General O'Leary, Narración,* I, 543 quoted in Hasbrouk, *Foreign Legionnaires*, 192

[21] General Pedro León Torres was a talented military leader whom Bolívar made commander of the Army of the South which knew hm as the 'Lion of the *Llanos*'. He died of wounds received in battle in 1822 at the age of 34. He and his six brothers all died in the war for independence; they are referred to as 'The Seven Sons of Lara', Lara being the state in which they were born.

[22] Vowell, *Campaigns,* 157

[23] Vowell, *Campaigns,* 157

[24] Vowell, *Campaigns,* 159

[25] O'Leary, *Narración,* I. 547, quoted in Hasbrouck, *Legionaries*, 193

[26] Vowell, *Campaigns,* 160

[27] Vowell, *Campaigns,* 160

[28] Vowell, *Campaigns,* 163

[29] Vowell, *Campaigns,* 163

[30] Vowell, *Campaigns,* 166

[31] Irene Nicholson, *The Liberators*, London: Faber & Faber, 1969, 189; see also Terry Hooker and Ron Poulter, *The Armies of Bolívar and San Martín*

[32] O'Leary, *Narración*, I, 561; quoted in Hasbrouk, *Foreign Legionaries*, 196, 197

[33] Pérez Tenreiro, *Campaña Libertadora, 142*

[34] Nicholson, *The Liberators*, 189

[35] Lambert, *Voluntarios*, 347

[36] Hiram Bingham, *The Journal of an Expedition Across Venezuela and Colombia in 1906-07*, New Haven: 1909, 200-223, cited in Hasbrouk, *Foreign Legionaries*, 195

[37] John Keegan, *A History of Warfare*, 63

Chapter Ten

[1] General José Antonio Anzoátegui, was a loyal and able military leader. When he died Bolívar declared: 'What a soldier the army has lost and what a man the Republic has lost!' He died in Pamplona and was buried in the cathedral, which later was ruined in an earthquake.

[2] Coronel Tomás Pérez Tenreiro, *Campaña Libertadora de la Nueva Granada- Estudio Historico-Militar*, en *La Campaña Libertadora de 1819*, Caracas: Academia Nacional de la Historia, 1969, I:133

[3] Hooker & Poulter, *Armies of Bolívar,* 39

[4] Sergeant Major John McIntosh arrived in Venezuela with Wilson's Red Hussars in 1818 and went on to serve with distinction in the Patriot Army, eventually leading the British Legion.

[5] Vowell, *Campaigns*, 169

[6] Eric Lambert, *Irish Soldiers in South America 1818-30*, in 'The Irish Sword', 29

[7] Lambert, *Voluntarios*, I: 349

[8] Hasbrouk, *Foreign Legionaries,* 394

9   Pérez Tenreiro, *Campaña Libertadora*, I: 173

10   Hasbrouk, *Foreign Legionaries*, 248

11   Lambert, *Voluntarios*, I: 350

12   Lambert, *Voluntarios*, I: 350

13   Lambert, *Voluntarios*, I: 357

14   Lambert, *Voluntarios*, 549–350; Hasbrouk, *Foreign Legionaries*, 204–210; José Nucete Sardi,
     'Projecciones Políticas de la Invasión a Nueva Granada y de la Victoria de Boyacá, in, 'La Campaña
     Libertadora de 1819', Caracas: Academia Nacional de la Historia, Ministerio de Educación, 1969,
     341–353; O'Leary, *Memorias*, 159–167

15   Keegan, *The Face of Battle*, 202

16   Hasbrouk, *Foreign Legionaries*, 202

17   Lambert, *Voluntarios*, I: 352

18   Keegan, *History of Warfare*, 45

19   Daniel Florence O'Leary, *Memorias*, tomo XVI, 421 (724), Boletín del Ejército, 25 julio 1819;
     Alexander Walker, *Colombia*, II:420–422; cited in Lambert, *Voluntarios*, 351

20   Cundinamarca is the ancient name of Nueva Granada, which is now the Republic of Colombia.

21   Vowell, *Campaigns*, 169

22   Hooker & Poulter, *Armies of Bolívar*, 11; Jacqueline Banks, *Historical Text Archive*,
     http://historicaltextarchive.com/sections.php?op=viewarticle&artid=631; Lambert, *Voluntarios*,
     355–360

23   Hasbrouk, *Foreign Legionaries*, 386

24   Rufino Blanco Fombona, *Memorias de un Oficial de la Legión Británica*, Bogotá: 1974, Prólogo, 8–9

25   Lambert, in *Voluntarios*, I: 361, states that Vowell was not at the battles of Pantano de Vargas or
     Boyacá, but was at Angostura. It is clear from *Campaigns and Cruises* that Vowell did cross the Andes
     with the army, so it would have been impossible for him to get to Angostura after crossing them.
     The only way he could have missed the battles was if he had been wounded or ill; but he does not
     state this in his book.

26   Keegan, *The Face of Battle*, London: Pimlico, 1976, 72

27   Keegan, *The Face of Battle*, 39–49

28   Keegan, *The Face of Battle`*, 129

29   Vowell, *Campaigns*, 171

30   Báez, *Saqueo cultural*, 37–39

31   Baez, *Saqueo cultural*, 109

32   Vowell, *Campaigns*, 176

33   Vowell demonstrates some confusion about the heroine's name. Today she is referred to as
     Policarpa Salvarrieta, but was also known as Apolonia.

34   Vowell, *Campaigns*, 172

35   Vowell, *Campaigns*, 66; Vowell is confused, Bolívar lived for a while under the protection of the
     Marqués de Ustáriz (not Uztaron), but his wife's father was Don Bernardo Rodríguez del Toro y
     Ascanio.

36   Hasbrouk, *Foreign Legionaries*, 221

37   Vowell, *Savannas of Varinas*, 14

38   Vowell, *Campaigns*, 171

39   José Nucete Sardi, *Projecciones Políticas*

40   Fitzpatrick, *Latin America*, 65

41   Lambert, *Voluntarios*, I: 344

42   Fitzpatrick, *Latin America*, 65

43   Lambert, *Voluntarios*, 361

Chapter Eleven

[1]   Lambert, *Voluntarios*, III, 357; Hasbrouk, *Foreign Legionaries*, 379

[2]   Bolívar was designated President, and Santander named vice-President.

[3]   Vowell, *Campaigns,* 192

[4]   Vowell, *Campaigns,* 180

[5]   Vowell, *Campaigns,* 185

[6]   Today Tequedama Falls is a major tourist attraction. It is a 132-metre waterfall on the Bogotá River, 30 km south-west of Bogotá.

[7]   Vowell, *Campaigns,* 189

[8]   Captain Basil Hall, *Extracts from a Journal written on the coast of Chili, Peru and, Mexico in the years 1820,1821 and 1822*, Edinburgh, 1824, vol. I, 104

[9]   The Army of the South was composed of the Albion, Neiva, Bogotá and Cundinamarca Battalions, and three cavalry regiments, the Guides (led by Carvajal), Huzares and Escolta.

[10] Hasbrouk, *Foreign Legionaries*, 220-221

[11] Vowell spells the name with a 'z', but it is properly spelled with an 's'. General Valdés, originally from Trinidad, joined the Patriot forces very early on. While his leadership of the Army of the South left much to be desired, he did go on to have a more successful military role, and ultimately he became a politician. He died in 1845.

[12] Hasbrouk, *Foreign Legionaries,* 262

[13] Vowell, *Campaigns,* 203

[14] The attitude of Lorenzo coincides with the comment made by Fray Felix de Villanueva in 1778 about the missions in Venezuela: that the Indigenous people never forgot '…the cruelties visited upon their ancestors by the first Spaniards'. Cited in F. Baez, *El saqueo cultural de America Latina*, 109

[15] Hasbrouk, *Foreign Legionaries,* 264

[16] Lambert, *Voluntarios*, III: 366

[17] Vowell, *Campaigns,* 210

[18] Vowell, *Campaigns,* 218

[19] Lambert, *Voluntarios*, III: 368-369

[20] Vowell, *Campaigns,* 214

[21] Author Unknown, *Recollection of Three Years Service*, 67

[22] Keegan, *The Face of Battle*, 104, 186,

[23] Letter of Sucre to Bolívar dated Callao, 25 June 1823, Archivo de Sucre, Caracas: Fundación, Lecuna, III:201

[24] R.A. Humphreys (ed), *The Detached Recollections of General D.F. O'Leary*, University of London, Athlone Press, 1969, 37-38

[25] The source of the Orinoco River is the Cerro Delgado Chalbaud in the Parima range on the Venezuelan/Brazilian border. It was explored only in 1951, 453 years after Columbus discovered the Orinoco Delta. The source of the Magdalena River is in southern Colombia between the Andean sub-ranges of Central and Oriental Cordilleras. The Cauca River is the chief tributary of the Magdalena River.

[26] Vowell, *Campaigns,* 216

[27] Vowell, *Campaigns,* 220

[28] This massive destruction of works of art in gold by the original peoples is well documented. For example, F. Baez, states, 'The expeditions were not distracted from the aim of obtaining riches, and art made from precious metals were examined not for their creative values, but for their materials.' *El saqueo*, 80–83

[29] Vowell, *Campaigns,* 220

[30] Vowell, *Campaigns,* 223

[31] Vowell, *Earthquake of Caracas,* 372

32   Vowell, *Campaigns,* 224

33   General Antonio José de Sucre liberated Quito and then Perú in decisive military battles. He was the most brilliant Patriot leader after Bolívar, and his most trusted friend and ally. He went on to be President of Bolivia and then of Perú. Unfortunately, he was assassinated in Berrucos in 1830 at the age of 35. His body is buried in the Cathedral of Quito.

34   Hasbrouk, *Foreign Legionaries,* 265

35   Quoted by Lambert, III, 379; Sucre's letter at Archivo Nacional de Colombia, Bogotá: Guerra y Marina, Secretaría, CCCXXIX, f 837; Mercaderes, febrero 8 de abril de 1821; informe sobre la fuerza del Albión.

36   The armistice lasted from 25 November 1820 to 28 April 1821.

37   O'Leary, *Memorias,* 108

Chapter Twelve

1   Guayaquil is located in what is now Ecuador.

2   The officers were Captains Richard L. Vowell, John Bendle and Henry Dunkin; Lieutenants Laurence MacGuire and Hugo MacManus; Sub-Lieutenant James Sutherland; plus seven sergeants and corporals. Lambert, *Voluntarios,* III, 379

3   Lambert, *Voluntarios,* III, 380

4   Since there were not enough vessels in any one port, the rest of the Army of the South, which included the Albion Battalion (numbering only 199 men at this point), left towards the port of Esmeralda.

5   Vowell, *Campaigns,* 234

6   Vowell, *Campaigns,* 235

7   Vowell, *Campaigns,* 136

8   Vowell, *Campaigns,* 238

9   Vowell, *Campaigns,* 238

10   Mary Graham, *Diario de su residencia en Chile (1822),* Madrid: Editorial America, 141

11   Carlos López Urrutia, *Chile: A Brief Naval History,* Historical Text Archive, http://www.historicaltextarchive.com/books.php?op=viewbook&bookid=16&cid=2 and www.bbslaguan.com.mx/CarlosLopez/introduccion.htm

12   This phrase means, 'The sea wolf', as quoted in Donald Thomas, *Cochrane,* 97

13   Thomas, *Cochrane,* 133

14   It was Don José Alvarez, the Chilean representative in London who asked Cochrane.

15   Carlos López Urrutia, *Historia de la Marina de Chile,* El Ciprés Editores, 2008; *Derroteros de la Mar del Sur,* #10, 2002

16   José de San Martín (1778-1850) great hero of Argentina who liberated Argentina and Chile, and parcially, Peru.

17   Carlos López Urrutia, *Historia de la Marina de Chile*

18   Brian Vale in *Memoirs of a Fighting Captain: Admiral Lord Cochrane* by Lord Thomas Cochrane, London: Folio, 2005, Introduction, xi

19   Alamiro de Avila Martel, *Cochrane y la Independencia del Pacífico,* Santiago: Editorial Universitaria, 1975, 152

20   Lawrence Sondhouse, *Naval Warfare 1815-1914,* Routledge, 2001

21   Thomas, *Cochrane,* 245

22   Carlos López Urrutia, *Historia de la Marina de Chile*

23   Vowell, *Campaigns,* 254

24   Before Richard Longfield Vowell, the former captains of infantry of the Chilean Squadron had been the Englishmen, James Charles and William Miller, and the German Eduard Gutike.

25   Vowell, *Campaigns,* 254

[26] Fernando Alegría in *La Escuadra Chilena en México (1822),* Carlos López Urrutia, Editorial Franciso de Aguirre, 1971, Prólogo xii

Chapter Thirteen

[1] A frigate was a warship, next in size to the largest warships known as ships of the line. They featured a raised main deck and a quarterdeck, and carried anywhere between 28 to 60 guns. A corvette was a flush-decked, fast warship, with one tier of guns, usually used to escort larger ships. A brig, or brigantine, was a two-masted warship with square sails, smaller than a corvette. A schooner was a fast naval vessel, smaller than a brig, originally with two masts, later with three or more.

[2] Cochrane, *Memoirs*, 245.

[3] The ships were the frigate *O'Higgins* (50 guns), commanded by Captain Crosby; the frigate *Valdivia* (formerly *Esmeralda*) (44 guns), commanded by Captain Cobbett; the frigate *Lautaro,* commanded by Captain Delano; the corvette *Independencia* (28 guns), commanded by Captain William Wilkinson; the brig *Galvarino,* commanded by Captain Brow; the brig *Araucano,* commanded by Captain Robert Simpson – all with between 20 and 24 guns each; and the schooner *Mercedes* (8 guns), commanded by Lieutenant Sheppard.

[4] Carlos López Urrutia, *La Escuadra*, 52.

[5] de Avila Martel, *Cochrane y la Independencia,* 152

[6] Vice-Admiral Ismael Huerta Díaz, 'El Elemento Humano en el Primer Medio Siglo de la Armada de Chile', Boletín de la Academia de Historia Naval y Marítima de Chile, Año II, No. 2, 1997, 89.

[7] de Avila Martel, *Cochrane y la Independencia,* 159

[8] Greg Dening, *The Face of Battle; Valparaíso, 1814,* in *War & Society,* Vol. 11, Number 2 (October 1993), 37; Arthur Herman, *Rule the Waves*, 224

[9] Worcester, *Sea Power,* 17

[10] Worcester, *Sea Power,* 26

[11] Bobos are beautiful, small birds with piercing, red eyes surrounded by black and brilliant blue colours and their body feathers are green, brown and yellow.

[12] Lord Thomas Cochrane, Earl of Dundonald, *Narrative of Services in the Liberation of Chili, Peru, and Brazil,* Vol 1, London: James Ridgway, 1859, 175.

[13] Jorge Andrés Delano, *Captain Paul Delano,* The Lost World Balloon Society, 2000, 53.

[14] Vowell, *Campaigns*, 259.

[15] León Volcano is situated in Northern Chile, whereas Izalco Volcano is located in western El Salvador and is the one that Vowell most surely saw.

[16] Vowell, *Campaigns*, 260.

[17] Tehuantepec is an isthmus and a gulf on the western, Pacific side of México. There is an underwater ridge located there with a series of volcanoes called the Chipanecan Volcano Arc. Today the area is the Mexican state of Oaxaca which contains, as well, the city of Tehuantepec.

[18] Cochrane, *Narrative*, 176.

[19] On 24 February 1821 the tenuous political situation of México was cobbled out in the Plan of Iguala which established the independent nation, but under a constitutional monarchy. On 21 July 1822, the conservative and opportunistic Agustín de Iturbide managed to become Emperor of México. His reign was short-lived; he was shot on 19 July 1824.

[20] According to López Urrutia (*La Escuadra,* 45), Captain Sheppard of the *Mercedes,* instead of having a close look at the ships anchored in Panamá, just reconnoitred the masts from afar, and thus failed to see that the *Prueba* and *Venganza* were indeed anchored there.

[21] Vowell, *Campaigns*, 262.

[22] Cochrane took the *Esmeralda* on 3 November 1820 when she was anchored off Callao. It is still considered one of the most astonishing feats of war in the age of sail.

23 Worcester, *Sea Power*, 53. Cochrane took Valdivia on 18 January 1820.
24 Cochrane, *Narrative,* 176.
25 Cochrane, *Narrative*, 177; López Urrutia, *La Escuadra* , 49
26 de Avila Martel, *Cochrane y la Independencia, 239-240.*
27 Cochrane, Lord Thomas, *Memorias*, Santiago de Chile, 1941, 87, cited in López Urrutia, *La Escuadra*, 27.
28 Vowell, *Campaigns,* 268.
29 Vowell, *Campaigns,* 271.
30 Vowell, *Campaigns,* 273.
31 Vowell, *Campaigns,* 274.
32 López Urrutia, *Escuadra*, 69.
33 According to Avila de Martel, (*Cochrane y la Independencia*, 158) the men who held the position of Captain of the Marines were James Charles, William Miller, Eduard Gutike, and, finally, Richard Longfield Vowell.
34 Vowell believed that the mutineers sailed the *Araucano* to the Sandwich Islands where the king of those islands seized it. The mutineers, turned pirates, did sail to Hawaii, but according to López Urrutia (*La Escuadra*, 72) later sailed towards French Polynesia where they were captured trying to take a missionary ship. The *Araucano* remained in Tahiti where eventually it rotted.
35 Carlos López Urrutia, *Chile: A Brief Naval History*, http://historicaltextarchive.com/books.php?op=viewbook&bookid=16&cid=2

Chapter Fourteen

1 Maria Graham/Lady Calcott, *The Captain's Wife – The South American Journals of Maria Graham 1821-23,* Elizabeth Mavor (ed), London: Weidenfeld & Nicolson, 1993, 77
2 Amasa Delano, *Delano's Voyages of Commerce and Discovery – 1817* (ed) Eleanor Roosevelt Searaves, Mass:Berkshire House, 1994, 221-222. Captain Amasa Delano was a relative of Captain Paul Delano, commander of the *Lautaro.*
3 Vowell, *Campaigns*, 316
4 Maria Graham/Lady Calcott, *The Captain's Wife,* 79
5 Maria Graham, '*An account of some effects of the late earthquakes in Chili: Extracted from a letter to Henry Warburton*' London: Trans. Geol. Soc. Ser.2, 1, 413-415, 1824
6 *South American Cities Destroyed*, originally published in 1906. See http://www.oldandsold.com/articles27n/volcanoes-earthquakes-11.shtml
7 Vowell, *Campaigns,* 294
8 José Toribio Medina, *Memorias de un oficial inglés al servicio de Chile*, xi
9 Vowell, *Campaigns,* 313
10 Vowell, *Campaigns,* 304, 341. Vowell spells *Huasos* with a 'z': *Huazos.*
11 The *estrado* was '… a platform, usually facing the door, about half a foot high, and four or five feet broad, covered with mats or carpeting, in which all the ladies of the family, and their visitors, sit by themselves; while a row of very low chairs is appropriated to the use of the gentlemen, in a different part of the room.' Vowell, *Campaigns, 316*
12 Vowell, *Campaigns,* 317
13 Vowell, *Campaigns,* 318
14 Vowell, *Campaigns,* 244-245
15 Vowell, *Campaigns,* 288-289
16 Vowell, *Campaigns,* 333
17 Vowell, *Campaigns,* 333
18 Vowell, *Campaigns,* 347
19 Vowell, *Campaigns,* 372
20 Avila Martel, *Cochrane,* 240

Chapter Fifteen

1 Quoted in Arthur Herman, *Rule the Waves*, 252.
2 Vice-Admiral Ismael Huerta Díaz, *El Elemento Humano en el Primer Medio Siglo de la Armada de Chile*, Boletín de la Academia de Historia Naval y Marítima de Chile, Año II, No. 2, 1997, 83.
3 Vowell, *Campaigns*, 351.
4 Ovidio Lagos, Chiloé, *A Separate World*, 8 (undated).
5 Valdivia was guarded by forts on either side of the bay, which were able to cover the entrance to the harbour. Cochrane surprised the Spanish with a land attack of marines on two key forts; he lost 26 men, but the Spanish lost one hundred before they surrendered.
6 Vowell, *Campaigns*, 357.
7 Bernardo O'Higgins was the illegitimate son of a wealthy Irishman and an upper class Chilean woman. He was educated in England, used his wealth for the Patriot cause, and went on to become the Supreme Director of Chile.
8 Vowell, *Campaigns*, 358.
9 Thomas, *Cochrane*, 277.
10 Thomas, *Cochrane*, 278.
11 López Urrutia, *Brief Naval History*, 1.3
12 Vowell, *Campaigns*, 394.
13 Vowell, *Campaigns*, 394.
14 Rodrigo Fuenzalida Bade, *La Armada de Chile*, Chile, 1975, 335.
15 Vowell, *Campaigns*, 396.
16 Carlos López Urrutia, *Historia de la Marina de Chile*, Editorial Andrés Bello, 1969, 153.
17 López Urrutia, *Marina de Chile*, 153.
18 Rodrigo Fuenzalida Bade, *La Armada de Chile*, Chile, 1975, Apendice 17.
19 Vowell, *Campaigns*, footnote 38, 471.
20 Arthur Herman, *Rule the Waves*, 414.
21 Vowell, *Campaigns*, 398.
22 Vowell, *Campaigns*, 398.
23 Guillermo A. Toledo Leal, *La Infantería de Marina en la Armada de Chile*, 1999. See www.revistamarina.cl
24 Vowell, *Campaigns*, footnote 29, 254.
25 Carlos López Urrutia, *Brief Naval History*, 2.
26 Vicente Lecuna (ed), *Selected Writings of Bolívar*, NY: The Colonial Press, 1951, II: 504.
27 Vicente Lecuna, *Selected Writings*, II:523.
28 Toledo Leal, *La Infantería*, 124.
29 Toledo Leal, *La Infantería*, 130.
30 Agui refers to the Castle of Agui – one of the forts.
31 Vowell, *Campaigns*, 412.

Chapter Sixteen

1 Vowell, *Campaigns*, 418.
2 Vowell, *Campaigns*, 434.
3 Vowell, *Campaigns*, 412.
4 Vowell, *Campaigns*, 458.

Chapter Seventeen

1 *The Bath Chronicle*, 6 October 1831
2 *The Bath Chronicle*, 6 October 1831
3 Susan and Rev. Michael H. Becher lived in a substantial, well-appointed country home, Clyda House, that still exists today outside Mallow, overlooking the Downs.

4   Mary died at Susan's house in Cork in 1835. Susan died in 1853. Catherine and Ann died in 1854, and each left Vowell an annuity of 18 pounds in their wills.

5   The quarantine was lifted on 10 March 1833. Most of the passengers' belongings were burnt to prevent spread of the disease, but the passengers were compensated. Vowell's belongings included mattress, blanket and pillows, clothes worn during the voyage – property in whole worth just under six pounds. Letter from Joseph Steret RH to Hon. Alexander McLeary, Spring Cove, 5 March 1833; NSW State Records, File 33/1581

6   All three letters of reference can be found in the NSW State Records, Colonial Secretary papers, 4/2/84

7   The Colonial Secretary's papers indicate that on 27 March 1833 the Colonial Secretary recommended the appointment of Richard Longfield Vowell as clerk and constable of the 2nd Cox's River Stockade. On 15 April 1833 his hiring as clerk and constable was approved with a salary of two shillings and three pence per diem. NWS State Records, File 4/2/84

8   Christopher Sweeney, *Transported: In Place of Death – Convicts in Australia*, Macmillan, 1981, 23

9   Robert Hughes cites L.L. Robson, who in 1965, was able to show that one-half to two-thirds of the convicts had previous convictions. Robert Hughes, *The Fatal Shore*, N.Y: Alfred A. Knopf, 1987, 159

10   David Mackay, *A Place of Exile – The European Settlement of NSW*, Melbourne: Oxford University Press, 1985

11   A.G. L. Shaw, *Convicts and the Colonies*, London: Faber and Faber, 1966

12   A ticket of leave granted the bearer's freedom in a designated locality, which they could not leave without permission and where they had to report twice a year to the police. This freedom could be revoked on the slightest misconduct. Pardons soon follow the granting of a ticket of leave, but people were led to believe that even if pardoned, they would still be felons in the UK. In fact, no Act of Parliament was passed forbidding a pardoned man to return to Britain.

13   www.tocal.com/homestead/vandv/vv34.htm

14   An authoritative account of Australia's history is Robert Hughes' book *The Fatal Shore*, NY: Alfred A. Knopf, , 1987

15   Frank Crowley, *Colonial Australia*, Nelson, I: 484

16   John Clay, *Maconochie's*, 37

17   William Romaine Govett, *Sketches of New South Wales*, Saturday Magazine 1836-37, Melbourne: Gaston Renard Publisher, 1977, 49

18   William Romaine Govett, *Sketches*, 47

19   Sue Rosen & Michel Pearson, *No. 2 Stockade Cox's River – Its Life and Times*, Environmental Services, Pacific Power, 1997.

20   William Romaine Govett, *Sketches*, 48

21   Ollie Leckbandt, *The Mount Walker Stockade Cox's River*, Australia: Industrial Printing, 1997

22   Quoted in John Clay, *Maconochie's*, 141

23   *Sydney Herald*, February 1839, quoted by Ollie Leckbrandt in the Lithgow Mercury, 2005

24   John Clay, *Maconochie's*, 43

25   Colonial Secretary papers 4/3676, p. 507, 15 April 1833, states: 'Colonial Secretary's Office, Sydney 15 April 1833. Sir, Having submitted to the Governor your letter of the 27th ultimo No. 33/166 recommending R.L. Vowell, a free Emigrant as Clerk and Constable of No. 2 Stockade Cox River...'

26   Martin Sullivan, *Men and Women of Port Philip*, Hale and Iremonger, Southwood Press, 1985, 119

27   John Clay, *Maconochie's Experiment*, London: John Murray 2001, 71

28   Bishop Wiliam Ullathorne was sent to Australia to the Catholic mission. He was a severe critic of the transportation system and helped to abolish it.

29   John Clay, *Maconochie's*, 98

30 Colonial Secretary's papers, 4/3681 p. 99

31 The Colonial Secretary was perhaps the most important and powerful position in Australia while it was under British rule. He was the respresentative of the Colonial Office in England. The men who occupied this position during Vowell's encarceration were Peter Broun (1828-1846), George Fletcher Moore (1846-47) Richard Madden (1847-49).

32 Colonial Secretary's papers, letters sent 1835-36, 4/3681, 99-100, reel 1049

33 Colonial Secretary's papers, 223, May 1835, No. 35/266, 99

34 Colonial Secretary's papers, letters sent 1835-36, 4/3681, 99-100, reel 1049

35 The convicts were John Fisher, (age 32) William Bryant (age 17), James Monds (age 27), and John McCann (age 40); the soldiers of the 4th Regiment were Privates Samuel Powell (age 24), William Marsden (age 23), James Shawn (age 29), William Shaw (age 26). NSW Colonial Secretary, Letters received, file 35/4094 at 4/2287.2

36 Rosen and Pearson, *No 2 Stockade*, 75

37 Thomas Cook, *The Exile's Lamentations*, Library of Australian History, North Sydney, 1978, 34

38 Thomas Cook, *Exile's Lamentations*, 35

39 Personal communication from Australian historian and expert on Cox's Rriver Stockade, Sue Rosen, via email, 15 November 2002

40 Colonial Secretary's papers: letter from the Superintendent Constable's Office, 30 May 1835, file 35/284

41 Rosen and Pearson, *No 2 Stockade*, 75

42 Colonial Secretary's papers, 31 May 1935, file 35/4094 at 4/2287.2

43 Vowell, *The Savannas of Varinas*, 201

44 *United Service Journal*, London, December 1838, 521-2, quoted in Frank Crowley, *Colonial*, 485

45 Don Foster, *Author Unknown – On the Trail of Anonymous*, NY: Henry Holt and Company, 2000. The author examined many articles written at the time that could have possibly been written by Vowell, but none presented clear similarities with his style of writing as much as this one.

46 *State of Convicts in New South Wales*, 1835, broadsheet, D356-19, Mitchell Library, Sydney; quoted in F. Crowley, *Colonial*, 484

47 Richard Keefe

48 John Conlan

49 It was only in 1848 that defendants were held under the presumption of innocence.

50 Before 1837, lawyers for the accused were not allowed to question or cross-examine witnesses; only until the turn of the century were the accused able to testify on their own behalf.

51 *The Proceedings of the Old Bailey 1674-1834*, Trial Procedures, The Old Bailely Proceedings Online, 2003, see www.oldbaileyoline.org

52 Colonial Secretary's papers, 1840; reel A 1222, 1000

53 Australian Dictionary of Biography, see www.adb.online.anu.edu.au/A010171b.htm

54 Judge Burton's notebook, NSW State Records, 5-14 August 1835, container 2/2420

55 Letter of James Monds to the right Honourable Lord Gleneg, Principal Secretary of State for the Colonial Department, enclosure to No. 4179, dispatch 11 August 1837; 4/2429.3; 38/12997, NSW State Records.

56 Vowell, *Campaigns*, 103

Chapter Eighteen

1 Hughes, *Fatal Shore*, 365.

2 John Clay, *Maconochie's*, 114.

3 Quoted in John Clay, *Maconochie's*, 115.

4 History of Norfolk Island, http://www.discovernorfolkisland.com/norfolk/hell.html

5 Between 1800 and 1850, it is a conservative estimate that about 1,800 people were transported for political crimes. Robert Hughes, *Fatal Shore*, 195.

[6]   The Colonial Secretary's papers have a sheriff's list of 70 prisoners to be sent to Norfolk Island
      and it includes Vowell's name.
[7]   Thomas Cook, *Lamentations*, 44.
[8]   John Clay, *Maconochie's*, 137.
[9]   Raymond Nobbs (ed), *Norfolk Island and its 2nd Settlement 1825-55*, Library of Australian
      History, Sydney, 1991; Thomas Beagley Naylor, *A Tale of Norfolk Island*, 1845.
[10] Raymond Nobbs (ed), *Norfolk Island and its 2nd Settlement 1825-55*, Library of Australian
      History, Sydney, 1991; Thomas Beagley Naylor, *A Tale of Norfolk Island*, 1845.
[11] Australian Government Culture and Recreation Portal:
      www.cultureandrecreation.gov.au/article/convicts
[12] Journal of Rev. T. Sharpe (1837-39), 29 Dec. 1839, Mitchell Library, Sydney, CY reel 1255, ML
      B217 B218, p50 p.238, Sydney.
[13] Hughes, *Fatal Shore*, 169.
[14] Hughes, *Fatal Shore*, 482.
[15] Major Joseph Anderson governed Norfolk Island from April 1834 to April 1839.
[16] John Clay, *Maconochie's*, 128.
[17] *The Journal of Ensign Best* (1837-1843), Edited by Nancy M. Taylor, New Zealand, 1966.
[18] Major Thomas Burnbury governed Norfolk Island from April to September 1839, and Major
      Thomas Ryan from September 1839 to March 1840.
[19] Hughes, *Fatal Shore*, 484.
[20] John Clay, *Maconochie's*, 70-76.
[21] Hughes, *Fatal Shore*, 477-484.
[22] NSW State Records, Colonial Secretary's papers, Letter from Captain Maconochie to E. Deas
      Thomson, G. Gipp's dispatch, 1840, reel A 1222, p 1000.
[23] John Clay, *Maconochie's*, 6.
[24] NSW State Records, Colonial Secretary's papers, 27 January 1841, 41/344, pp 267-268.
[25] *Sydney Morning Herald*, 27 November 1845, 3.
[26] Vowell's Creek appears in the *Gazetteer of Victoria*, 1879; the entries were checked against *Place
      Names of Victoria* by Les Blake, Macbeth Genealogical Book Publisher, 1986.
[27] My husband and I found out about Vowell's Creek with the help of local historian, Joan Hunt, of
      the Ballarat Public Record Office on 24 December 2001. See Victoria Topographic Map 125000,
      7323-2-3 zone 54.
[28] Cobden was newly established in 1840, a small town then located east of Port Fairy and about
      200 km south-west of Melbourne (Port Philip).
[29] Jan Lier and Cheryl Elmes of the Casterton Historical Society informed me of this in conversation
      with them in Casterton in 2001.
[30] Rev. Michael Henry Becher, son of Vowell's sister, Susan, and Rev. Michael Becher, had
      emigrated to Australia in 1861, becoming rector of St. James Old Cathedral in Melbourne. Since
      his mother and aunts were aware that Vowell was alive and of his whereabouts, it is unlikely that
      Rev. Becher did not know that his uncle was living in Victoria. His brother – and Vowell's
      namesake – Richard Savage Fane French Becher, was also living in Australia at that time.
[31] Poem quoted in a pamphlet of the Royal Canadian Legion in Gananoque, Ontario for its
      exhibition of the Victoria Cross awarded to Private Harry Brown, August 2007.

A Personal Note

[1]   Vowell, *Campaigns and Cruises*, 44
[2]   F.A. Kirkpatrick, *Latin America*, Cambridge University Press, 1938

Bibliography

Archival Sources

Jacqueline Banks, *Historical Text Archive*:

    See http://historicaltextarchive.com/sections.php?op=viewarticle&artid=631

Hansard's Parliamentary Debates

Rooke Family documents, D1833, Gloucestershire Records Office, UK

Ballarat Public Record Office, Victoria, Australia

Colonial Secretary's papers, NSW State Records, NSW, Australia

Hamilton Historical Society

Casterton Historical Society

Records of the Genealogical Society of Victoria, Australia

State Library of NSW, Sydney, Australia

Jennings Family Manuscripts, State Library of Victoria, Melbourne, Australia

Victoria Public Records, Melbourne, Australia

Records of the Victoria Historical Society

Archives of the Church of Ireland (Anglican), Dublin

W. Maziere Brady, Records of Cork, Cloyne and Ross, , D.D., Dublin, 1863, Vol. II

Newspapers

The Bath Chronicle (Bath, UK)

Bell's Weekly Messenger (London)

Morning Chronicle (London)

The Times (London)

Correo del Orinoco (Venezuela)

NSW Government Gazette (Australia)

Sydney Morning Herald (Australia)

Published/Printed Sources

Academia Nacional de la Historia, Caracas, 1912-1964, No. 1 – 188

Adams, Captain W.J., *Journal of Voyage to Margarita,* etc., Dublin: Pub. R.M. Tims, 1824

Albi, Julio, *Banderas olvidadas: el ejército realista en America,* Madrid: Ediciones de Cultura Hispánica, 1990

Alexander, Alexander, *Life of Alexander Alexander, Written by Himself,* (ed) John Howell, Edinburgh and London: 1830

Annear, Robyn, *Nothing but Gold – The Diggers of 1852*, Melbourne: Text Publishing, 1999

Author Unknown, *Narrative of a Voyage to the Spanish Main in the Ship Two Friends,* London, Piccadilly: Printed for John Miller, 1819

Author Unknown, *Recollections of a Three Year's Service During the War of Extermination in the Republics of Venezuela and Colombia,* by an Officer of the Colombian Navy, London: Hunt and Clark, 1828

Australian Dictionary of Biography, at www.adb.online.anu.edu.au/A010171b.htm

Bateson, Charles, *The Convict Ships* 1787-1868, Sydney: A.H. &A.W. Reed, 1969

Bartlett, C.J., *Castlereagh*, MacMillan, London, 1966

Barry, John Vincent, *Alexander Maconochie of Norfolk Island*, Oxford University Press, 1958

Bastidas Padilla, Carlos, *Los Estados Unidos contra Simón Bolívar*, 4 January 2007,
     Argenpress, see www.argenpress.info

Beagley Nalor, Thomas, *A Tale of Norfolk Island*, 1845

Beckett, J.C., *The Anglo-Irish Tradition*, Faber and Faber, 1976

Bencomo Barrios, Héctor, *La Puerta y Semen; dos campos de ingrata recordación*, Bingham, Hiram,
     The Journal of an Expedition Across Venezuela and Colombia in 1906-07, New Haven, 1909

Blanco Fombona, Rufino, *El Capitán General Don Domingo Monteverde*, Caracas: Bloch, Marc,
     The Historian's Craft, Manchester University Press, 1954

Boletín de la Academia Nacional de la Historia, tomo XXXIX, abril-junio, 1956, #154, 123

Boletín Histórico, Caracas: Fundación John Boulton, enero 1977

Borsay, Peter, *The Image of Georgian Bath 1700-2000*, Oxford University Press, 2000

Brock, M.G. and Curthoys. M.C., *The History of the Universities of Oxford*, Vol. VI, 19th Century, Part I,
     Oxford: Clarendon Press, 1997

Brown, C., *Narrative of the Expedition to South America Which Sailed from England at the Close of 1817 for
     the Service of the Spanish Patriots*, London, 1819

Callcott, Lady Maria, *The Captain's Wife, The South American Journal of Maria Graham 11821-23,* (ed)
     Elizabeth Mavor, London: Weidenfeld & Nicolson, 1993

Chesterton, George Laval, *Peace, War and Adventure*, London: Longman, Brown, Green and Longman,
     1853

Clay, John, *Maconochie's Experiment*, London: John Murray, 2001

Cochrane, Admiral Lord Thomas,
     – *Memoirs of a Fighting Captain*, Folio Society, 2005
     – *Narrative of Services in the Liberation of Chili, Peru and Brazil*, Vol. I, London: James Ridgway, 1859

Cook, Thomas, *The Exile's Lamentations*, North Sydney: Library of Australian History, 1978

Costigan, Giovanni, *Sir Robert Wilson – A Soldier of Fortune in the Napoleonic Wars*, Madison, 1932

Cova, J.A., *Elogio del Almirante Brión*, Caracas: Boletín de la Academia Nacional de la Historia, tomo
     XXXIX, abril-junio 1956, #154

Crowley, Frank,
     – *A Documentary History of Australia* 1788–1840, Nelson, vol I, 1980
     – *Colonial Australia,* Nelson, vol. 1

Cunninghame Graham, Robert B., *José Antonio Páez*, NY: Books for Libraries Press, 1929 de Avila
     Martel, Alamiro, *Cochrane y la Independencia del Pacífico*, Santiago: Editorial Universitaria, 1975

Davies, David, *Fighting Ships, Ships of the Line, 1793-1815*, London: Robinson, 2002
     Amasa Delano, *Delano's Voyages of Commerce and Discovery*, (ed) Eleanor Roosevelt Seagraves,
     Berkshire House Publishers, 1994

Delano, Jorge Andres, *Captain Paul Delano*, The Lost World Balloon Society, 2000

Dening, Greg, *The Face of Battle: Valparaíso, 1814,* in War & Society, Vol. 11, No. 2, October 1993

Earle, Rebecca, '*A Grave for Europeans? Disease, Death, and the Spanish-American Revolutions*', in War in History Journal, vol 3, No. 4, 1966

Encina, Francisco A., *Bolívar y la Independencia de la América Española*, Chile: Editorial Nascimiento, 1962

Hon. Harold Finch-Hatton, *Advance Australia! An account of eight years work, wandering, and amusement in Queensland, NSW and Victoria*, London: W.H. Allen & Co, 1886

Fitzpatrick, F.A., *Latin America-A Brief History*, Cambridge University Press, 1938

Fortique, José Rafael, *John Roberton, Cirujano del Ejército de Bolívar*, 1972

Foster, Don, *Author Unknown, on the Trail of Anonymous*, Henry Holt & Co, 2000

Freide, Juan, *La Batalla de Boyacá, A través de los Archivos Españoles,* Bogotá: Banco de la República, 1969

Rodrigo Fuenzalida Bade, *La Armada de Chile*, 1975

Fundación Polar, *Diccionario de la Historia de Venezuela*

García Arrieche, Carlos, *La Legión Británica en la emancipación de Venezuela y Colombia*, Caracas: Boletín Histórico, Fundación John Boulton, 1971

García Reyes, Antonio

    – *Primera Escuadra Nacional 1866*

    – *Memoria sobre la Primera Escuadra Nacional*, Santiago, 1846

Glover, Michael, *A Very Slippery Fellow: The Life of Sir Robert Wilson 1777-1849*, Oxford University Press, 1978

Grases, Pedro, *El Archivo de Bolívar*, Ediciones Equinoccio, Caracas: Universidad Simón Bolívar, 1978

Green, V.H.H., *A History of Oxford University*, London: B.T. Batsford Ltd, 1974

Hall, Captain Basil, *Extracts from a Journal Written on the Coasts of Chili, Peru, and Mexico, in the years 1820, 1821 and 1822*, vol. I , II, Edinburgh, 1824,

Hackett, James, *Narrative of the Expedition Which Sailed from England in 1817 to join the South American Patriots,* London, 1818

Harvey, Robert, *Liberators,* Woodstock & New York: Overlook Press, 2000

Harvie, Christopher & Matthew, H.C.G., *Nineteenth-Century Britain*, Oxford: Oxford Paperbacks, 2000

Hasbrouck, Alfred, *Foreign Legionaries in the Liberation of Spanish South America*, Columbia University Press, 1928

Herman, Arthur, *To Rule the Waves, How the British Navy Shaped the Modern World*, London: Harper Perennial, 2005

Hippisley, Col. Gustavus, *Narrative of the Expedition to the River Orinoco and Apure in South America which sailed in Nov. 1817 and joined the patriot forces in Venezuela and Caracas*, London: John Murray, 1819

Hobsbawm, E.J., *The Age of Revolution –Europe 1789-1848*, Abacus, 1978

Hogg, Ian V., *The Story of the Gun*, London: St. Martin's Press, 1966

Holmes, Richard, *Redcoat,* London: Harper Collins, 2001

Holloway, Estelle, *Elinor with the Pleading Eyes*, Somerset: Williton Printers, (undated)

Hooker, Terry and Poulter, Ron, *The Armies of Bolívar and San Martin,* London: Osprey, No. 232, 1991

Howitt, Richard, *Australia Felix: historical, descriptive and statistic, with an account of a four years residence in that colony and notes of a voyage round the world, Australian poems, etc.* London: Longman, Brown, Green and Longman, 1845

Huerta Díaz, Vice-Admiral Ismael, *El Elemento Humano en el Primer Medio Siglo de la Armada de Chile,* Boletín de la Academia de Historia Naval y Marítima de Chile, año II, No. 2, 1997

Hughes, Robert, *The Fatal Shore,* NY: Alfred A. Knopf, 1987

Humphreys, R.A.

– (ed), *The Detached Recollections of General D.F. O'Leary,* University of London, Athlone Press, 1969

British Consular Reports on the Trade and Politics of Latin America, Vol. XIII, London: Offices of the Royal Historical Society, 1940

British Consular reports on the Trade and Politics of Latin America, Vol. LXII, London: Office of the Royal Historical Society, 1940

– *British Merchants and South American Independence,* Raleigh Lecture on History, 17 February 1965, in Proceedings of the British Academy, Vol. 51, 1965

Johnson, Paul, *Napoleon,* London: Phoenix, 2002

Kaufmann, William W., *British Policy and the Independence of Latin America 1804-1828,* Archon Books, 1967

Keegan, John,

– *A History of Warfare,* Vintage Canada, 1993

– *The Face of Battle,* London: Pilmico, 1976

Kirkpatrick, F.A., *Latin America – A Brief History,* Cambridge, 1938

Koebel, W.H., *British Exploits in South America,* NY: The Century Co. 1917

Ovidio Lagos, *Chiloé, A Separate World, online:* see http://www.ovidiolagos.com/english.html

Lambert, Eric,

– *Voluntarios Británicos e Irlandeses en la Gesta Bolivariana,* Volumes I, II, III, Caracas, 1993

– *Irish Soldiers in South America 1818-1830,* in *The Irish Sword,* Journal of the Military History Society of Ireland, Vol. XVI, No. 62, 1984

Langford, Paul, *Eighteenth-Century Britain,* Oxford: OUP, 1984

Leckbandt, Ollie,

– *The Mount Walker Stockade Cox's River,* Australia: Industrial Printing, 1997

– *Convict Stockades From Mount Walker to Mount Victoria,* Australia: Industrial Printing, 1998

Lecuna, Vicente,

– *Expedición de Los Cayos,* Caracas: Litografía y Tipografía Mercantil 1928, 1937; 2 Vols.

– *Selected Writings of Bolívar,* (ed) Vicente Lecuna, NY: Colonial Press, 2 Vols. 1951

– *Bolívar y el Arte Militar,* NY: The Colonial Press, 1955

– *Biografía de Aury por Stanley Faye,* Caracas: Boletín de la Academia Nacional de la Historia, tomo XXI, oct–dic, 1938, No. 84

– *Documentos inéditos para la historia de Bolívar, Campaña de 1818*, Boletín de la Academia Nacional de la Historia, tomo XXI, oct-dic, 1938

Lee, Steven J., Aspects of British Political History 1815-1914, London: Routledge, 1994

Lewis, Samuel, *Topographical Dictionary of Ireland*, MDCCCXXXVII

Lodge, Edmund, *The Peerage of the British Empire*, London: Saunders & Ofley, 1838

Longford, Elizabeth, *Wellington- the Years of the Sword*, London: Panther, 1971

López Urrutia, Carlos,

    – *La Escuadra Chilena en México 1822,* Editorial Francisco de Aguirre, 1971

    – *Historia de la Marina de Chile, El Cipres Editores, 2008 Los insurgents del Sur,*

    see www.bbslaguan.com.mx/CarlosLopez/introoduccion.htm

    Chile: A Brief Naval History, Historical Text Archive, See

    www.historicaltextarchive.com/book.php?op=viewbook&bookid=16&cid=2

Lynch, John, *The Spanish-American Revolutions,* NY: W.W. Norton & Co, 1973

Mackay, David, *A Place of Exile – The European Settlement of NSW*, Melbourne: Oxford University Press, 1985

de Madariaga, Salvador, *Bolivar*, London: Hollis and Carter, 1952

McNerney Jr., Robert F., (ed), *Memorias del General Daniel Florecio O'Leary*, University of Texas Press, 1970

Milford, Humphrey, *Britain and the Independence of Latin America,* 1912-1830, Oxford: Oxford University Press, 1944

Miller, General William, *Memoirs of General Miller*, Vol. II, London: Longman, 1829

Mitre, Bartolomé, *Emancipation of South America – Being a Condensed Translation by William Pilling of the History of San Martin,* London: Chapman & Hall, 1893

Mondolfi Gudat, Edgardo, *Páez Visto por Los Ingleses*, Fuentes Para la Historia Republicana de Venezuela, 2005

Moore Jr, Barrington, *Social Origins of Dictatorship and Democracy*, London: Penguin, 1967

Morris, Norval, *Maconochie's Gentlemen, The Story of Norfolk Island and the Roots of Modern Prison Reform,* Oxford, 2002

Morón, Guillermo, *A History of Venezuela*, London: Allen and Unwin, 1964

Mudie Spence, James, *The Land of Bolivar*, London, 1878

Murray, Venetia, *High Society in the Regency Period 1788-1830*, London: Penguin, 1998

Neale, R.S., *Bath 1680-1850, A Social History,* London, Boston & Henley: Routledge & Kegan Paul, 1981

Nicholson, Irene, *The Liberators,* London: Faber & Faber, 1969

Nobbs, Raymond, (ed), *Norfolk Island and its Second Settlement 1825-55,* Sydney: Library of Australian History, 1991

Nucete Sardi, José; Pérez Tenreiro, Col. Tomás; Iribarren Célis, Lino, *La Campaña Libertadora de 1819,* Caracas: Academia Nacional de la Historia, Ministerio de Educación, 1969, 108-109

O'Leary, Daniel Florencio, *Memorias del General Daniel Florencio O'Leary*, Tomo I, Caracas: Imprenta Nacional, 1952

Páez Chataing, Delfín Enrique, *Tratado de la Regularizacion de la Guerra a Muerte*, Caracas: Liceo Fermín Toro, 26 Noviembre 1945

Páez, José Antonio, *Páez, Las Razones del Héroe*, (ed) Edgardo Mondolfi, Caracas: MonteAvila Editores, 1990

Parry, J.H., *The Spanish Seaborne Empire*, London: Hutchinson, 1966

Paxson, Fredric L., *The Independence of the South American Republics*, NY: Cooper Square Pub, 1970 (originally published in 1903)

Pocock, Tom, *Captain Marryat, Seaman, Writer and Adventurer*, Stackpole Books, 2000

Polanco Alcántara, Tomás, *José Antonio Páez, Fundador de la República*, Caracas: Ediciones GE, 2000

Reid, Stuart, *Redcoat Officer 1740-1815*, Oxford: Osprey, 2002

Roberts, Andrew, *Waterloo, The Battle for Modern Europe*, London: Harper Perennial, 2005

Robinson, J.H., *Journal of an Expedition 1400 miles up the Orinoco and 300 miles up the Arauca, with an account of the country, the manners of the people, military operations, etc.* London, 1822

Romaine Govett, William, *Sketches of New South Wales*, Saturday Magazine 1836-37, Melbourne: Gaston Renard Publisher, 1977

Rosen, Sue, and Pearson, Michel, *No 2 Stockade Cox's River – Its Life and Times*, Australia: Environmental Services, Pacific Power, 1997

Rothenbert, Gunther, *The Napoleonic Wars*, (ed) John Keegan, London: Cassell & Co, 1999

Rourke, Thomas, *Simón Bolívar*, London: Michel Joseph Ltd, 1940

Rubinstein, W.D., *Britain's Century – A Political and Social History 1815-1905*, London: Arnold, 1998

Salamé Ruiz, Gil Ricardo, *Sucre – Algo Mas Que un Guerrero*, Caracas, 2009

Salcedo-Bastardo, J.L., *Bolívar, A Continent and Its Destiny*, Humanities Press International, 1977

Scott, Drusilla, *Mary English, A Friend of Bolivar*, London: The Book Guild, 1991

Semple, Robert, *Sketch of the Present State of Caracas*, London 1812

Shaw, A.G.L., *Convicts and the Colonies*, London: Faber and Faber, 1966

Sinclair, David, *The Land That Never Was: Sir Gregor MacGregor and the Most Audacious Fraud in History*, Cambridge, MA: Da Capo Press, 2003

Sitwell, Edith, *Bath*, Faber and Faber, 1932

Sociedad Bolivariana de Venezuela, *Cronología de Bolivar*, Caracas 1962

Sondhause, Laurence *Naval Warfare 1815-1914*, London: Routledge, 2001

Spence Robertson, William, *Rise of the Spanish-American Republics – As told in the Lives of their Liberators*, NY: Collier Books, 1961

Sturma, Michael, *Vice in a Vicious Society*, St. Lucia, London, NY: University of Queensland Press, 1983

Sullivan, Martin, *Men and Women of Port Philip*, Hale and Iremonger, 1985

Sunyer, Carlos Pi, *El autor de la obra Campañas y Cruceros en Venezuela: Richard Longfield Vowell*, Santiago: Revista Chilena de Historia y Geografía, julio-dic. 1952, No. 120

Sweeney, Christopher *Transported: In Place of Death*, London: MacMillan, 1981

Taylor, Nancy M. (ed), *The Journal of Ensign Best (1837-43)*, New Zealand, 1966

Thomas, Donald, *Cochrane – Britannia's Sea Wolf*, London: Cassell & Co, 2001

Toledo Leal, Guillermo A., *La Infantería de la Marina en la Armada de Chile*, 1999, Revista de la Marina de Chile, see www.revistamarina.cl

Toribio Medina (traductor), José, *Viajes Relativos a Chile*, Guillermo Feliú Cruz, (ed), Santiago: Fondo Histórico y Bibiográfico José Toribio Medina, 1962

Vargas, Francisco Alejandro, *La Guardia de Honor en La Campaña de los Llanos*, 1975

Velázques, María del Carmen, *Hispanoamerica en el Siglo XIX*, México: Editorial Pormaca, 1965

de Vere White, Terence, *The Anglo-Irish*, London: Victor Gollancz Ltd, 1972

Vowell, Richard Longfield,

– *Campaigns and Cruises, in Venezuela and New Grenada, and in the Pacific Ocean; from 1817 to 1830: with the Narrative of a March from the River Orinoco to San Buenaventura on the Coast of Chocó; and Sketches of the West Coast of South America from the Gulf of California to the Archipelago of Chiloé. Also, Tales of Venezuela: illustrative of revolutionary men, manners, and incidents. In three volumes.* London: Longman & Co. 1831

– *Memorias de un Oficial de la Legión Británica*, (traductor Luis Terán), Caracas: Editorial América, Prólogo de Rufino Blanco Fombona, 1916; edición de 1973, Caracas: Biblioteca de la Academia Nacional de la Historia,

– *The Sabanas de Barinas* , Caracas: Biblioteca de la Academia Nacional de la Historia, 1952, Prólogo de Juán Uslar Pietri

– *El Terremoto de Caracas, por Un Oficial de la Legión Británica*, Nota Preliminar del Traductor (A.R.V), Caracas: Banco Central de Venezuela, 1974

– *Campañas y Cruceros en el Océano Pacífico*, (traductor) José Toribio Medina, Buenos Aires, Chile: Editorial Francisco de Aguirre, 1968.

Webster, C.K., *Britain and the Independence in South America 1812-1830, Selections from the Foreign Office Archives*, two volumes, Oxford University Press, 1938

Webster, Sir Charles, *The Foreign Policy of Castlereagh 1815-22*, London: Bell & Sons, 1947

Whitaker, Arthur Preston, *The United States and the Independence of Latin America 1800-1830*, Baltimore: John Hopkins Press, 1941

Willis, David, *The Mallow Blackwater*, in Burke's Landed Gentry of Ireland, Journal No. 5

Worcester, Donald E., *Sea Power and Chilean Independence*, University of Florida Monograph No. 15, 1962

Index

Places

Military units & formations

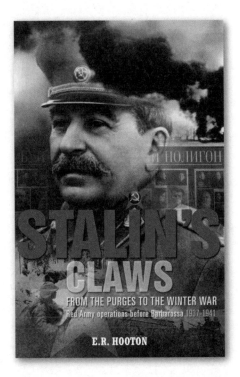

STALIN'S
CLAWS
FROM THE PURGES TO THE WINTER WAR
Red Army operations before Barbarossa 1937-1941

E.R. HOOTON

In the late 1930s the Soviet Union experienced a brutal Purge which swept through all levels of its society with millions arrested and tens of thousands shot for reasons lacking any form of ethics or justification.

As historian, E.R. Hooton describes in this absorbing and revealing history, the Soviet armed forces did not escape the bloody tidal wave which swept away the majority of their most experienced and gifted officers. Yet as the leadership of the Soviet forces was cut to pieces, the Red Army was deployed in operations at the extremities of Stalin's empire. Despite showing ominous signs of weakness, in every case it triumphed. The Japanese had been defeated on the Korean border at Lake Khasan in 1938 and a year later suffered a major defeat on the Mongolian border at the River Khalkin (Khalkin Gol) in an offensive directed by the future Marshal Zhukov. These guns had barely ceased fire when there was a major invasion of eastern Poland following the Ribbentrop Pact. On the back of that, the Baltic States were compelled to allow the Russians to base forces in their borders.

But as the Purges eased and Moscow became overconfident, the massive Red Army became enmeshed in the disastrous Winter War with Finland of 1939-1940 which saw its military prestige shattered and its invasion not only stopped, but dealt a series of major defeats. Victory of a kind, when it came, was pyrrhic.

In the aftermath, the Red Army hurriedly sought to modernise and to expand in order to meet the growing threat from Nazi Germany. It invaded Rumania's eastern province of Bessarabia in June 1940 to provoke 'Barbarossa'. Yet the Purges and the Purge mentality continued to wreak slaughter and fear from 1939 to 1941, culminating in a mini massacre of Soviet generals even as Hitler's armies approached Moscow.

Hooton provides a vivid and important insight into the operations conducted by the Red Army from 1937 to 1941 and makes some surprising conclusions about the impact of the Purges.

ISBN: 978-0-9543115-5-1
Hardback 234 x 146 mm and eBook
228 pp plus b/w photographs

www.thetatteredflag.com

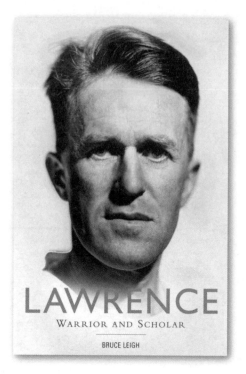

LAWRENCE
WARRIOR AND SCHOLAR

BRUCE LEIGH

M any books have been written about T.E. Lawrence, exploring the man and his deeds. Just about every aspect and the many incarnations of his life, his campaigns, the geo–politics of the Arab world, and the influence of the West in it, as Lawrence experienced them, have been examined.

However, to date, nobody has gone in search of the mind of the man himself – of his formation and his deep beliefs. Nobody has asked the question, *What, really, is the source of the extraordinary power of this little man?* – not only in terms of his incontestable qualities of leadership, but also in regard to the sheer range of his activities and accomplishments.

Archaeologist, writer, guerilla warfare theorist and practitioner, diplomat, soldier and airman, Lawrence also possessed an unusual ability to cross boundaries of class, race, culture, and religion. On top of this, he demonstrated the ability to walk away from power and wealth and the accumulation of things – to change his name more than once; to begin again at the bottom of the heap in the RAF, and stay there, with only a few friends and books and a motorcycle.

Lawrence – Warrior and Scholar is a quest. It examines how a slight Oxford academic combined two of the most challenging paths a man can choose. Drawing upon what Lawrence and those who knew him wrote, and did, and said, Bruce Leigh delves into Lawrence's personal philosophy and practices, examining and analysing his library, and his close relationship to the world of classical scholarship and chivalry, emphasising that Lawrence's views were not abstractions only, but intimately tied to his actions and deeds.

ISBN 978-0-9543115-7-5
Paperback 234 x 146 mm
120 pp plus photographs

www.thetatteredflag.com

'Andrew Simpson's "Ops" bears all the hallmarks of becoming the definitive work on bomber operations during World War Two.'
Military History Monthly

This is the story of RAF Bomber Command from its highest levels of leadership to the experiences of the lowest WAAF; it is a book which reveals, truthfully, the grim, dogged and often humorous human side of the bomber crews' experience. *The Times* commented: 'These pages do not do self-pity.'

Between 1939-1945, of 125,000 men who volunteered for operations with Bomber Command, 55,573 were killed, the slaughter being at the almost unprecedented level. Total British Empire and Commonwealth fatalities from 1939 to 1945 were 452,000..

Based upon many personal interviews, *'Ops - Victory at All Costs'* is an important, compelling and absorbing documentary record of what the men of RAF Bomber Command went through – from initial training, to descriptions of life on squadron and on their extremely dangerous and draining operations, to the numbing effect of morale breakdown. The book also examines the technology of bombing and how this form of aerial warfare evolved in terms of aircraft design, navigation, bombing methods, tactics and gunnery.

After the fighting was over no campaign medal was ever struck for the air and ground crews of Bomber Command, and Air Marshal Arthur Harris, its Commander-in-Chief, never forgave the British government.

This book, written by the son of a Lancaster pilot, is the result of years of intense research.
For anyone with a desire to learn more about Britain at war or for those seeking to understand more about the operations of Bomber Command, this book offers a unique and extraordinary insight into a momentous period of history.

ISBN: 978-0-9555977-6-3
Hardback 234 x 146 mm and eBook
288 pp plus ca 60 b/w photographs and maps

www.thetatteredflag.com

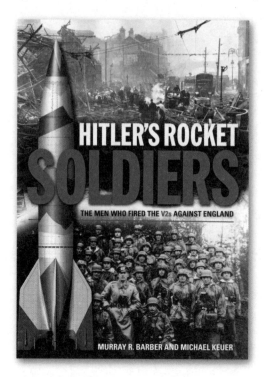

HITLER'S ROCKET SOLDIERS

THE MEN WHO FIRED THE V2s AGAINST ENGLAND

MURRAY R. BARBER AND MICHAEL KEUER

In the final, desperate months of World War Two, at a time when the German war machine was considered by the Allies to be an almost spent force, Adolf Hitler unleashed a new weapon against England and Western Europe which fell from the silence of the Earth's upper atmosphere and the edge of space. It was a weapon that struck fear into the hearts and minds of wartime civilians; it came without warning and defence was impossible – an unseen threat that fell at supersonic speeds, levelling suburban streets to dust in seconds, terrorising the residents of London and Antwerp: this was the V2 Rocket.

The V2, designed at the secret Nazi research centre at Peenemünde, by the renowned rocket scientist and engineer, Wernher von Braun, was the most sophisticated weapon developed in Europe during the war. Following the end of hostilities, von Braun and many in his team transferred their allegiance to the United States and subsequently went on to design the mighty Saturn V that took the Americans to the moon. The experiences of von Braun's rocket team are well documented, but aspects of the V2 story remain largely uncovered.

For the first time, this book tells the story of the rocket through the eyes and experiences not only of the men who fired the missiles at targets in Britain and France, but also of some of the military scientists and technicians involved in its development. The authors of this book spent many years tracking down and interviewing the few surviving veterans of these little-known and secretive units, and have unearthed rare information from first-hand accounts. These are the unique recollections of Hitler's Rocket Soldiers and they form an important contribution to our understanding of the German war machine and its technology.

ISBN: 978-0-9555977-5-6
Hardback 234 x 146 mm and eBook
284 pp plus b/w photographs and maps

www.thetatteredflag.com

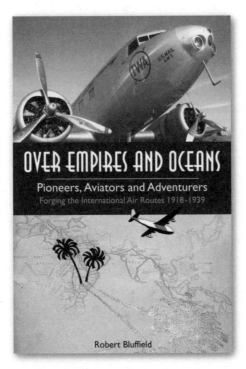

This a story of pioneers, intrepid aviators, adventurers, tycoons and innovators. It is also a story of dedication and determination, for despite fixed-wing aircraft proving their value over the battlefields of the the First World War, convincing governments and public alike that they had a role in peacetime proved far more challenging. The Americans, as inventors of heavier-than-air powered flight, courted with a passenger airline across Tampa Bay in 1914, yet it took a further nine years for mail to be flown coast-to-coast. In 1919 a British company made the first international scheduled flight between London and Paris, but regular services were thwarted by a less-than-enthusiastic government.

Eventually, the British realised that fast links with their Empire were vital, and followed the example of the French and Dutch who had forged air links with their cousins in North Africa and the Far East. Meanwhile, in South America, the Germans, forbidden from any major aircraft-building, were establishing cunning supremacy by forming airlines throughout South America and in China. While America awaited a transcontinental passenger service, Pan American Airways was crossing swords with NYRBA for air supremacy between the US and Latin America that led to the formation of arguably the world's greatest airline.

In Russia, Sikorsky had built a vast passenger-carrying aircraft, but the mighty German airship, *Hindenburg*, exploded while mooring at Lakehurst in 1937.

Robert Bluffield's highly researched account tells the dramatic stories of explorers and flamboyant entrepreneurs who risked fortunes and reputations to follow their dreams of reaching and ruling the skies over empires, continents and oceans. Against bewildering adversity, corruption, underhanded deals and dwindling resources, these tenacious individuals braved the elements using primitive, entirely unsuitable equipment to establish earth-shrinking aerial services that criss-crossed the great oceans and the globe's most inhospitable territories. These are the stories of those pioneers – of Aéropostale, CNAC, Air Orient, Imperial Airways, KLM, Deutsche Luft Hansa, Pan Am, SCADTA, The Condor Syndicat, Qantas and others that had a far-reaching impact on the way the modern world would travel.

ISBN: 978-0-9543115-6-8
Paperback 234 x 146 mm and eBook
ca 284 pp plus b/w photographs and maps

www.thetatteredflag.com

TATTERED
FLAG
Tattered Flag Press East Sussex

A Box of Sand
The Italo-Ottoman War 1911-1912

Charles Stephenson

In September 1911 Italy declared war on the declining Ottoman Empire and attempted to add to her growing African empire by attacking Ottoman-ruled Tripolitania (Libya). The Italian action began the swift fall of the Ottoman Empire, which would end with its disintegration at the end of the First World War. It was a conflict that saw many 'firsts' and pointers to the awful future that lay ahead: the first aerial reconnaissance and bombing, and use of armoured vehicles; war fever whipped up by the Italian press; military incompetence and stalemate; immense difficulties in penetrating the Dardanelles; lessons in how not to fight a guerilla war; and mass death from disease and executions. Historian Charles Stephenson has written a graphic account of the struggle in which thousands would die for little more than 'a box of sand'.

This is the first book to be written in the English language on The Italo-Ottoman War – a stark example of the futility of armed conflict in recent history. It was a war which left Italy with a huge monetary cost and it halved the population of Libya through emigration, casualties and famine.

Britain's Bomb
The RAF's Atomic and Nuclear Strategies
From the Manhattan Project to Weapons of Mass Destruction

Tim McLelland

Acclaimed aviation historian Tim McLelland reveals the chilling story of how the Royal Air Force prepared and armed itself for nuclear warfare during the militarily and economically uncertain years after the Second World War, through the Cold War and beyond. From the physics behind the atomic bomb and the Manhattan Project to Britain's unilateral path culminating in Operation Hurricane; from the genesis of the jet age to the emergence of the V-Force. Britain produced some impressive and formidable aircraft, such as the Canberra, the Valiant, the Vulcan and the Victor. It is a story of 'Megaton Might', of secret thermonuclear weapon development on a terrifying scale. Later would come TSR2, the Blue Steel missile, the switch to low-level operations and the abandoned Skybolt programme as well as the Thor system and Blue Streak. This is an essential and compelling book for those with an interest in the Cold War and Britain's post-war political and military history.

Friends and Enemies
The Natal Campaign in the South African War 1899-1902

Hugh Rethman

In this exhaustive and provocative new account of the Boer War, Hugh Rethman explores how many British commanders failed to heed local advice and opinion, a fault which was to convert a campaign in which casualties should have been measured in hundreds into a war in which Britain suffered 80,000 casualties, of whom 20,000 lost their lives. In negotiating the Peace Treaty of 1902, the peoples of Natal and the Cape were denied any say in the proceedings, with the result that the Boers were given exclusive control over all the peoples in South Africa, a situation which was to last for almost 100 years. While they ruled the country, Boer propaganda manipulated information emanating from South Africa to such an extent that commentators have come to rely almost exclusively on British and Boer sources for information. This has, in turn, resulted in histories of that conflict becoming progressively more skewed. *Friends and Enemies* takes into account, for the first time, the experience of, and contribution to, the war of all the people of Natal, whose Volunteers had trained specifically to meet the threat of a mounted enemy armed with modern, long-range rifles.

Using archival resources in both Britain and South Africa, as well as private sources, Rethman offers a refreshing and detailed perspective of the Natal Campaign.

A Shield Twice Broken
The Battle of the Hindenburg Line 1918

E.R.Hooton

In the summer of 1918 the tide of battle finally turned against the German Army. The numerical superiority it had possessed, having transferred troops from the Russian Front, was now offset by the thousands of American troops reaching France each month. Even as they arrived, the French and British staged a series of operations which steadily drove the Germans from their gains in the spring and the summer. With the Allied success at Amiens, the Germans were driven from the territory they had first gained in 1918 and back to their start line.

However, this line was the great series of fortifications known to the Allies 'The Hindenburg Line' which had held off the enemy throughout 1917. It was Germany's great shield and provided a sanctuary from which it might still gain some political success from the war which was, by this time, exhausting the German Empire. But on 27 September 1918 the British Army, after a brief pause, smashed its way through the defences in a single day and by 10 October, it had driven a deep salient into the German lines. Successful Allied attacks from the Ypres Salient exposed thousands of German troops between Lille and Douai, forcing the Germans to abandon a substantial bloc of territory in the second half of October and leading to a fighting retreat which did not cease until 11 November.

Historian, E.R. Hooton recounts the breaking of the Hindenburg Line and the liberation of most of Belgium. The operations in many ways heralded the battles of the Second World War, with the British seeking to exploit their breakthroughs using mobile forces of cavalry, motorised troops and light armour, while air power harassed the enemy retreat. This new study offers an important and fresh perspective on an important campaign.

www.thetatteredflag.com